*Culture, Religion, and Demographic Behaviour*

# Culture, Religion, and Demographic Behaviour

## Catholics and Lutherans in Alsace, 1750–1870

KEVIN MCQUILLAN

Liverpool University Press

McGill-Queen's University Press
Montreal & Kingston · London · Ithaca

© McGill-Queen's University Press 1999
ISBN 0-7735-1860-6
Legal deposit third quarter 1999
Bibliothèque nationale du Québec

Printed in Canada on acid-free paper

Published in the European Union
by Liverpool University Press
ISBN 0-85323-864-2 (cloth)

This book has been published with the help of a grant
from the Humanities and Social Sciences Federation of
Canada, using funds provided by the Social Sciences
and Humanities Research Council of Canada. Publication has also been assisted by a grant from the J.B.
Smallman and Spencer memorial Fund, University of
Western Ontario.

McGill-Queen's University Press acknowledges the
financial support of the Government of Canada
through the Book Publishing Industry Development
Program (BPIDP) for its activities. We also acknowledge the support of the Canada Council for the Arts
for our publishing program.

**Canadian Cataloguing in Publication Data**

McQuillan, Kevin
    Culture, religion, and demographic behaviour:
    Catholics and Lutherans in Alsace, 1750–1870
    (McGill-Queen's studies in the history of religion)
    Includes bibliographical references and index.
    ISBN 0-7735-1860-6
    1. Alsace (France) – Population – History – 18th
    century. 2. Alsace (France) – Population – History –
    19th century. 3. Alsace (France) – Religion.
    4. Catholics – France – Alsace – History –
    18th century. 5. Lutherans – France – Alsace –
    History – 18th century. 6. Catholics – France –
    Alsace – History – 19th century. 7. Lutherans –
    France – Alsace – History – 19th century. I. Title.
    II. Series.
    HB3594.A48M37 1999    304.6'0944'38309033
    C99-900233-3

**British Cataloguing-in-Publication Data**
A British Library CIP record is available

This book was typeset by Typo Litho Composition Inc.
in 10/12 Palatino.

*To Marilyn, Sarah, Daniel, and Liam*

# Contents

# Tables

# Figures

Alsace, showing the villages included in the analysis

# Acknowledgments

It is a pleasure to have the opportunity to thank the many people and institutions who have helped me with this project. Compiling the demographic information that this study is based on could not have been accomplished without the generous assistance of the staff at the Archives Départementales du Bas-Rhin, the Archives Départementales du Haut-Rhin, and the Bibliothèque Nationale et Universitaire de Strasbourg. I was able to acquire microfilm copies of some of the parish and civil registers from the Genealogical Library of the Church of Jesus Christ of Latter-Day Saints in Salt Lake City, Utah, and I thank the staff of the library for their efficient response to my requests. A project of this scope requires financial aid, and I wish to express my gratitude to the Social Sciences and Humanities Research Council of Canada, the Humanities and Social Science Federation of Canada, and the J.B. Smallman Publication Fund of the Faculty of Social Science at the University of Western Ontario for providing the resources needed.

Assistance with the time-consuming task of recording the information from the original sources and putting the data in computerized form was provided by Tracey Adams, Henny Westra, Lisa Parsons, Ingrid Day, Brenda Vidal, Jiajian Chen, and Cheryl McNeil. Their careful work made the analysis presented here possible. Sylvia Coté, Sue Shiel, and Denise Statham provided excellent administrative support for this project. My thanks also to Lesley Barry, Joan McGilvray, and John Zucchi for their superb editorial work.

Many colleagues offered invaluable advice and assistance along the way. In Strasbourg, Jean-Pierre Kintz, Christian Wolf, and especially Bernard Vogler provided guidance on the sources of Alsatian history. My friends at the Université de Montréal, particularly Jacques Légaré and Bertrand Desjardins, were a source of support throughout this project. George Alter, Steven Messner, Daniel Scott Smith, Richard Smith, Charles Tilly, Frans Van Poppel, Susan Watkins, and Frances Westley also provided helpful suggestions at various stages.

I have been fortunate to be surrounded by wonderful colleagues at my own university. My associates in the Population Studies Centre, T.R. Balakrishnan, Roderic Beaujot, Danièle Bélanger, Tom Burch, Eddie Ebanks, Rajulton Fernando, Carl Grindstaff, and Paul Maxim have always offered good counsel and encouragement. Many others at Western, especially Michael Carroll, George Emery, Ed Grabb, Peter Neary, and Jim Rinehart provided important assistance at various points. My two good friends, Sam Clark and Ron Gillis, have been steadfast supporters over the years, and I am certain this book would not have been completed without their help.

Finally, and most importantly, I thank my family. My brother and sister, Michael and Maggie, have always taken pride in my achievements, and I am grateful to them for all the help they have given me. My largest debt is to my wife Marilyn, and our children Sarah, Daniel, and Liam. Marilyn spent many hours helping me to decipher barely legible records and match them to form accurate family histories. Most of all, she had unwavering confidence that the project was worth doing and would eventually be completed. She and our children made many sacrifices over the years while also coming to enjoy the gastronomic pleasures of living in Strasbourg. I dedicate this book to the four of them as a sign of the gratitude I feel for their love and support.

ABBREVIATIONS
USED IN THE TEXT

ADBR  Archives Départementales du Bas-Rhin

ADHR  Archives Départementales du Haut-Rhin

*Culture, Religion, and Demographic Behaviour*

# CHAPTER ONE

# Culture, Religion, and Demographic Behaviour

The Protestant Reformation divided the population of Alsace into two major religious communities, one Catholic, the other Lutheran.[1] From that time forward, the two groups lived side by side in the cities and countryside of the region, their communities shaped by similar economic and political circumstances. And yet the two groups differed in important ways. Whether one looks at economic activity, voting patterns, or, as this study does, demographic behaviour, Catholics and Lutherans went their separate ways. This book explores the role of religion in shaping the demographic patterns of these two groups and, in doing so, seeks to contribute to a wider appreciation of the influence of culture on population patterns. The role of culture in demographic behaviour has attracted increasing attention in recent years, as demographers have turned away from the economic models that once dominated the field of population studies. Before looking at the specifics of the Alsatian case, then, it is helpful to examine the debate between economic and cultural approaches, in hopes of arriving at a better understanding of the effect of religion on the population patterns of a society.

## TRANSITION THEORY AND CULTURAL DIFFERENCES

The theory of demographic transition has been, without question, the most influential approach to understanding modern population change,[2] and much of the theoretical literature that has blossomed in demography in recent years has grown out of a dialogue with the ideas it contains. Originally a description of the Western experience as much as an attempt to account for it, transition theory outlined a now familiar three-stage model of demographic change in which populations pass from an equilibrium based on high rates of fertility and mortality through a stage of transitional growth towards a new equilibrium based on low vital rates. While early statements of the theory were vague concerning causality, subsequent versions have regarded economic factors as the primary source of population change (Alter 1992). Yet, as Chesnais (1992, 4) noted, in its original form transition theory accorded cultural factors a significant role in shaping demographic behaviour. For Notestein, culture provided critical support for the high fertility regimes of pre-transitional societies: "Their religious doctrines, moral codes, laws, education, community customs, marriage habits, and family organizations are all focused toward maintaining high fertility" (1945, 39). It seems fair to infer from this statement that Notestein believed economic incentives alone might be insufficient to insure a birth rate high enough to offset the unavoidably high mortality such populations faced, and that societies (consciously or unconsciously) evolved a set of beliefs and practices to reinforce the desire of couples to have large families.

Transition theory also credited culture with an important role in the timing of fertility decline. In considering why fertility rates do not immediately adjust to declining mortality, Notestein referred not to socio-economic variables but to the power of values and customs. The impressive array of forces society had marshalled to support high fertility could not be so quickly dismantled, and nor were individuals likely to change their values and beliefs in a short period of time. Thus, the spread of contraception and corresponding lower fertility could occur only when people were "freed from older taboos" (Notestein 1945, 40). Although Notestein did not say so, it seems reasonable to conclude that the length of the waiting period would vary with the strength of the cultural forces that supported high fertility.

More recent work on both historical and contemporary societies has supported the view that demographic change does not follow simply from economic and technological development, and that cultural variables also influence both the timing and nature of demographic change. The Princeton studies of the decline of fertility in Europe, though arguably launched on the basis of an "economist" reading of transition theory, nevertheless conclude by emphasizing the significance of cultural factors in the timing of the fertility transition (Anderson 1986). Others have taken up a similar theme with respect to fertility change in the developing world (Cleland and Wilson 1987; Caldwell and Caldwell 1987). And Lesthaeghe (1983, 1989; Lesthaeghe and Surkyn 1988), in particular, has extended the argument to include not only marital fertility but other components of demographic behaviour as well. Variation among present-day

European societies in patterns of nuptiality, cohabitation, divorce, and non-marital fertility are best explained, he argues, by those cultural features that have deep historical roots.

If the result of this growing body of research has been to accord greater respect to the influence of cultural variables on demographic behaviour, it has not yet produced a satisfactory explanation of exactly how that influence affects such behaviours as marriage and childbearing. Although economic theories of demographic behaviour have been found wanting on empirical grounds, the logic behind them is impressive. Beginning from the assumption that people act in their own material interest, they are able to outline how economic and social changes alter the calculus of costs and benefits accruing to individual households, and thereby change the incentives for certain forms of behaviour (Easterlin 1978). Cultural approaches, by contrast, can point to empirical evidence that suggests a significant role for cultural variables but have a harder time tracing the path that leads from culture to the demographic behaviour in question (McQuillan 1989; Kertzer 1995). Demographers are thus left with economic models that provide compelling arguments but do not fit the data, and cultural models that appear more in line with the empirical record but lack a convincing interpretation for their findings.

## OBSTACLES TO A CULTURAL THEORY

Certain problems face all efforts to understand the influence of culture on demographic behaviour, and two issues in particular appear important. One involves identifying the elements of culture that are critical for demographic behaviour. A second and related problem centres on the mechanisms through which culture comes to influence demography. Support for the cultural approach comes from empirical research, both historical and contemporary, that has identified significant differences among social groups defined by such traits as ethnicity, religion, language, or region of residence. But one does not marry earlier or have a larger family simply because one speaks a certain language or lives in a particular area. The traits that correlate with certain patterns of behaviour merely signify membership in some form of community. The question remains: how does membership in a community influence the demographic behaviour of individuals?

The most common answers to this question stress the importance of values, the generalized statements of belief that have been internalized by group members and serve as a reference in their evaluation of action. Hammel (1990), for example, has argued that culture always entails some evaluation of behaviour, and that individuals shape their actions in anticipation of such evaluation. McNicoll, approaching the issue from a somewhat different angle, has emphasized the role of institutions, by which he means "behavioural rules governing ... human actions and relationships in recurrent situations" (1994, 201). The values that people internalize surely play a significant role in shaping behaviour, especially with regard to intimate matters touching on marriage, sexuality, and childbearing. But this emphasis on ideational factors has led some critics to complain that proponents of a cultural approach have removed culture from its historical setting (Greenhalgh 1990, 1995). As a result, culture becomes "an ethereal arena of 'meaning-worlds'" (Kertzer 1995, 45), cut off from the social structures which support it and with which it interacts. A convincing explanation of the association between culture and demographic behaviour must do more than show consistency between a set of values and a particular pattern of behaviour. It requires exploring the origins of values and their evolution over time. This, in turn, demands attention to the actions of individuals and groups as they redefine and reshape elements of received culture, often in an effort to advance the interests of their group in society. It also requires examining the social mechanisms that transmit values to group members and promote compliance.

To date, demographers have paid little attention to the first issue, the ways in which values are shaped, more often simply taking their existence as a given element of culture.[3] In perhaps the most significant instance, students of the Western European marriage pattern emphasize the importance of the norm dictating that married couples establish an independent household, yet the origin and institutionalization of this behavioural rule remain poorly understood (Hajnal 1965; Macfarlane 1986). Demographers frequently focus not on the internal social processes that shape values but instead on the diffusion of new values from one cultural setting to another. This approach is not without its problems, as Kreager (1993) has noted. New ideas or values do not simply replace older ones but are integrated into an ongoing cultural and social structure, and are likely to be transformed in the process. Nevertheless, work in this area has directed attention to the ways in which social structures can reshape values and, ultimately, behaviour. Watkins (1990, 1991), for example, has identified sources of value change in the critical years of the nineteenth century when marital fertility rates declined in many European societies. In doing so, she emphasized the role of political and economic forces. National states made increasing efforts to integrate the populations living in their territory, which typically involved the growth of those institutions that touched the lives of ordinary citizens. Chief among them was education, which transmitted new ideas and values to citizens in all regions of the nation. At the same time, national markets were becoming increasingly integrated as well. The penetration of new, standardized products into villages and towns of even remote regions helped to reshape the aspirations of both urban and rural dwellers. Often supported by the earliest forms of modern advertising, the new retail trade was in a powerful position to supplant established forms of commerce and to bring in its wake new signs of social status and new ways of looking at the world. A similar process has been at work in much of the developing world in recent decades, and Caldwell (1976, 1980), in particular, has identified the importation of a Western world-view as an important source of value change that can ultimately lead to fertility decline.

Other work has examined the process by which new values are adopted in local communities. High-status persons are often initiators and exemplars of new forms of behaviour. Caldwell (1976), for example, noted the tendency of highly educated urban dwellers in some developing countries to lead the way in accepting a "Westernized" view of family life. Livi-Bacci (1986), in reviewing findings of the Princeton project, also pointed to the role played by key groups such as the nobility as precursors of a shift in values and behaviour. Hammel (1990) has taken this point further, noting that the circumstances that lead high-status people to alter their behaviour may not be shared by others in the society. Nevertheless, their status may support a change in behaviour by those in different circumstances.

Diffusion of new values and new forms of behaviour occurs most easily, of course, where people share membership in some form of community, and where the communication of new ideas and ways of behaving is possible. It is this point that analysts of fertility transition have stressed when trying to account for regional variations in the timing of fertility decline. Cultural boundaries obstruct the transmission of new knowledge – concerning contraception, for example – and new forms of evaluating behaviour. Language can block the spread of new information, but the significance of cultural boundaries may go beyond this. High-status persons in one group are unlikely to be held in the same respect in a different cultural milieu. As a result, members of other ethnic or religious groups may ignore their example or even see it as an affront to their own cultural traditions.

In sum, despite the formidable difficulties standing in the way of culture-based theories of demographic change, a good deal of theoretical and empirical work has helped to point the way forward. While the heavy emphasis on the diffusion of "modern" values to traditional settings has downplayed the role of existing structures, it has also raised some important issues. In the next section, we draw on these insights to describe the ways in which religion may shape demographic behaviour.

## RELIGION AND DEMOGRAPHIC BEHAVIOUR

### Elements of Religious Influence

This section explores situations in which religion has a direct influence on demography,[4] that is, where it can be argued that features of a religion itself affect demographic behaviour. In his careful consideration of this question, Goldscheider (1971) pointed to two possible sources of religious influence: first, a "particularized theology" that supports a certain type of demographic behaviour, and second, a more generalized value orientation or world-view.[5] In the latter case, a distinctive demographic pattern may be a part of a quite different orientation to social life even though specific teachings relating to marriage, sexuality, or contraception are either absent or ignored.

Goldscheider's perspective calls attention to a number of issues. The "particularized theology" approach is often dismissed rather quickly, and, indeed, Goldscheider himself tends to see it as a naive and limited attempt to capture the religious dimension. To be sure, it is easy enough to cite variation in fertility rates among groups belonging to a common faith as proof that theological principles do not determine behaviour. It would be a mistake, however, to move from this to the conclusion that religious dogma can be ignored when trying to understand religious influences on demographic action. I would argue instead that religious teachings touching on demographic issues form an important part of a religious world-view, and are a necessary, though not sufficient, condition for the formation and continuation of a distinctive demographic pattern.

A full understanding of religious influence on values and, ultimately, behaviour requires attention to a broader set of concerns. Due, in part, to demographers' concern with the decline in marital fertility, attention to the role of religious doctrine has too often focused narrowly on the permissibility of contraception. Mason (1992), in her critique of cultural approaches to fertility transition, has argued that demographers must extend their interest beyond the problem of fertility control and examine how culture influences the demand for children as well. Seccombe (1993), echoing the criticisms of many feminist writers, has pointed to the central role of sexuality in any explanation of fertility patterns and wonders why demographers often seek to avoid the issue. Beliefs about sexual relations, he suggests, may be as important as norms related to contraception in understanding fertility trends. A woman, fearing a new pregnancy but influenced by norms regarding her conjugal duty, may agree to sexual relations even though her husband refuses to cooperate in the use of contraception. Here, it is not so much norms about contraceptive use *per se* that are important (the husband's refusal to cooperate may not entail any moral objection to the use of fertility control), but beliefs about when sexual relations should occur and under what conditions it is appropriate for a woman to refuse her husband. And these are issues that have often been the focus of religious teaching. Flandrin (1983) has noted the numerous prohibitions that the pre-Reformation Church placed on sexual relations between spouses, calculating that a couple that rigorously followed the Church's teaching could engage in sex only about once a week. Tentler (1977), in his remarkable study of the practice of confession on the eve of the Reformation, explored changing ideas in Catholicism about the sinfulness of various sexual practices and the role of the confessor in questioning married penitents about their sex lives. The Church, in the post-Reformation era, maintained a strong interest in using the confessional to monitor sexual activity both inside and outside of marriage (Haliczer 1996). The leaders of the Reformation, on the other hand, while continuing to condemn extramarital sexuality, introduced several significant changes. They rejected celibacy as a superior state in life and accepted sexual pleasure among spouses as a positive good. Corresponding to this was a denial of the Catholic ideal that procreation was the sole licit purpose of sexual relations (Hull 1996, 20). They also virtually abolished the sacrament of confession: no longer would men and women be subjected to questioning by their ministers about their sexual behaviour.

Parent-child relationships, and particularly parental authority, have also been the territory of religious doctrine (Ozment 1983). Here, too, though religious teachings do not directly address demographic questions, the more general issues of parental authority and filial obligation may well have important implications for marriage patterns and the demographic regime of the society. The debate that raged during the Reformation over the issue of parental consent to the marriage of their children is one striking example of this.[6]

In sum, the teachings of major religious traditions are complex and touch many aspects of the lives of their followers. Some, including rules governing contraception, have an obvious and direct link to demography. But demographers are mistaken if they limit their consideration only to such teachings. Religious views on the proper ordering of the family and sexual relations may also affect the demographic patterns of society. The challenge is to identify those components of the religious value system that hold importance for particular groups.

The existence of religious doctrine or a more generalized religiously inspired world-view does not, of course, guarantee a role for religion in the construction of a demographic regime. Two other elements, I would suggest, are critical. One concerns the ability of religious institutions to communicate their message to ordinary people and to promote compliance. The second is the degree to which religious values are internalized, which in turn depends on the salience of religious membership for personal identity.

The role of social organization in transmitting cultural influence is often ignored in demographic discussions. In some instances, this reflects the difficulty of identifying the institutional mechanisms responsible for communicating and reinforcing cultural values. However, in the case of religion, particularly in a European context, this is not a serious problem. The Christian churches of Europe had put in place structures designed to communicate their teachings and to promote conformity with them (Kertzer 1995, 46; Smith 1995). Several aspects of religious organization made it possible for churches to have special influence, particularly in the period before widespread urbanization and the emergence of the modern state. One was the proximity of religious leaders to ordinary people. In the Alsatian case, even the smallest villages were adorned with a church and, in the vast majority of instances, a clergyman who lived amongst the people. Moreover, there was a determined effort to link the priest or pastor in his village to the larger structures of the churches. A wealth of archival materials testifies to the regular communication between religious authorities and local ministers. Parish priests and ministers informed their superiors of goings-on in their parishes and received both advice and instruction in return. This allowed church leaders a significant measure of influence among local populations, though, as historians of popular religion have shown, the lower clergy and their parishioners often strayed from the paths approved by the hierarchy. Nevertheless, the network of parishes provided a key mechanism by which the teachings of the churches could be brought to even isolated communities.

The church also managed, through a series of ceremonies and regulations, to insert itself into the daily routine of the common people. Certainly in Alsace, and probably in most parts of Europe before the nineteenth century, attendance at religious worship was high, and often supported by a web of regulations that carried material penalties along with them. The size and structure of rural communities made supervision relatively easy, and local officials did not hesitate to use their power to discipline violators. But participation was not limited to a traditional Sunday service. Churches created a host of traditions and institutions – holidays, processions, organizations of the laity (Châtellier 1989) – that insured exposure to religious influences. Through such practices as the blessing of crops and prayers for good weather, the churches encouraged their followers to view the material world through a religious filter (Hufton 1979). Perhaps most important were religious practices that placed the church at the centre of life's demographic events. Birth, marriage, and death were imbued with religious significance and surrounded by religious ceremony. Goody (1983) has outlined the efforts of the Catholic Church to extend its control over marriage. The struggle took on a new dimension, as we will discuss below, with the emergence of Protestantism and its very different view of the place of marriage in society (Carlson 1994; Harrington 1995). With birth and death as well the church sought to form people's understanding of the significance of these events and to place itself at the centre of the ceremonies that marked them. Baptism opened the door to salvation and legitimized the newborn in the community. Proper preparation for death and burial in consecrated ground were intimately linked in the minds of believers to one's fate in the afterlife. The accompanying religious rituals lent these occasions dignity while also providing the church with a regular opportunity to communicate their beliefs to the faithful. Their power to withhold the approved rites gave religious authorities a lever with which to encourage conformity with church teaching.[7]

The power to influence or even coerce people to comply with codes of behaviour is of obvious importance but alone may be limited in effect. In the face of authoritarian structures, individuals can be remarkably resourceful in evading regulations or developing strategies that fit the letter if not the spirit of the law. Clearly, religious values are most likely to influence behaviour when people see conformity to principle as something worth struggling to attain. This tends to occur, I would argue, when religion rather than other social traits plays a central role in people's sense of identity. Typically, religion is only one aspect of a person's sense of self. Membership in a family or lineage, an ethnic or linguistic group, may also exert demands on the individual. Indeed, a variety of cross-cutting or overlapping social groups often compete for the loyalty of individuals. In some settings, people may continue to see themselves as belonging to a religious group, even though their involvement has little or no impact on their behaviour. In others, individuals may place their religious affiliation before all else. Religion is especially likely to assume a central role in personal identity when it marks one group off from another, particularly in situations of group competition or conflict. In such cases, conformity to group norms reinforces a sense of identity and strengthens internal solidarity and the boundaries between groups.[8] Conformity then becomes a sign of virtue, one that differentiates and contributes to a sense of superiority in the face of the competing group. Indeed, articulating a different set of values or ideology can be a crucial part of the conflict or competition. As recent work in the sociology of culture suggests, culture can be seen as more than a "passive" instrument, internalized by members of a group (Swidler 1986; Wuthnow 1987); it can be an active agent, manipulated by members of a group to strengthen the group's position. In this case, cultural prescriptions or proscriptions take on a special force and play an important role in shaping behaviour.

### The External Environment

Recent efforts to understand the influence of culture on demographic behaviour have often started from a critique of economic models, with the unfortunate effect of polarizing the two approaches (Pollak and Watkins 1993). Yet, any realistic assessment of cultural influences must recognize that the cultural system interacts with other elements of social structure, helping to shape aspects of social organization while being itself refashioned over time by economic, environmental and political forces. Studying the effects of culture in a specific setting, then, requires examining how cultural influences are mediated by the economic and political setting of society. While the crucial issues will vary from one situation to another, two general points can be mentioned here: the "fit" between religious values and material interests, and the relations between churches and other institutions in society.

The relationship between cultural values and economic interests is most commonly approached from an assumption of conflict between the two. For example, is the commitment to cultural values strong enough to lead people to act against their economic interests? The two need not, of course, be opposed. Indeed, Notestein (1945) assumed that, in the pre-transition era, they reinforced one another. Cultural values that favoured large families and/or prohibited contraception supported behaviour that was beneficial to society and, in most circumstances, the individual as well. At the same time, it is reasonable to assume that the greater the conflict between the material interests of individuals and the values of their group, the greater the likelihood that the values will be ignored or, more likely, change in response to circumstance. The now near-universal acceptance of some form of fertility control in technologically advanced societies would seem to support this point. Seldom, however, do individuals find themselves in a situation where following a normatively approved demographic pattern brings dire consequences. The path followed will certainly have implications for the people themselves and the society as a whole, but only rarely will it place individuals in positions where conforming to social traditions threatens their livelihood. Hajnal (1982), for example, has argued that the convention in Western European societies of setting up an independent household at the time of marriage had far-reaching demographic consequences, most notably concerning age at marriage and proportions marrying. Following the norm may well have entailed significant costs for at least some individuals – delayed sexual gratification, a longer period of submission to parents, or periods of domestic service to amass the resources needed to marry. It probably also brought certain rewards: young people no doubt felt that a separate household would bring greater happiness to them as a couple than might be achieved living under a parent's roof. It did not, however, place people in an intolerable situation that forced them to choose between observing the rules of the group and prosperity or personal happiness. Rather, the broadly agreed-upon rules of social life are likely to influence the strategies people follow in dealing with their economic and social environment (Kreager 1986). As Swidler has argued, "a culture has enduring effects on those who hold it ... by providing the characteristic repertoire from which they build lines of action" (1986, 284). The challenge for demographers, then, is to understand how culture shapes the demographic responses of individuals to the demands and limitations placed on them by the environment in which they live out their lives.

The second issue of general importance concerns the relationship between churches and other institutions in society. As was the case with values, religious and non-religious institutions may reinforce one another or be at odds. This issue is critical to this study because the relationship between church and state in Alsace, and indeed throughout much of Europe, changed dramatically during this period. Certainly in the seventeenth and eighteenth centuries, church and state worked together in many regions of Europe with each drawing benefit from the actions of the other (Hsia 1989). Churches were often seen by civil rulers as instruments to discipline populations and promote obedience to civil authority.[9] With the growing power of national states, however, this relationship was often transformed into one of opposition, and the nineteenth century was characterized by simmering conflict as the new state apparatus sought to intervene in areas of social life previously dominated by religious authorities. The situation was even more complex in areas like Alsace where civil authorities carried on relationships with competing religious denominations. While a "union of throne and altar" might be expected to exact greater compliance with official standards of conduct, the implications of conflict between religious and civil authority are not so clear. Active opposition to religious teachings might weaken conformity and would certainly provide individuals at odds with the values of their religion the chance to strike out on new paths. It is also possible, however, that civic repression would increase solidarity among religious followers, thereby strengthening the commitment of members to the teachings of the faith. As I will argue later on, evidence suggests that the repressive treatment of the Catholic Church in Alsace during the French Revolution had just such an effect. Several prominent examples from present-day societies, perhaps most notably the role of the Catholic Church in Eastern Europe, point to this possibility as well (Michel 1991; Weigel 1992). The uncertainty inherent in the often complex relationships among social institutions underlines the need for demographers to attend to the interplay of forces in the societies they study.

CONCLUSION

This chapter highlights some of the most significant ideas advanced in recent discussions of the role of culture as a determinant of demographic behaviour. I have also outlined the conditions under which religious values are particularly likely to influence the population patterns of society. It is worth repeating that the need for a more fully developed approach to culture in demography does not imply the rejection of theories that attribute a role to other variables, particularly economic ones. It would be a mistake to substitute a univariate model based on culture for one that focuses almost exclusively on economics. The position advanced here simply argues that while economic factors shape aspects of demographic behaviour, they do not determine the particular patterns that will be followed. Technological growth and a high standard of living may make it unlikely that a society will be marked by high fertility. But just how low fertility rates are likely to be, whether marriage is universal or not, whether most childbearing occurs inside or outside marital unions are issues that vary significantly among advanced industrial societies. Culture almost certainly plays a role in shaping these patterns, just as it did under different economic and environmental circumstances in the past.

More specifically, religion can be a powerful cultural influence on demographic behaviour. This is especially likely to be the case when several conditions are met:

1 The religion pays particular attention to demographic questions. This implies the construction of a set of religious values that promote or prohibit forms of behaviour that have demographic consequences. As was emphasized above, this entails not only rules regarding the permissibility of contraception, but the whole set of teachings and norms that touch on family life, gender roles, sexuality, and related issues.
2 The religion constructs a set of institutions that can convey the teachings to the faithful, and a set of sanctions that will promote compliance and punish deviance.
3 The religion forms an important part of the personal identity of its members. This, in turn, is most likely to occur under conditions of inter-group competition and/or conflict. In such situations, the rewards for compliance and the punishments for deviations are likely to be greater.

As the material in subsequent chapters makes clear, these conditions prevailed to a remarkable extent in Alsace in the period from 1750 to 1870 and, in fact, beyond. The next chapter provides a brief overview of the history of the region and the characteristics of the communities studied. The following four chapters give a detailed analysis of demographic patterns in the region, emphasizing the differences between the Lutheran and Catholic communities, but also touching on the role played by other social and economic factors. Finally, in the last chapter, I examine the evolution of religious identity and religious conflict in the region and demonstrate how this influenced the behavioural patterns of the two communities.

# CHAPTER TWO

# Alsace: Economic and Social Structures

## POLITICAL INTEGRATION

The French region of Alsace comprises the *départements* of the Bas-Rhin and Haut-Rhin, stretching from the mountains of the Jura in the south to the German Palatinate in the north, and from the Vosges Mountains in the west to the Rhine (see map). Although the precise boundaries are easily defined today, the region has only gradually taken shape through a long evolutionary process. War, revolution, armistices and peace treaties have redefined not only the territory of the region, but its political and administrative structures as well. With several interruptions, most of the region's current area has been a part of France for more than three centuries. Yet for an even longer period before this, Alsace was a part of the Holy Roman Empire. Indeed, from the fall of Rome until the Thirty Years War in 1618, Alsace was culturally and economically, as well as politically, a part of the Germanic world. During this long period of development, the features that even today mark the unique culture of the region were etched.

The Treaty of Westphalia, signed in 1648, ended the Thirty Years War and assigned most of what is now Alsace to the French Crown. It was an outcome not clearly sought by either party (Dreyfus 1979, 151). France evinced little interest in annexing the territory until the late stages of the peace negotiations. Preoccupied by its continuing struggle with Spain, France's main interest lay in controlling the flow of traffic through the region and along the Rhine and in opening a gateway to Germany. Its original intention was to hold the region as a fief, thereby giving the French king a seat in the Diet of the Holy Roman Empire. For Alsatians as well, union with France was not a desired outcome. Prior to the outbreak of the war in 1618, the region was a patchwork of seigneurial lands and free cities loosely attached to the Empire. Efforts by the Habsburgs and their Austrian allies to unify the region and tighten the bonds to the Empire provoked considerable unease, particularly in the independent cities of Strasbourg and Mulhouse, which not only jealously guarded their independence but, having converted to Protestantism, also feared religious repression. When Sweden under Gustavus Adolphus entered the war against the emperor and Swedish troops moved into Alsace, most of the nobility in the region moved to distance itself from the Empire. Protestant seigneurs rallied to the Swedish side and the free (and Protestant) city of Strasbourg broke with the emperor (Livet 1970a, 274). The death of Gustavus Adolphus in 1632, followed by a series of military victories by the forces of the emperor, caused considerable dismay among the nobility, and they sought the protection of the king of France.

Beginning with the Protestant count of Hanau-Lichtenberg, and spreading gradually throughout the region, a series of agreements were signed with the French Crown, and by 1636, virtually the entire region was under French protection. These agreements were explicitly designed to be short-term (Parker 1984, 146), but as negotiations to end the war proceeded, the French gradually came to see the value of extending their authority over the area, and when the Treaty of Westphalia was signed, France was given jurisdiction over nearly all of Alsace except for the cities of Strasbourg and Mulhouse.

If France now had title to Alsace, exerting effective control and integrating the new province into the kingdom proved a difficult task. The diverse status of the various regions under the Empire meant that no uniform administrative system was in place that the French could take over and turn to their advantage. The devastation of the war further complicated matters, adding basic problems of feeding the population and restoring economic activity to those related to the change in administration. Moreover, the ambiguity of the treaty, particularly concerning the status of the formerly independent cities, encouraged resistance to the new order in some regions.

In response, French officials moved slowly. Their basic strategy was to leave local institutions and customs in place except where pressing need forced change (Livet 1970a). This did much to allay fears among the local nobility, particularly among Protestants who feared heavy-handed attempts to restore the power of the Catholic Church supported by "his most Christian Majesty." Then, in 1672, war between France and Holland left Alsace in the midst of hostilities once again. The fighting caused both the Crown and the Alsatian nobility to see the advantages in a closer relationship. For the French, the military value of the region, and particularly its vital position on the Rhine, grew in importance. For the indigenous nobility, again exposed to devastation from conflicting armies crossing their territory, the benefits of French military protection became clearer. The result was a strengthening of French control. Strasbourg finally accepted incorporation into France in 1681. Mulhouse, on the other hand, remained a part of the Swiss confederation until 1798, when a combination of economic pressure and popular enthusiasm for the French Revolution resulted in this last major part of present-day Alsace joining with France (Oberlé 1985).

Now more closely united to France, the region enjoyed almost uninterrupted peace throughout the late seventeenth and eighteenth centuries. During this period, French influence spread gradually, though the region remained distinctive in many ways. When Strasbourg joined France in 1681, it became the administrative centre of the region (Kintz 1981a). As a result, a variety of French officials took up residence in the city, changing the nature of the local elite. While efforts to establish French as the working language of new institutions fell short of success, being bilingual now became a valuable tool for a successful career. As a frontier area, the army was conspicuous, and the soldiers and officers from the interior also served to extend the French influence. As the eighteenth century progressed, the privileged classes began to feel a stronger attachment to the kingdom, earlier among Catholic notables, later among the Protestant elite. Among the ordinary people, however, French influence was muted. German remained the common language and, religion aside, the French policy of using existing local institutions meant that the average person was far less affected by the change in sovereignty than might have been expected. Thus, on the eve of the French Revolution, the province, though now firmly linked to France, remained a distinctive part of the kingdom.

In contrast to many other parts of France, the local clergy and nobility had good reason to support the Crown as the crises preceding the Revolution began to unfold. The Catholic hierarchy, preoccupied by the continuing struggle with Protestantism, needed the assistance of the French monarchy. The nobility had also benefitted from the policies of the Crown and had no history of involvement in efforts to weaken the monarchy (Marx 1970). Nevertheless, as the Revolution progressed, Alsace, even more than most other regions, was transformed. The revolutionary drive to centralize and harmonize administrative procedures across the country had far-reaching effects on a province that had retained a special status. Following the historic division between Upper and Lower Alsace, the region was divided into two *départements*, the Bas-Rhin with Strasbourg as its administrative centre, and the Haut-Rhin with Colmar as its *chef-lieu*. The Catholic Church too was reorganized, with the boundaries of dioceses redrawn to fit the new limits of the *départements* and the links to the episcopal centres of Spire and Basel, previously responsible for regions of the province, were severed. Protestants gained equal status with Catholics under the new, secularized regime. Perhaps most importantly, a customs barrier was established on the Rhine, completing the economic integration of Alsace while at the same time weakening its role as an *entrepôt* and point of transit for goods moving along the Rhine. These changes drew the province even more closely to France and eliminated some of the distinctive characteristics that had set it apart from the interior (Marx 1970).

The local population responded positively if not enthusiastically to all these changes. The peasantry, in particular, suffering after a run of bad harvests and crushed under the weight of increasing taxes and seigneurial dues, welcomed the new regime. Among the bourgeoisie of the towns, the Revolution found fairly broad support. Of special importance in Alsace was the government policy to sell the land held by the Catholic Church and noble emigrants, the *biens nationaux*. The Church was a substantial landholder under the old regime with the bishop of Strasbourg being the single largest landholder in Lower Alsace. Altogether, the Church probably controlled about one-quarter of the land in what became the *Département du Bas-Rhin* (Marx 1970, 57). Selling off these lands thus held the promise of significant social and economic change. Both farmers, albeit the wealthier ones, and city-dwellers responded enthusiastically. There was some hesitation among Catholics in buying up land seized from the Church, but this dissipated over time and Catholic farmers eventually purchased Church lands "second-hand" from speculators who had snapped them up initially. This, combined with favourable harvests in 1790 and 1791, built support for the new order among the common people.

As elsewhere in France, however, support began to weaken as the Revolution continued and produced more radical policies. Critical for Alsace, who as a frontier region, had suffered grievously in the past, was the outbreak of war. In October of 1793, Austro-Prussian forces entered from the north and were soon at the gates of Strasbourg. The arrival of Louis-Antoine Saint-Just, leading member of the Committee of Public Safety, led to the reorganization of the army of the Rhine, and the foreign troops were driven from Alsace by the end of the year. But the war had other effects on the populace, some of which would leave long-lasting scars. As elsewhere, the peasantry resented the conscription of their sons and the requisitioning of food and live-stock for the army (Palmer 1969, 177–201). In Alsace, however, the issue was complicated by language. Revolutionary officials sent from Paris had no knowledge of the local language, while the ability to speak French was still largely limited to the more privileged elements of the population. As supplies began to run short and peasant resis-tance to further demands sharpened, the accusation that elements of the local population were unpatriotic and even traitorous came to be heard (Dreyfus 1979, 195–8). An additional source of contention was the treatment of the Catholic Church. Although many peasants had suffered at the hands of ecclesiastical landlords and had purchased church lands, the increasing repression of the Church provoked a strong reaction among a population known for its devotion, and fur-ther dampened support for the revolutionary regime. Nevertheless, the effects of the Revolution on the area cannot be underestimated: the redistribution of land had lasting economic consequences, and above all, the radical political and social changes the Revolution unleashed accelerated the integration of Alsace into France.

The Napoleonic era is seen, with justice, as a prosperous one for Alsace, and the emperor (as later, Napoleon III) enjoyed considerable support in the region. The reasons are not hard to find. Although men continued to be recruited into the army, the region was largely spared direct involvement in the fighting. The new administrative regime succeeded in producing order and reasonably good govern-ment. Napoleon's negotiations with the Church, culminating in the Concordat of 1802, provided a new framework for relations between Catholics and Protestants. Best of all, the region saw considerable economic development: Napoleon's continental blockade increased Strasbourg's role as a point of entry into France and provided new opportunities for Alsatian industrialists, especially in the rapidly growing textile industries in the Mulhouse region, to ship their prod-ucts to the interior (Ellis 1981). This not only enriched the populace but also tightened the economic bonds between Alsace and the rest of France. In particular, stronger links developed between the Mulhou-sian industrialists and Paris-based financiers (Schmitt 1980).

Not surprisingly, then, the collapse of Napoleon's empire caused dismay in Alsace. Aside from the feared economic consequences, the region had once again to deal with military invasion; from 1813 to 1818, foreign troops were once again on Alsatian territory. In addi-tion, the spectre of severance from France was raised throughout negotiations. Nothing came of this, however, and the region was con-fronted with adapting to the Restoration. This provoked particular fear on the question of land ownership. Many farmers worried that the land purchased under the Revolution might be taken away from them and handed back to the Church and nobility. A number of claims were filed and some upheld, but no significant change in land-holding occurred. As a result, the population gradually adjusted to the latest regime even if it did not gain widespread support.

France, of course, experienced unparalleled political turbulence during the nineteenth century, and as an integral part of the country, Alsace could not help but be affected. More significant than the polit-ical turmoil, however, was the gradual growth of the administrative apparatus of the modern state. Many of Napoleon's initiatives were preserved and extended by subsequent regimes, and the Napoleonic code, military conscription, and the spread of public schooling helped to reshape the lives and habits of the people. As the state gradually expanded its role in society, ordinary Alsatians were drawn into closer contact with the French nation. To be sure, progress in this area should not be overestimated. Alsace remained distinctive in many ways, most of all in terms of language. Many French regions continued to be marked by local dialects well into the nineteenth cen-tury (Weber 1976), but the fact that Alsatians spoke a German dialect linked them to Germany's large and growing population and influen-tial culture. French language and culture made noticeable inroads in the nineteenth century, especially in the cities and among the elites. Bilingualism was now the *sine qua non* of a successful career in poli-tics, administration or commerce. Among ordinary working people, however, and especially in rural areas, the use of French remained limited, to say the least. The public school was seen as the best vehicle for the spread of French but progress was slow (Vogler 1993, 282). Getting children into school and finding a sufficient number of teach-ers qualified to give instruction in French were formidable obstacles. As late as 1859, a school inspector in the area complained that "too often French is the language of the school only on the day we visit" (quoted in L'Huillier, 1970, 428).[1] In addition to the practical difficul-ties, the spread of French encountered ideological obstacles as well. Part of the intelligentsia strongly supported retaining German as both an essential part of the regional identity and as a means of making Alsace a bridge between French and German cultures. Moreover, the churches, both Catholic and Protestant, also supported the use of German. For the Catholic clergy, French culture was tainted by ratio-nalism and atheism and the local language was seen as a way of solidifying the faith. The Protestant clergy felt an attachment to the language of Luther and to the German liturgy that had developed since the Reformation (Vogler 1994, 215), and the fact that many of the Protestant clergy had studied in Germany or Switzerland strengthened their attachment to the language as well.

## POPULATION GROWTH IN ALSACE, 1648–1870

Although the historical literature on Alsace is exceptionally rich, there has been relatively little research on the demographic evolution of the region. A number of studies of the social and economic development of Alsace have touched on population questions (Boehler 1995; Juillard 1953; Kintz 1977; Leuilliot 1959; Hau 1987; Marx 1974; Peter 1995), but, in contrast to many other French regions, analysis of demographic change has been limited. Virtually none has employed family reconstitution methods to examine the components of demographic change. As a result, our knowledge of population movements in the area is lacking in detail.

The outbreak of the Thirty Years War clearly marked a turning point in the demographic history of Alsace. The period before the war was a prosperous one, leading to a relatively high density of population, but the devastation wrought by the war led to demographic collapse. The few parish registers that survived the period show a huge surplus of deaths, especially during the 1630s when several hard winters added to the effects of war and plague. Writing in 1636, the curé of the parish of Dambach-la-Ville noted that those who were not dying by the sword were being carried off by famine or plague (quoted in Schmitt 1983). In some regions, whole villages were abandoned. Boehler's analysis of twenty-four villages in the Sundgau, located in the southernmost part of the region, indicates that the population declined by 75% (Boehler 1995, 182). For the region as a whole, as much as half the population may have disappeared.

With the return of peace and the departure of foreign troops, economic production began to revert to normal levels and the population increased rapidly. Parish registers for the late seventeenth century show an excess of births to which was added a significant number of immigrants. Union with France brought a number of French officials as well as military personnel, though they tended to concentrate in the cities. More substantial was the inflow of Swiss and German immigrants who helped to repeople the countryside. The combination of natural increase and immigration probably raised the population total of the region to somewhere near 350,000 by the end of the seventeenth century (Dreyfus 1979, 166; Boehler 1995, 371).

We are better informed about the demographic pattern of the eighteenth century, though again knowledge of the specific components of population growth is limited. Nevertheless, existing studies clearly indicate that population grew steadily throughout the century. Among the best studies is Marx's 1974 analysis of seventy-eight villages in lower Alsace. His data show that 80% of the villages saw their population at least double in size between 1723 and 1791, and about one-quarter had their population triple. Juillard (1953), on the basis of a smaller sample, also sees significant growth, and suggests that after 1766, growth of about 1% per annum was the rule in the countryside of lower Alsace. Our own analysis of four villages shows a similar pattern of growth with deaths exceeding births in each decade of the period 1750–90. This growth seems to have been based on a high rate of fertility and moderately high mortality. Marx suggests that in the early 1780s, the crude birth rate was somewhat over forty per thousand while the death rate was near thirty per thousand. The cities also experienced significant growth throughout the eighteenth century. Strasbourg grew from around 28,000 in the 1690s to nearly 50,000 at the time of the French Revolution (Dreyer-Roos 1969). As a consequence, the population of the region reached approximately 650,000 on the eve of the French Revolution.

Among other changes introduced by the Revolution were procedures that greatly increased our knowledge of population trends. A civil system for registering births, marriages and deaths was begun in 1793, and though it was several years before it was fully functional (Bernardin 1990), the result was a considerable improvement in demographic accounting. The revolutionary period also saw the first tentative attempts at carrying out censuses. The accuracy of these early surveys left something to be desired, but they began the process which would lead to high-quality, quinquennial censuses later in the nineteenth century. Surprisingly, given these data, even in the nineteenth century our knowledge of population trends is limited to the broad outlines. It seems clear that the disruption caused by the Revolution and Napoleonic Wars that followed slowed population growth, in part through emigration. Nevertheless, the population of the region as a whole stood at approximately 825,000 in 1815.

The years 1815–70 were marked by constant population growth. In contrast to many other regions of France, where fertility control spread rapidly and birth rates declined, there is little evidence of any significant downturn in the birth rate for Alsace (Coale and Treadway 1986). Mortality rates, too, remained high, with the infant mortality rate among the highest in France. In addition to high mortality, the countryside continued to be marked by significant emigration. Much of this flowed to the cities, Strasbourg and Mulhouse in particular, but, again in contrast to other French regions, Alsace was a key point of departure for North America. Thus, despite continued high fertility, the population of the two Alsatian *départements* stood at only 1.1 million at the time of the 1866 census, the last one conducted before the transfer of sovereignty to Germany.

## THE ALSATIAN ECONOMY, 1750–1870

Understanding the structure of the Alsatian economy is critical for our analysis of demographic change. Although Alsace covers an area of just over 8000 square kilometres, its economy, particularly in the late eighteenth and nineteenth centuries, was characterized by a remarkable diversity. Throughout the period of this study, agriculture was dominant, as was true in most other regions of Europe. Yet the agricultural sector was itself diverse and underwent far-reaching changes. Prior to the mid-eighteenth century, the majority of the land was committed to cereals with a smaller but important segment dedicated to wine production. The bulk of the territory followed the traditional three-field system with a smaller area in the north relying on a biennial system of rotation (Juillard 1953; Boehler 1995, 733). In the grain-growing regions, a variety of crops was grown including rye, oats, and wheat, though the production of wheat, once seen as a luxury crop, increased throughout the eighteenth century. The major wine-growing area was located along the eastern slopes of the Vosges Mountains, though some wine was also produced in the northern region bordering the German Palatinate.

Landholding patterns varied considerably across the area depending on the quality of land and the kind of crops grown. By far the richest area was the fertile plain to the west of Strasbourg known as the Kochersberg. Here cereals predominated under the control of small owner-operators. Although the size of holdings obviously varied, the range was relatively narrow with few large landholders and few landless workers. In areas with poorer quality soil, such as the marshy region known as the Ried which runs north-south along the Rhine, there was more diversity. Poorer grains such as barley were more popular, and there was greater variation in the size of holdings with an identifiable class of large landowners and a significant population of landless or near-landless workers who often supplemented their earnings with non-agricultural work (Juillard 1953). In the wine-growing regions, the intense labour required meant that holdings were generally small. Beside this class of small-holders existed a significant group of day-workers (*journaliers* or *Taglöhner*) hired to help with the pruning and harvesting of the crop. While keeping in mind this variability, it is nevertheless fair to conclude that, in contrast to many other regions in France and the neighbouring German states, Alsace was marked by relatively high levels of productivity and peasant ownership (Juillard 1953; Marx 1974; Boehler 1995). These characteristics would remain despite the wide-ranging changes that began to occur around the middle of the eighteenth century.

As with any such process, the agricultural revolution in Alsace was a gradual one. Yet Etienne Juillard, the foremost analyst of agriculture in the region, felt that 1750 marked a turning point. He points to three significant developments which transformed the agricultural system and allowed it to support a much larger population. The first was the gradual introduction of new crops, especially the potato. Although known in the area since the seventeenth century, it was only after 1750 that it began to be widely planted and used for both human and animal consumption. Second, the introduction of fodder crops led over time to the elimination of the fallow field. This in turn had important implications for both productivity and social organization. The spread of fodder crops and consequent feeding of animals in the stables rather than using open pastures boosted productivity. With more land in use, more grain was produced and, at the same time, the supply of meat increased while the price declined. This change in feeding methods led to another change as well, the sell-off or renting of the commons. Small landholders were the most eager to purchase or rent these lands that communities now saw as disposable. This trend, along with increased clearing of forest lands and draining of marshes in the region by the Rhine, significantly increased the amount of arable land. Taken together, these changes may not have constituted a revolution in agricultural practice but they did materially increase production while at the same time strengthening the hold of owner-operators. Perhaps most importantly, they allowed the land to support a growing population. As a result, Juillard (1953) sees the century 1750–1850 as constituting the apogee of the traditional system of agriculture.

Although small owners played a larger role in the agrarian system of Alsace than in many other areas, this did not necessarily translate into a higher standard of living. While the high level of ownership allowed many to escape rent payments, in the period before the Revolution peasants staggered under a heavy weight of taxes, seigneurial dues, and tithes (Marx 1974). Moreover, while productivity was high, high population density limited the benefits accruing to the rural population. Revolutionary legislation eliminated some but not all of these problems. The abolition of seigneurial dues and the tithe eased the fiscal burden, and, as we have seen, the sale of lands held by the Church and noble émigrés allowed many peasants to increase the size of their holdings (Marx 1974). Nevertheless, continued population growth depressed the standard of living of rural dwellers. As Hau and Hau (1981) have shown, though output per hectare in Alsace was among the highest in France, output per employed person in agriculture was far lower. By the mid-nineteenth century the system based on intensive land use and abundant labour began to founder. The rural exodus, which had already begun, gathered strength with the increasing mechanization of production. To be sure, the area continued to be an important producer right up until the First World War, but the balance of economic activity began to shift away from agriculture towards industrial production.

The centrepiece of industrial production in Alsace was unquestionably the textile industry. As early as the eighteenth century, Mulhouse was a centre of textile production. The first factory in the city began operations in 1746 and was quickly followed by others. By 1787, the number of firms in the city itself had grown to twenty-six (Oberlé 1985, 186), and others began to spread into the surrounding regions of the Haut-Rhin. The factory at Husseren-Wesserling, one of the communities included in our analysis, was established in 1762. From its beginnings the industry had a high level of technical sophistication and a concern for high-quality production. Dominated by a relatively small group of Calvinist families and buoyed by strong financial backing from Basel and other parts of Switzerland, Mulhouse soon came to be known as the "Manchester" of the continent.

The textile industry in the last half of the eighteenth century was marked by rapid growth but by considerable turbulence as well (Levy 1912). The factory at Wesserling, for example, passed through a number of changes in ownership and personnel (Schmitt 1980). Nevertheless, the base was created for extraordinary growth in the nineteenth century. Hau (1987) saw the decades 1800–40 as the highpoint of the textile industry. In the late eighteenth century, the industry had relied heavily on the immigration of skilled labour, first from Switzerland and later from Germany. But in the nineteenth century, it was local workers who held the dominant position. Indeed, Hau (1987, 89) estimated that the textile industry was able to absorb virtually all of the population increase of the Haut-Rhin in the years from 1800 to 1840. And, while the bulk of production was located in the southern *département*, the industry attracted a substantial number of migrants from the Bas-Rhin as well. According to his estimates, by 1844 as much as 17% of the labour force in Alsace was employed in the textile industry (Hau 1987, 89). At the same time, the industry accounted for over 60% of exports from the region.

Two characteristics of the industry proved of particular importance. First, though the business was largely built around the production of printed calicoes, an extensive operation of spinning and weaving operations developed to feed production. In the countryside around Mulhouse, this entailed a large amount of domestic labour. Isaac Koechlin, a member of the great family of Mulhousian capitalists, noted in an 1850 report on operations at his factory in the town of Willer-sur-Thur that the factory employed over 1000 employees, then added as a footnote that it provided work for another 150–200 who worked in their homes (ADHR 9M 21). Similarly, the Gros, Davilier and Roman factory in Wesserling was a large source of employment for those in the surrounding villages in the canton of Saint-Amarin, and even some living in villages on the western slopes of the Vosges in Lorraine.

A second critical feature of the industry was the commitment to technological improvement (Fohlen 1956; Landes 1970). While not as productive as the English, Mulhousian capitalists were leaders on the continent in the development of new techniques of production. The *Bulletin de la Société Industrielle de Mulhouse*, begun in 1828, published a stream of technical articles on topics relevant to the industry and demonstrated the commitment of the Calvinist entrepreneurs to introducing new products and production techniques. In this they were no doubt aided by a relatively high-quality work force. While some skilled workers continued to be brought in from Switzerland, Germany, and even England, by the nineteenth century local workers had developed a high level of skill. Moreover, the local population was highly literate. In 1866, for example, recruits into the French Army from the Bas-Rhin had the highest level of literacy in all France while those from the Haut-Rhin ranked eighth of eighty-seven *départements* (Hau 1987). In spite of this, the industry was marked by relatively low wages. The textile factories of Normandy and the Nord, not to mention the English industry, paid substantially higher salaries. As was noted above, high population density in rural areas had depressed rural incomes and this apparently carried over into industry as well (Hau 1987). With a large surplus population to draw from, mill owners were under little pressure to raise wages in order to attract labour. As a result, the industry reaped substantial profits, particularly in the first half of the century, and this in turn provided a base for further investment.

While textiles dominated *grande industrie* throughout the period of this study, the nineteenth century saw the growth of several other significant initiatives in industry, particularly in metallurgy. Concentrated in the Bas-Rhin, they benefitted from both the increasing demand for machinery in the textile business as well as the growth of railways. In addition, expansion in both the tobacco and brewing industries in the latter half of the nineteenth century provided significant employment to those leaving the land. In the northern part of Alsace, however, small industry was far more important in providing work for the surplus population of the countryside. Centred in rural areas and often combined with work in agriculture, Stoskopf (1987, 196) estimated it may have provided work for as many as one in five workers in the 1860s. The type of work involved varied from that of small craftsmen – shoemakers, blacksmiths, millers – working for their neighbours, to veritable industries that from small workshops produced goods for regional and even international consumption. Most important for this study was the rural branch of the textile industry. Alongside the great factories of the Mulhouse region, the textile business flourished around the small town of Sainte-Marie-aux-Mines, located near the border of the two Alsatian *départements*. Up until the last decades of the nineteenth century, when the industry finally succumbed to lower-cost competition, the small firms in the area managed to carve out a distinctive niche within the market by concentrating on the production of goods subject to rapid change in fashion. The absence of investment in costly machinery allowed them to adjust quickly to produce relatively small quantities of goods that fit with current fashions (Stroh 1914; Stoskopf 1987). The industry was organized along what might be called classic "protoindustrial" lines (Mendels 1972, 1984; Medick 1981). *Fabricants* from Sainte-Marie travelled to the surrounding villages, bringing with them the raw materials and instructions for the workers and collecting the finished product. In the villages they might deal directly with workers or go through a local contact who acted as a depot for the area. In the villages themselves, the industry was organized rather loosely. The individual family was the basic unit of production, but family members might choose to work in their own home or, if they lacked space, join with others in a common workshop. The owner of the workshop would charge rent and might also serve as an agent for the *fabricant*, but otherwise exercised no direct control over the workers who were free to come and go as they pleased. Families varied in terms of their involvement in the industry (Stroh 1914; Juillard 1953). Some worked full-time in the trade while others combined weaving with agricultural work, either on their own plot of land or as a hired labourer, especially at harvest time. Even within families, the degree of participation varied. Often it was the mother and children who worked for the *fabricant* while the father devoted his efforts to the land or another trade. The numbers involved varied with the ups and downs of the industry, but it continued to be an important source of rural employment throughout the period of this study.

## RELIGIOUS CHANGE AND CONFLICT

Religion plays a critical role in this study and its effects on demographic behaviour will be discussed at length. Here our goal is to provide a brief history of the evolution of religious organizations and religious conflict in the region. Alsace was among the first regions of Europe to be deeply touched by the Reformation, and Strasbourg was an important centre of development for the new religious ideas (Strohl 1950; Abray 1985). Sympathy for Luther's teachings grew quickly in Strasbourg among both lay people and the clergy, and the efforts of influential figures such as Martin Bucer led to widespread acceptance of reform. By 1529, Strasbourg was fully committed to Luther's ideas. Support for the Reform also gained strength in Wissembourg in the north and in Colmar, while in Mulhouse the definitive break with Catholicism occurred in 1529 and was followed by adoption of a statement of beliefs influenced by the teachings of Ulrich Zwingli. The success of the Reformation in the towns exceeded its influence in the rural areas. Protestantism did establish roots in parts of the countryside, especially in the north and central regions, but the majority of the rural population remained committed to Catholicism. The religious geography of the region was largely set with the signing of the Peace of Augsburg in 1555. By establishing the principle *cuius regno, ejus religio*, the treaty solidified the religious attachment of communities. Strasbourg and Mulhouse remained Protestant as did perhaps one-third of rural communities (Strohl 1950, 107). Aside from the region around Mulhouse, this entailed a commitment to an orthodox Lutheranism as established in the Confession of Augsburg. The remainder of the countryside, much of which belonged to the diocese of Strasbourg or to powerful religious communities such as the Abbey of Murbach, and many of the smaller towns continued to be Catholic.

What this division of territory meant for the common people in the initial stages of the Reformation is hard to decipher. Châtellier (1981) claims that religious differences were not widely felt in the early decades following the Reformation, and that close relations, including intermarriage, between Catholics and Protestants continued for some time. It is certain that religious authorities in the new Protestant areas struggled for a long time to eliminate religious practices and traditions that reflected older, Catholic influence. The centrality of religion to political and military struggles in Europe inevitably led to a hardening of differences however, and these were exacerbated by the Thirty Years War which, as we have seen, devastated the area.

The union of the region with France further complicated the situation. Although the French Crown had been content to lend support to Protestant nobles in their struggle with the emperor, on gaining control of Alsace the new administration moved to strengthen the position of Catholicism. This did not involve the direct suppression of Protestantism – freedom of worship was guaranteed and Alsace was excluded from the effects of the Revocation of the Edict of Nantes. It did, however, lead to a series of initiatives which threatened the Protestant position. Foremost among them was the introduction of what came to be called the *simultaneum*. This practice entailed granting Catholics use of Protestant churches in villages where at least seven Catholic families lived. In Strasbourg and other Protestant towns, Protestant domination of political and administrative functions was limited by the *alternation*, which directed that many positions be held alternately by a Catholic and Protestant, while in the countryside administrative offices had to be filled by Catholics (Livet 1956, 449). Conversions to Catholicism were encouraged and rewarded while conversions to Protestantism were punished by banishment and seizure of goods. Children of mixed marriages had now to be raised as Catholics and illegitimate children were to be baptized in the Catholic faith. Added to this was the growing strength of the Counter-Reformation. As early as 1580, the Jesuit order was established at Molsheim, a town some twenty kilometres from Strasbourg, and played a critical role in the renewal of Catholicism in the region. The number of conversions to Catholicism grew and whole villages once again shifted their religious affiliation. The immigration of French administrative and military officials and Catholic clergy further consolidated the position of Catholicism even in Strasbourg, the bastion of Lutheranism. Entirely Protestant when united with France in 1681, by the middle of the eighteenth century the city's Catholic population had surpassed the Lutheran total (Dreyer-Roos 1969, 98).

The turmoil of the revolutionary period created grave difficulties for both major denominations, though its effects were greater for the Catholic community. The seizure of church property did not extend to the Protestant churches, while the civil constitution of the clergy drove large numbers of Catholic priests out of the area. The Bas-Rhin led France in the proportion of priests who refused to take the oath pledging allegiance under the new constitution (Epp 1990), and the increasingly radical legislation enacted under the Terror hardened resistance in the Catholic community and weakened support for the Revolution among Lutherans as well. The Concordat signed in 1801 between Napoleon and Pope Pius VII established a new set of ground rules for the Catholic Church in the region. The Church recovered quickly from the devastation of the revolutionary period and carried out an extensive reorganization which tightened its links with the Church in France (Muller 1986). Prior to the Revolution, the territory of Alsace had been carved up among four different dioceses, two of which were centred outside of the region. After 1802, the entire region was attached to the diocese of Strasbourg while the territory in Baden, which had previously belonged to the diocese, was transferred to the diocese of Freiburg. Religious orders operating in the region now had to be linked to a French motherhouse. The Catholic population continued to grow as well, partly as a result of immigration, and partly due to a more rapid rate of natural increase. At the beginning of the nineteenth century, approximately two-thirds of the population was Catholic; by 1870, this had risen to almost three-quarters.

The increasing integration of the region into France had important consequences for the Lutheran Church as well. Although the link to German culture remained strong, French administrative control influenced the evolution of the Protestant churches. At Napoleon's urging, a new, more hierarchical form of administration was established culminating in the General Consistory (Vogler 1994, 196). The use of French within the Church, though modest, increased and, perhaps most importantly, the proportion of Protestant pastors trained in Germany declined steadily (Lienhard 1981). The Concordat provided a framework for stability in Protestant-Catholic relations but certainly did not eliminate conflict. Competition and suspicion continued to prevail, occasionally breaking out into open conflict. The effect was to produce a high level of religious consciousness among members of both denominations.

## THE COMMUNITIES IN THIS STUDY

The demographic analysis presented in the chapters to follow is largely based on a family reconstitution study of five villages located in the countryside of Alsace.[2] Analogous to tracing one's family tree, the method of family reconstitution makes use of religious and civil registers of births, marriages and deaths to recreate the history of family units. Important as this technique has been in expanding our knowledge of populations in the past, it is not without its limitations.

The strict rules used in deciding on the families to be included in the analysis mean that a significant proportion of the population is excluded from study. This is particularly true of mobile families and may well be true of disadvantaged groups in the community as well. The absence of such families, who may differ in important ways from the more stable families of the community, leaves the analysis with only a partial view of the demographic life of the community. Beyond that, the community itself may be unrepresentative of the larger regions or nations we wish to study. The extraordinary amount of time required to assemble data for even relatively small communities has tended to limit reconstitution studies to a small number of modest-sized communities. Moreover, the need for complete and legible registers has led many researchers to select populations for study not on any theoretical basis, but rather because the community was blessed with a long run of high-quality parish or civil registers.

The value of family reconstitution studies would seem to outweigh the effects of these limitations, some of which are inherent in the method. Moreover, careful planning can offset a number of these problems; two steps were taken in the analysis that follows to address some of the traditional limitations. First, the communities included have been chosen on the basis of explicit theoretical concerns. This has, at times, made missing or defective data unavoidable. These problems are relatively small, however, and the negative consequences are outweighed by the advantages which flow from a sample that allows us to address important theoretical issues. Second, we have attempted to improve the representivity of the sample by supplementing the reconstitution study with an analysis based on aggregate data for a wider range of communities. The remainder of this chapter provides background on the particular communities chosen for inclusion in the study.

As the discussion in chapter 1 indicated, much of the debate on the determinants of population patterns has focused on the relative importance of economic and cultural variables. Alsace is a good testing ground on which to examine these competing claims because of the tremendous variability in the economic and social structure of the region. As such, it allows us to examine the demographic history of communities with a common administrative and political structure, but which differed with respect to vital economic and cultural characteristics.

Aggregate data were collected for a sample of twenty-six villages and small towns located across Alsace, of which five were chosen for the family reconstitution study. The sample of communities can be divided into three groups on the basis of their primary economic

Table 2.1
Villages included in the aggregate sample by type of economic activity and dominant religious affiliation

|  | Agricultural | Rural-Industrial | Industrial |
|---|---|---|---|
| CATHOLIC VILLAGES | Avolsheim* | Bindernheim | Husseren-Wesserling* |
|  | Bernolsheim | Breitenbach | Masevaux |
|  | Bischoffsheim | Hilsenheim | Willer-sur-Thur |
|  | Dambach-la-Ville | Mussig* |  |
|  | Dossenheim | Urbeis |  |
|  | Eschbach |  |  |
|  | Hegeney |  |  |
|  | Hohatzenheim |  |  |
|  | Niederlauterbach |  |  |
|  | Rangen |  |  |
|  | Reutenbourg |  |  |
| LUTHERAN VILLAGES | Daubensand | Baldenheim* |  |
|  | Goxwiller* | Muttersholtz |  |
|  | Pfulgriesheim |  |  |
|  | Retschwiller |  |  |
|  | Volksberg |  |  |

Note: Villages in the reconstitution sample are marked by an asterisk.

activity. For the first group, which includes sixteen villages (two of which were selected for the reconstitution analysis), agriculture was the dominant economic activity. None of these communities were home to any significant industrial activity throughout the period of study: the labour force was almost entirely devoted either to farming or to trades designed to satisfy the needs of the local population. Although all were agricultural, the type of farming differed. Twelve of sixteen concentrated on cereal production. These villages were spread across the *département* of the Bas-Rhin, both on the fertile Plaine d'Alsace as well as in the less productive northern and eastern regions of the province. The other four villages were located in the wine-producing belt located on the eastern slopes of the Vosges Mountains. While some land was used for grain-growing and pasture land, grapes used for wine-production was the primary crop. Farms in the area tended to be small as vine-growing required intensive labour.

In the second group of communities agriculture was combined with the domestic production of textiles. Seven villages were involved in the network of textile firms centred in the town of Sainte-Marie-aux-Mines, but they were spread across two different regions, both marked by poor-quality arable land. Five of the villages (of which two are included in the reconstitution sample) were in the canton of Marckolsheim, a marshy area that runs along the western bank of the Rhine. Some families in these villages were involved on a full-time basis in weaving. The majority of families, however, combined weaving with agricultural work. The other two villages were located in the mountainous canton of Villé. This was one of the poorest regions in Alsace with little good farmland. Here weaving was often combined with seasonal work in the surrounding forests. Many men worked at least part of the year as loggers or in the small mills and woodshops which depended on the lumber business. Families frequently spent part of the year gathering wild berries which were either sold on the market or distilled into *eaux-de-vie*. In both areas, weaving was a family undertaking. Mother and children played an important role in production and, at times when the father was involved in farming or logging, other family members might carry the whole burden of the trade.

The final group of communities includes three small towns in the vicinity of Mulhouse that were home to textile factories. In all three towns, one of which was used for the family reconstitution study, factories were established in the late eighteenth century and grew rapidly in the nineteenth. In each case, the textile business dominated the life of the town, and the majority of the working population was employed in the production of printed cloth. Much of the labour force was relatively unskilled and depended heavily, particularly in the early decades of the nineteenth century, on child labour. There were, in addition, a core of skilled workers who cared for the machinery or performed the more complex tasks involved in the preparation and dying of the cloth. The remainder of the labour force – tradesmen, shopowners and the small professional class – provided services to the factory workers.

The second dimension on which the communities in this study divide is religion. Although the majority of the rural area remained Catholic after the Reformation, Lutheranism did take root in some regions. Seven of the twenty-six villages included here had overwhelmingly Lutheran populations throughout the nineteenth century. At least 85% of the population was Protestant, a figure that usually understates the dominance of Lutheranism since many of the Catholics in these communities were domestic servants who were unmarried and seldom established permanent roots in the village. Five of these seven Protestant villages were included in the group of sixteen agricultural communities while two were centres of the domestic textile trade. Protestantism established no real base in southern Alsace except in the city of Mulhouse, and thus the three factory towns included here were overwhelmingly Catholic. Only a small number of families in each town were Protestant, and these were almost invariably involved in the direction or ownership of the mill. Unlike Protestants elsewhere in Alsace, the families in this region were Calvinist rather than Lutheran. Most had moved to the towns either from Mulhouse or parts of Switzerland where they had developed a strong attachment to a rather severe form of Protestantism. Thus the bourgeoisie in these towns were separated from the working class not only by huge differences in wealth and status, but by religion as well. The remaining sixteen communities were overwhelmingly, and in many cases, homogeneously Catholic. Eleven were agricultural while five were rural industrial villages.

The majority of the analysis in this study is based on the subset of five villages used for the family reconstitution. In the following section, we provide a brief introduction to each of the five villages. More detail on the economic and social structure of these communities follows in the substantive chapters.

## The Agricultural Communities

*Avolsheim*   Avolsheim is a small, agricultural village on the northern extreme of the valuable strip of wine-producing land that runs through the centre of Alsace along the eastern slopes of the Vosges Mountains. Located some twenty kilometres west of Strasbourg, the village lies on the main route leading from the south and west towards the city. In pre-revolutionary times, the village, like much of the surrounding territory, was the property of the bishop of Strasbourg. Population data for the eighteenth century are sketchy, but records from 1766 counted forty-eight households in the village, suggesting a population of perhaps 250 (Kintz 1977, 81). Significant growth occurred during the late eighteenth century: a census done in 1791 indicated the population had risen to 448. By 1866 the population total stood at 742.

Throughout the period of our study agriculture was the leading form of economic activity. The 1851 census indicates that 74% of the male labour force was involved in agriculture. Wine was the major product of the region, and certainly the most lucrative, though some land in the village was given over to cereal production as well. As was typical of the wine-growing region, landholdings were relatively small. Yet the labour-intensive nature of wine production provided employment for a large number of *journaliers*, or day-workers. In the mid-nineteenth century, the census recorded roughly three times as many *journaliers* as farmers. Even among heads of households, day-workers outnumbered farmers by almost two to one.

Table 2.2
Characteristics of the five villages used for the reconstitution analysis

| Name | Dominant Religion | Dominant Economic Activity | Beginning of Birth Registration | Beginning of Accurate Infant Death Registration | 1836 Population |
|---|---|---|---|---|---|
| Avolsheim | Catholic | Agricultural | 1786 | 1786 | 700 |
| Baldenheim | Lutheran | Rural-Industrial | 1684 | 1750 | 1040 |
| Goxwiller | Lutheran | Agricultural | 1590 | 1750 | 657 |
| Husseren-Wesserling | Catholic | Industrial | 1676 | 1785 | 906 |
| Mussig | Catholic | Rural-Industrial | 1722 | 1750 | 755 |

Aside from agriculture, a number of families in the village worked as boat-builders, and this number increased throughout the nineteenth century. Avolsheim was located on the Canal de la Bruche which led to the river Ill near Strasbourg and onto the Rhine. This activity was artisanal in nature and, judging by the marriage records, was passed down from father to son. In addition to the artisans one would expect to find in a village this size – bakers, butchers, shoemakers, etc. – a small number of men travelled to the nearby town of Mutzig and worked in a large factory that produced rifles for the French Army.

The population of Avolsheim was almost entirely Catholic throughout the period of this study. Indeed the 1841 census, which asked about religious affiliation, identified every resident of the village as Catholic. The fact that no villages in the immediately surrounding area held significant numbers of Lutherans probably limited the amount of contact Avolsheim residents had with members of the other major faith. The consciousness of religious identity that developed among those who shared communities with Protestants may well have remained muted here.

*Goxwiller*   Like Avolsheim, Goxwiller was located in the Vignoble, the wine-producing region of central Alsace. Lying some fifteen kilometres south of Avolsheim and closer to the slopes of the Vosges, Goxwiller was even more heavily involved in the production of wine. There is little evidence of economic activity other than farming and, aside from some limited cereal production and livestock for local consumption, grapes were the leading crop. As in Avolsheim, farms were small in size but, in contrast to Avolsheim, labour was organized on a rather different basis. Goxwiller was dominated by small landowners who worked their own land. Additional labour was provided by domestic servants who lived in the households of their masters rather than by day-workers who formed their own households and often had small plots of land as well. The 1866 census recorded sixty-eight households headed by farmers and a total of sixty-three domestic servants, both male and female, who resided with their masters.

Goxwiller had a somewhat larger population than Avolsheim in the eighteenth century but growth was slower here during the period of our study. From a population of perhaps 400 in the 1760s, the number of inhabitants crept up to only 486 in a census conducted in 1792. Growth continued to be relatively modest during the first half of the nineteenth century, and, by the census of 1866, the total number of residents stood at just 656.

Unlike Avolsheim, Goxwiller was a largely Protestant village. In the pre-revolutionary era, the village had belonged to the independent city of Strasbourg. When Strasbourg opted for the Reform in 1529, the population of Goxwiller and the other small villages in the *bailliage* of Barr became followers of Luther. In the nineteenth century, the village had a small Catholic population and, by the middle years of the century, just over 10% of the population listed their religion as Catholic. Few of these belonged to families established in the village, however, most being employed as servants by the Protestant landowners of the village. Only three families in the 1866 census were Catholic.

### The Villages with Rural Industry

*Baldenheim*   Located in the canton of Marckolsheim near the Rhine, Baldenheim, was, in the pre-revolutionary period, a possession of a powerful family belonging to the nobility. The village had long been sparsely populated, owing to the poor quality of the land and a substantial amount of marshland. Settlement in this and neighbouring villages was given an important boost, however, by the immigration of a large number of Swiss families in the early seventeenth century. By 1760, just over one hundred households existed in the village and the population continued to expand throughout the last decades of the century, reaching a total of approximately 800 during the revolutionary period. Growth continued until the early 1820s, when the total rose to just over 1000 inhabitants, but throughout the rest of the nineteenth century, the population remained remarkably stable. Population growth came to a virtual halt not because of a marked decline in the rate of natural increase, but because of the growing stream of migrants leaving the village. Strasbourg and other cities in the region attracted some residents, but a substantial number moved to the

United States and North Africa as well. As a result, the 1871 census, conducted just after the takeover by Germany, recorded only 1074 residents.

Farming played a central role in the village economy and concentrated on cereal production, supplemented from the eighteenth century on by potatoes. It is the growth of the textile trade that makes the village especially important for this study, however. The local textile industry was a tributary of the firms centred in the town of Sainte-Marie-aux-Mines, some twenty kilometres away. The trade served as a blessing for the region, providing critical additional income to families attempting to scratch out a living from the poor-quality land. The textile industry may have established deeper roots in Baldenheim than in any of the neighbouring villages. Although census records for the mid-nineteenth century show that the majority of family heads considered themselves to be farmers, an analysis of the manuscript censuses shows that almost all families had some involvement in weaving, and many family heads probably contributed to production in the off-season. Some men in the village seemed to be responsible for a significant number of looms producing for the *fabricants* of Sainte-Marie, though the degree of control they exercised is open to doubt. A Michel Bucher, for example, requested permission from the authorities to establish some forty looms in Baldenheim in 1835 while George Burghart asked for permission to set up twenty more in the same year (ADBR 5M 214). The letters requesting permission in these two cases were virtually identical, however, and both cited their connection to the same firm in Sainte-Marie. Whether they were local entrepreneurs or simply agents for the merchants of Sainte-Marie is thus unclear, but the records do suggest that weaving was well established in the community throughout the first half of the nineteenth century.

Baldenheim committed to Lutheranism in the sixteenth century and, according to a short history of the village written by a nineteenth-century pastor, the Reform was firmly established following the Peace of Augsburg in 1555. As with a number of Protestant villages in the region, Baldenheim held a small but significant number of Catholic families. The *simultaneum* was established in the village in 1749, testifying to the presence of at least seven Catholic families. As elsewhere, their numbers were bolstered by a certain number of servants and labourers who worked for Protestant families in the village. The extent of contact between people of the two faiths is hard to determine. Certainly there seems to have been very little intermarriage between the two groups. Given the tiny number of Catholic families, one might have expected that some of their children would marry into the majority Lutheran population. This was not the case, however. An astonishing number married the children of the few other Catholic families in the village while others seem to have married Catholics from the nearby villages. Almost none, throughout the whole period of our study, married a son or daughter of the Protestant families.[3] The existence of the *simultaneum*, here as elsewhere, was a source of tension between the communities. In the pastor's chronicle of the village, he maintains that relations were generally good, though a major controversy erupted in 1843 when the Catholic curé embarked on a renovation project without consulting the Protestant pastor or community (ADBR 2G 19 9). The conflict attracted considerable attention even in Strasbourg and resulted in a ministerial order forbidding any changes in the churches without prior approval by both groups (Muller 1986, 634).

*Mussig* Located only two kilometres from Baldenheim, Mussig obviously shared many of the same economic characteristics. Weaving for the merchants of Sainte-Marie and farming were the major forms of economic activity, though involvement in the textile industry was somewhat less extensive than in Baldenheim. In particular, a smaller proportion of household heads identified themselves as weavers than was the case in Baldenheim, suggesting that weaving played more of a supplementary role in Mussig.

In pre-revolutionary times, Mussig was a property of the duc des Deux Ponts and formed a part of the Grand Bailliage de Ribeaupierre. Initially smaller in size than Baldenheim, the village counted only forty households in the 1760s. In contrast to Baldenheim, however, the village experienced almost continuous growth throughout the latter half of the eighteenth century and the first half of the nineteenth century. From a recorded population of 445 in 1792, barely half the size of Baldenheim, the population climbed to 755 in 1836, and to 918 in 1871. The chapters that follow explore the reasons for this difference but it is worth noting here that Mussig was less affected by emigration. While numerous families from Baldenheim can be found among the lists of passengers headed for America, only a very small number of Mussig residents seem to have been tempted by the prospect of a better life outside Alsace.

Throughout the period of this study, Mussig remained solidly Catholic. Aside from Baldenheim, a number of villages in the region were predominantly Lutheran, but there seems to have been very little contact across confessional lines. Remarkably few interfaith marriages occurred, and virtually no Protestants came to take up residence in the village. The census of 1851, for example, recorded 779 Catholics and only six Protestants, Anabaptists who had come from Switzerland. Taken together, then, Baldenheim and Mussig, situated side by side and sharing many economic traits, provide a good basis for observing the effect of religious affiliation on the evolution of demographic behaviour.

### A Factory Town

*Husseren-Wesserling*   The development of what was, in the early nineteenth century, one of the most important textile factories in all of France allows us to follow in detail the history of Husseren-Wesserling, a village that grew into a small industrial town.[4] The commune of Husseren-Wesserling comprised two small hamlets fused into one in the aftermath of the Revolution. Located in the valley of Saint-Amarin at the foot of the Vosges and some thirty kilometres northwest of Mulhouse, both hamlets were the property of the powerful Abbey of Murbach. Prior to the development of the textile trade, the small population scratched out a living from some farming and the exploitation of the abundant resources of the surrounding forests. These same resources, combined with the settlement's location on the road from Switzerland to Lorraine and strong supply of inexpensive labour, attracted the interest of Swiss and Alsatian entrepreneurs. The first effort to create a factory devoted to the production of printed calicoes occurred in 1762. The enterprise was short-lived, however, and fell into bankruptcy in 1768. A new effort was undertaken in 1776 by Nicolas Risler, a member of a wealthy family of Protestants from the region of Porrentury. Work began in 1777 and was accompanied by the immigration of a number of skilled workers from Switzerland and Germany. The firm prospered and Schmitt (1980, 341) claims that by 1788 some 1400 persons were employed, divided more or less equally into groups working at the mill and those in the surrounding area as spinners and weavers in their homes. About half of the production of the factory was sold in France while the other half was exported to Germany, sometimes for resale in the lands to the east.

The factory experienced a number of changes of ownership over the decades that followed, but it continued to be an important centre of the Alsatian industry. In 1802, the firm, then known as Gros, Davillier, Roman et Compagnie, embarked on a major effort at expansion and modernization. New buildings for weaving cloth were constructed at Wesserling and in several surrounding villages, and the first mechanized spinning machine in Alsace was installed. By 1806, the company employed more workers and produced a larger quantity of printed cloth than any other factory in Alsace, including the workshops of Mulhouse. While the periodic crises that marked the nineteenth-century economy affected the fortunes of the firm, the directors nevertheless continued to pursue an aggressive policy of technical innovation. Throughout the Restoration and the July Monarchy the firm continued to expand despite the generally sluggish economic climate. Interestingly, the introduction of mechanized spinning and weaving did not eliminate the use of domestic labour. As a result the company continued to be the dominant employer not only in the commune of Husseren-Wesserling but throughout the canton of Saint-Amarin. Schmitt (1980, 291) shows that by 1850 the company employed almost 4000 people, or about one-quarter of the total population of the canton.[5]

This commitment to continuous innovation helped the firm survive the crises of the 1860s, when the American Civil War interrupted the flow of raw cotton to the region. The factory continued to prosper after the Treaty of Frankfurt and, indeed, under different ownership and producing a different line of products, the operation continues to this day.

The hamlets of Husseren and Wesserling were a part of the diocese of Basel in the years before the Revolution. As a part of the domain of the Abbey of Murbach, the population was entirely Catholic, the Abbey forbidding non-Catholics to settle on its lands. Despite this prohibition, no objections were raised to settling the skilled immigrants needed for the operation of the mill, many of whom were Protestant. The local curé reported no religious-based conflict between the immigrants and the local Catholic population, though both groups were highly conscious of their confessional identity. The combination of class and religious differences between the new immigrant groups and the local population insured that virtually no intermarriage occurred. In any event, with the explosive growth of the textile industry in Alsace, many of the skilled immigrants moved on, attracted by offers from the other companies springing up in Mulhouse or in the Alsatian countryside. Their places were gradually taken by the offspring of the local population, and by the early decades of the nineteenth century the local population was again overwhelmingly Catholic. A small Calvinist community existed, including members of the families that owned the mills as well as a limited number of specialized workers and managers. Despite the growth of the factory and the heavily Catholic character of the population, no church existed in the community until 1857, when the Roman family, Calvinists and part-owners of the factory, supported the construction of a Catholic parish. Prior to that, the workers attended services in neighbouring villages.

The intermittent growth of the textile trade had a marked effect on the evolution of the community's population. Prior to the founding of the first textile enterprise, the community likely numbered no more than a few hundred inhabitants. The village grew slowly through the first decades of the factory's existence with many of those employed working in their homes in the surrounding villages or commuting to the factory. At the beginning of the nineteenth century, the local population stood at perhaps 400. With the success and increasing mechanization of the business, the population began to grow rapidly. By 1841, the population totalled more than 1000 and peaked at 1272 in 1861. This seemingly steady growth through the first half of the nineteenth century occurred alongside considerable immigration and emigration that produced volatility in population totals. The erratic nature of the textile industry led to frequent layoffs, leading some workers to quit the village and return to their home villages. A serious slump in the early 1850s also led to a surge in the number of families from the village and the valley of Saint-Amarin leaving for America. The more unstable nature of the local population makes demographic analysis via family reconstitution more challenging here than was the case for the other four villages.

### THE TIME FRAME OF THE STUDY

Most of the demographic analysis presented in the following chapters covers the period from 1750 to 1870. However, limitations in the data set occasionally forced us to either begin the analysis at a somewhat later date or cut it short of the usual termination date. Only rarely does the study reach beyond 1870, though information on births and deaths occurring in the post-1870 period is linked to couples in the study who married prior to that date.

Demographic patterns of human populations are usually deep-rooted and change rather slowly. As a result, the starting and ending points for a demographic study are perhaps more arbitrary than is true for some other types of historical investigations. That said, the time frame used here makes sense in light of the demographic and political history of the region: the French Revolution has often been seen as a vital turning point in the region's history, and it seemed important to be able to examine the demographic patterns of the generation that married and bore children in the decades prior to the revolutionary upheaval. To be sure, this should not be taken to imply that demographic patterns were unchanging in the earlier historical period, but using this starting point allows us to chart the behaviour of the two religious communities prior to the political turbulence of the late eighteenth century, and to examine the evolution of their demographic behaviour in the light of the far-reaching economic and social change that reshaped the region in the nineteenth century. The absence of reliable data, it should be added, precludes us from pushing the start date much further back in time.

It is harder to justify using 1870 as our closing date. It was, of course, a critical time in the history of Alsace, with sovereignty passing to Germany as a result of the Treaty of Frankfurt. From a demographic perspective, however, it seems a bit too "early" to close our study. Aggregate data presented by Knodel (1974) suggest that important changes in demographic behaviour took place in the last decades of the nineteenth century. Unfortunately, the availability of data and the limitations imposed by family reconstitution methods make it impossible to extend the study that far. The civil registers of birth are kept secret for one hundred years in France. As such, it is impossible to trace the histories of the couples who married in the post-1870 period. Indeed, as is explained in the appendix, even following the cohorts that married in the years after 1840 becomes difficult. Thus, 1870, with its symbolic significance for the region, seemed a reasonable cut-off point for most of the analysis to be presented. It must be emphasized, however, that neither the starting nor the closing date should be seen as turning points in the demographic development of the region.

CONCLUSION

As chapter 1 made clear, much discussion of demographic change and adaptation has emphasized the competing influence of economic and cultural variables on the behaviour of individuals. Marked by considerable economic diversity, with a population divided into two self-conscious religious communities, Alsace provides an ideal setting in which to examine the influence of these factors. The particular villages selected for analysis illustrate, I believe, the influence of economic structure and religious affiliation on nuptiality, fertility, and mortality in an era of rapid economic and social change.

# CHAPTER THREE

# Marriage and Remarriage

Historical demographers have often taken a rather narrow and mechanistic view of marriage. Limited by sources to only readily quantifiable aspects, such as age at marriage and the age difference between spouses, demographers have largely avoided a fuller consideration of the role of marriage in the village community, and explanations of variability in marriage patterns have usually emphasized material factors. John Hajnal (1953, 1965), in his classic work on European marriage patterns, argued that the relatively late age at marriage and high rate of permanent celibacy in Western European societies reflected the difficulty young people faced in acquiring the means to establish an independent household, a prerequisite for marriage in these societies. More recently, analysts of English nuptiality have explored the effect of changing real wages and employment opportunities on age at marriage and the proportion of cohorts ever marrying (Weir 1984; Schofield 1985; Woods and Hinde 1985). In a similar vein, proponents of a protoindustrial model of marriage have suggested that the growth of wage labour led to a younger age at marriage in communities where rural industry took root (Levine 1977; Medick 1981).

Marriage in the village communities of eighteenth- and nineteenth-century Europe did involve issues of great economic consequence to the couple themselves and to their families. Control over property, the work patterns of the couple and their relatives, and responsibilities for the care of other family members might all be transformed by the marriage of two young people. There is ample evidence from both novelists and social historians that not only the bride and groom, but their families as well, were keenly aware of the material implications of a proposed marriage (Medick and Sabean 1984; Sabean 1990). At the same time, the significance of marriage went well beyond its economic effects. Norms touching on marriage reflected broader community sentiments about the place of young people in village society, and embodied the community's attempts to control their behaviour, particularly in matters involving sexuality and childbearing. As Segalen (1980) has emphasized, the existence of households containing mostly nuclear families should not lead us to conclude that the married couple and their children formed an isolated unit, standing apart from the larger community. In observing family life in nineteenth-century Brittany, she underlined the broad role played by village society in regulating issues that, today, might be thought of as private matters. In such a setting, it seems inevitable that the ideas people held about appropriate conduct in the formation of marriage would reflect not only narrow material concerns but broader religious and moral understandings about the world.

This chapter examines the evolution of marriage patterns in eighteenth- and nineteenth-century Alsace, looking first at how the economic and religious character of the region might have influenced nuptiality. This is followed by a consideration of the data on marriage, marriage dissolution, and remarriage, with a special emphasis on the differences between the Catholic and Lutheran communities of the region.

### THE RELIGIOUS CONTEXT: LUTHERAN AND CATHOLIC VIEWS ON MARRIAGE

Marriage was a topic of great importance to the first generation of reformers, and their ideas profoundly altered the view of marriage and celibacy that had held sway among Catholic theologians of the pre-Reformation period. Traditional Catholic teaching had viewed the celibate life as superior in virtue to marriage. In contrast, Luther, Zwingli, and Martin Bucer, the great leader of the Reform in Strasbourg, exalted the married state and rejected the view that celibacy was more pleasing to God than a faithful marriage (Phillips 1988). In doing so, they recommended marriage not only for the laity but for the clergy as well. And they put their views into practice in their own lives. Luther, who not only extolled the virtues of marriage but attacked the existence of communities of celibate priests and nuns, married a woman who had fled from the convent in the early years of the Reformation (Oberman 1992). Marriage rapidly became the norm among the clergy of the new church, and the example set by their pastors may well have made a greater impression on the new Protestant communities than did their theological writings (Karant-Nunn 1986).[1]

From a demographic perspective, the greater status accorded to married life might have been expected to encourage earlier and more universal marriage. Yet other aspects of this new theology of marriage pointed in a different direction. Despite the "second-class" status given to marriage in traditional Catholic thought, the Roman Church had always insisted on the sacramental character of marriage (Gillis 1996, 1277). This not only gave a certain dignity to the married state but also allowed the Church a greater role in its regulation. In the pre-Reformation era, the Church had struggled to exert control over the process and fought consistently against efforts to accord greater influence to parents or secular authorities (Ozment 1992; Carlson 1994). One focus of these struggles was the issue of consent (Smith 1986; Harrington 1995). Against considerable opposition, the Church maintained the validity of marriages, including those conducted clandestinely, if they were performed by an authorized minister even if parental consent was not obtained. Stepping into this conflict, the reformers affirmed the right of civil authorities to draw up regulations governing marriage. They also upheld the right of parents to a say in the marriage decisions of their children by asserting the necessity of parental consent to the marriage of minors. Some defenders of the reformers' position, notably Ozment (1992), argue that this view should not be taken as evidence of support for a more patriarchal or authoritarian model of the family on the part of Luther and other early Protestant leaders. Luther's insistence on parental consent, he suggests, was intended to protect immature young people from contracting inappropriate marriages, and he points to Luther's admonitions to parents that they had a duty both to make a suitable match for their children and to respect their choice of marriage partner. Nevertheless, this aspect of the new Reformist theology of marriage did allow for greater familial and social influence, and raised the possibility that material factors could come to play a larger role in decisions concerning marriage. If parents had an interest in keeping their children in their own household, a greater say for parents might serve to increase age at marriage.

As we argued in chapter 1, ideological changes do not automatically produce changes in behaviour, particularly when the behaviour in question touches on intimate matters that are regulated by deeply held values. Yet the leaders of the Reform saw themselves as bringing about a profound change in the popular perception of marriage, and as the new churches began to take root their leaders worked hard to put their beliefs into practice (Abray 1985). Our analysis of marriage patterns in Alsace picks up the story in 1750, by which time confessional differences were well established. The Lutheran communities had long come to take for granted a married pastor, and the differing rituals surrounding marriage were well known. As we shall see, these developments had implications for the demography of marriage in the two religious communities.

## SOCIO-ECONOMIC FACTORS AND MARRIAGE PATTERNS

In describing the Western European marriage pattern, Hajnal (1953) emphasized the convention that a couple should establish their own separate household at the time of their marriage. In this respect, Western European beliefs and practices differed sharply from those of many other cultures. The need to establish their own household placed on young people the heavy burden of accumulating a significant amount of resources before they could marry. How were young adults to obtain these resources? Two options were usually available. One could inherit property from one's parents, or one could try to save the funds necessary to marry and set up house. In the former case, young people might have to wait a long time until parents either passed away or decided to transfer control of their property to their children. In the latter case, many years of work might be necessary to save the amount of money needed to buy land, establish a trade, or amass a dowry (Hufton 1981, 1996). In either case, marriage would likely be delayed to a later date than would be the case in societies where young people could marry and cohabit with their parents.

Within this broad framework that linked independent households to later marriage and higher levels of celibacy, varying economic conditions might either reinforce or undermine the pattern. The classic peasant farming situation was thought to have been particularly conducive to later marriage and greater celibacy. In this context, where the family farm was the sole means of support, the future of young people depended almost entirely on their parents who controlled the property. Children who continued to work on the family farm were in no position to gather the resources of their own that would allow them to marry. They had to rely on their parents to make available to them, through inheritance, a grant of land, or a dowry, the resources needed to marry (Goody et al 1976). But since parents benefitted from the use of their labour, it was in parents' interest to forestall the marriage of their children for as long as possible. In areas where peasant agriculture predominated, then, we should expect to find a relatively late age at marriage and significant proportions remaining unmarried. Two of the villages in the reconstitution sample, Avolsheim and Goxwiller, were primarily agricultural communities in which independent ownership of relatively small plots of land was the rule, and it is here that one might expect to find a pattern of constrained nuptiality.

In economies not based on the family farm, however, the system might work differently. In particular, the growth of employment prospects that offered a wage to young people might make it easier for them to save, and thereby limit the power of parents to influence the marriage decisions of their children (Mendels 1972; Levine 1977; McQuillan 1984). Greater independence for young people would translate into earlier and more universal marriage. The other three communities included in the reconstitution study were the site of textile-producing industries that offered opportunities to earn wages. As outlined in more detail in chapter 2, in Mussig and Baldenheim a significant proportion of the population was involved in the household production of cloth goods, while Husseren-Wesserling was the location of one of the first textile factories in Alsace. If the introduction of wage labour led to earlier marriage, we should expect to find evidence of it in these three communities.

### AGE AT FIRST MARRIAGE

Demographic attention to the question of age at first marriage has focused largely on the effects of nuptiality on fertility. In an era of uncontrolled marital fertility and low levels of illegitimacy, age at marriage is one of the most important determinants of completed fertility (Bongaarts and Potter 1983). But variation in age at marriage has other important effects on social behaviour. The work patterns of young people and control over property are likely to vary with the timing of marriage, all the more so in a context where marriage entails the establishment of a separate household. A pattern of late marriage also raises hard questions about the social control of sexuality (Flandrin 1979). The harsh treatment of unmarried mothers and their offspring in many Western societies of the past can be seen as a reflection of the difficulty involved in controlling sexual behaviour in a context of late marriage and the absence of contraception.

Before we look at the data on marriage ages in Alsace, we should note that age at marriage is an imperfect indicator of the time at which couples began to live together (Smith 1986, 44). To be sure, it seems likely that the wedding marked the beginning of married life for most people, but in Alsace as in other parts of Europe (Hufton 1974; Smith 1986) evidence indicates that a not insignificant number of couples lived together outside of marriage. In the village of Mussig, for example, Anne Marie Ottenwelter bore two children by Francois

Table 3.1
Mean age at first marriage by sex, village and time period

| Village | 1750–89 | 1790–1815 | 1816–35 | 1836–50 | 1851–70 | Total |
|---------|---------|-----------|---------|---------|---------|-------|
| | | | MEN | | | |
| Avolsheim | — | 28.1 | 26.4 | 29.4 | 29.7 | 28.5 |
| Husseren | 26.7 | 27.9 | 28.0 | 28.7 | 28.6 | 28.0 |
| Mussig | 28.3 | 26.5 | 27.2 | 28.6 | 29.0 | 28.1 |
| CATHOLICS | 27.5 | 27.5 | 27.3 | 28.9 | 29.2 | 28.2 |
| Baldenheim | 26.9 | 26.8 | 26.8 | 27.7 | 27.9 | 27.2 |
| Goxwiller | 24.1 | 25.8 | 27.2 | 27.7 | 27.6 | 26.1 |
| LUTHERANS | 25.5 | 26.4 | 26.9 | 27.7 | 27.4 | 26.7 |
| | | | WOMEN | | | |
| Avolsheim | — | 26.2 | 24.9 | 26.4 | 27.7 | 26.4 |
| Husseren | 26.0 | 25.3 | 25.9 | 26.1 | 26.6 | 26.0 |
| Mussig | 24.8 | 25.0 | 25.7 | 26.5 | 25.7 | 25.6 |
| CATHOLICS | 25.4 | 25.5 | 25.6 | 26.3 | 26.6 | 26.0 |
| Baldenheim | 24.2 | 23.3 | 24.6 | 25.0 | 25.2 | 24.4 |
| Goxwiller | 22.2 | 24.2 | 25.1 | 24.5 | 24.4 | 23.8 |
| LUTHERANS | 23.3 | 23.7 | 24.8 | 24.8 | 24.8 | 24.1 |

Joseph Schwamberger before they eventually married in 1865 (ADBR 4E 310 2). In Avolsheim, Catherine Vetter bore a number of illegitimate children, at least two fathered by a Louis Dietrich. In the 1846 census, she lived in his household and was listed as his housekeeper, while in 1851 the census taker identified her as his "concubine" (ADBR 7M 237). Sometimes, an impediment that might have prevented marriage led couples to simply live together. Francois Joseph Untz's first wife died in Mussig in October 1840. In March 1842, he and her sister Thérèse produced a child, and over the next ten years four more followed before they finally married in February 1857 (ADBR 4E 310 5). Untz acknowledged all five of the children at the time of their births, which suggests the relationship was probably perceived by the couple, and perhaps by the rest of the village, as something similar to a legally recognized marriage.

It is impossible to know how common such relationships were, but it is noteworthy that cases like the ones mentioned here can be found in all five of the villages studied. Moreover, in some regions they seem to have been even more common. A police report for the village of Illkirch-Grafenstaden, located on the outskirts of Strasbourg, noted the presence of twelve couples known to be living together without the blessings of church or state. The local curé, when questioned about this, volunteered that he had regularized many more such unions, often using church funds for couples who said they could not

Age in years

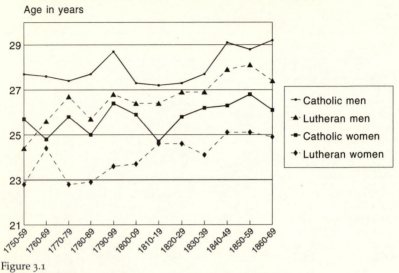

Figure 3.1
Mean age at first marriage for reconstituted villages by religion
*Note:* Primary marriages only

afford to marry (ADBR 3M 892). It is unlikely that these cases seriously distort the picture supplied by data on age at marriage, but it is important for historical demographers to remember the limitations of relying almost completely on official records to track the intimate behaviour of men and women.

Table 3.1 as well as figures 3.1 and 3.2 provide basic data on age at marriage in Alsace between 1750–1870.[2] The table presents data for the individual villages, while the graphs group the data by religious affiliation for finer periods of time. Broadly speaking, the results confirm that Alsace fit within the confines of the Western European marriage pattern described by Hajnal. Marriage for men and women occurred, on average, in the mid- to late twenties. There were, however, significant differences by religion. The data for the five reconstituted villages, as well as those for the broader sample based on aggregate data, indicate that Lutheran men and women married significantly earlier than their Catholic counterparts. In the reconstituted sample, Catholic men married about eighteen months later than Lutheran men, while for women the difference was almost two years. It is interesting to note as well that the differences among villages sharing the same faith were modest despite the very different geographic and economic settings. Among Catholic women, for example, average age at first marriage ranged from 28.0 in the industrial town of Husseren to only 28.5 in the agricultural village of Avolsheim. For both men and women, marriage

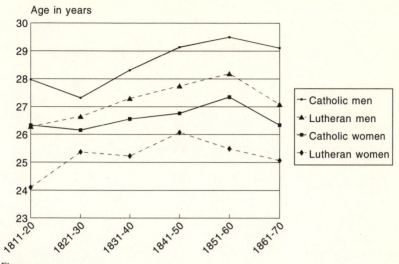

Figure 3.2
Mean age at first marriage for aggregate sample by religion
*Note:* all first marriages

age was lower in the two Lutheran villages than in any of the three Catholic villages.

Figures 3.1 and 3.2 allow us to look more closely at change over time. The data point to a gradual upward trend in age at marriage for both religious groups. The high point for males and females of both denominations occurred in the decades from 1840 to 1860. This trend is interesting in that Juillard (1953) and Hau (1987) have argued that the Alsatian countryside entered into a period of crisis towards the middle of the nineteenth century. Increasing population density and stagnant or falling real incomes called into question the organization of the agricultural system that rested on the heavy use of labour. At the same time, many of the industrialized villages, including Husseren-Wesserling, an almost purely industrial town at this point, also saw an increase in age at marriage. For men, in particular, the average age at marriage rose noticeably, from 26.7 in the pre-revolutionary period to almost 29 years in the middle decades of the nineteenth century.

Table 3.2 provides an additional perspective on marriage patterns in the Protestant and Catholic villages, focusing this time on the distribution of marriage ages. Given the younger average age at marriage in the Lutheran communities, it is not surprising to find a higher proportion of teen brides and grooms than in the Catholic villages. What is striking, though, is the virtual elimination of these marriages

Table 3.2
Mean age at first marriage, standard deviation, and distribution of marriages by age, sex, religion and time period

| Year | Men | | | | Women | | | |
|------|-----|-----|--------|--------|-------|-----|--------|--------|
| | Mean | sd | % < 20 | % > 30 | Mean | sd | % < 20 | % > 30 |
| | | | | CATHOLICS | | | | |
| 1750–89 | 27.5 | 4.8 | 0.0 | 22.3 | 25.4 | 4.6 | 11.7 | 13.3 |
| 1790–1815 | 27.5 | 5.8 | 4.8 | 21.7 | 25.5 | 4.7 | 7.0 | 14.4 |
| 1816–35 | 27.3 | 4.6 | 1.5 | 19.3 | 25.6 | 4.2 | 7.4 | 13.0 |
| 1836–50 | 28.9 | 5.2 | 0.0 | 33.3 | 26.4 | 4.8 | 4.4 | 16.2 |
| 1851–70 | 29.1 | 4.6 | 0.3 | 33.8 | 26.6 | 4.7 | 5.0 | 18.5 |
| Total | 28.2 | 5.1 | 1.2 | 26.9 | 26.0 | 4.6 | 6.6 | 15.5 |
| | | | | LUTHERANS | | | | |
| 1750–89 | 25.5 | 4.3 | 5.9 | 10.3 | 23.3 | 4.2 | 18.6 | 6.9 |
| 1790–1815 | 26.3 | 5.2 | 6.3 | 21.0 | 23.7 | 3.8 | 13.6 | 7.2 |
| 1816–35 | 26.9 | 4.5 | 1.1 | 18.4 | 24.7 | 4.9 | 11.5 | 9.8 |
| 1836–50 | 27.6 | 3.9 | 0.6 | 22.4 | 24.8 | 3.7 | 7.1 | 9.0 |
| 1851–70 | 27.7 | 4.7 | 0.0 | 22.3 | 24.8 | 3.9 | 6.9 | 6.9 |
| Total | 26.7 | 4.6 | 3.0 | 18.2 | 24.2 | 4.2 | 12.4 | 7.6 |

from all five villages over time. In the pre-revolutionary period, a small but not insignificant proportion of Lutheran men and almost one in five Lutheran women married before age twenty. By the last period covered in this study, however, teen marriage was a rare event among Protestants as well as Catholics. Indeed of 992 first marriages conducted in the five villages between 1836 and 1870, only two involved a man less than twenty years of age and just fifty-five a teen bride. At the other end of the spectrum, marrying for the first time at a relatively late age became more widespread, especially for men. In the years from 1851 until the outbreak of the Franco-Prussian War, approximately one in five grooms in the Protestant villages and one in three in the Catholic villages was thirty years of age or older. Despite this upward trend in marriage age, there is no evidence of increasing dispersion in the ages at which people married. The standard deviations for all groups fluctuated somewhat over time but show no clear direction toward either increased dispersion or concentration in marriage age.

Data on average age at marriage as well as on the proportion of late marryers seem to point to a gradual tightening of the marriage system that influenced both religious groups. We explore this notion further in the analysis of fertility, especially fertility outside of marriage.

*Occupational Differences*

It would appear that differences in marriage patterns between agricultural and more industrialized areas were limited. Given our discussion above of the potential effect of the growth of wage labour on
marriage patterns, it would be more appropriate to look at differences
in marriage age by the occupation of the marriage partners. Although
women played a critical role in the household economy of both peasant and wage-earning families, the marriage registers unfortunately
provide little data on the occupations of women. In table 3.3, then, we
examine occupational differences in age at marriage by the occupation of the groom. As is discussed more fully in the appendix, there
are a number of problems involved in using the information on occupation supplied by priests and civic officials. Nevertheless, the results
that follow give us some insight into variations in marriage patterns
among the different social groups in the village.

The differences in age at marriage by occupation were not huge, but
they do follow an interesting pattern. Among both Catholics and Protestants, the youngest brides were those who married professionals and
farmers, while the brides of *journaliers* and domestic servants were the
oldest at marriage. This suggests that the timing of marriage was
related to the status hierarchy of the village. Men with professional
occupations – typically teachers, merchants, lawyers, and, in the Protestant villages, ministers – were often joined by wealthier farmers and
the occasional master artisan in forming the elite of village society. The
mayor of the village, the village councillors, and the *kirchenpfleger* or
church elders in the Lutheran villages were almost invariably drawn
from these groups. Their privileged status no doubt strengthened their
position in the local marriage market. This did not generally translate
into early marriage for them – only farmers in the Protestant villages
were among the early marryers – but it may have given them first
choice of the desirable mates within the community. The result was a
markedly younger age at marriage among their brides.

By contrast, domestics and *journaliers*, arguably the most economically disadvantaged within the rural community, tended to be late
marryers themselves and to select brides who were also older.[3] In
part, this may have reflected the greater difficulty they and their
brides encountered in accumulating the necessary resources needed
to marry. It may also, of course, be a reflection of their less desirable
status within the local marriage market.

A brief note should be added on the marriage pattern of workers in
the textile industries, whether factory workers in the town of Husseren, or rural weavers in the villages of Baldenheim and Mussig. The

Table 3.3
Mean age at first marriage by religion and occupation of the groom

| Occupation | Catholics | | | Lutherans | | |
|---|---|---|---|---|---|---|
| | Men | Women | N | Men | Women | N |
| Farmer | 28.0 | 25.0 | 249 | 25.7 | 23.0 | 351 |
| Journalier | 28.6 | 27.2 | 195 | 28.9 | 25.9 | 77 |
| Artisan | 28.5 | 26.3 | 283 | 27.1 | 24.1 | 290 |
| Weaver | 28.0 | 26.5 | 85 | 26.7 | 24.9 | 203 |
| Worker | 26.9 | 26.0 | 195 | — | — | — |
| Domestic | 28.7 | 26.9 | 18 | 27.3 | 26.5 | 25 |
| Professional | 30.7 | 24.1 | 61 | 29.2 | 23.3 | 21 |

male factory workers did marry somewhat earlier than men from other occupational groups but the difference was modest. Their brides, on the other hand, were very close to the average age for all Catholic women. Similarly, weavers who were involved in the household production of textiles did not stand out as either early or late marryers. If anything, the marriage patterns of rural weavers placed them closer to the *journaliers* and domestics, reflecting their lower economic standing in the community and, perhaps, their disadvantaged position in the local marriage market. These findings provide no support for the argument that wage labour or a household mode of production encouraged early marriage.

Beyond the occupational differences, what is striking about the figures in table 3.3 is the consistent difference between Catholics and Lutherans. Average age at marriage in almost every category of the table was lower in the Protestant communities. While occupational status exerted a significant influence on marriage, perhaps through a supply and demand effect played out in local marriage markets, its influence was felt within the confines of a marriage system peculiar to each of the religious communities.

## AGE DIFFERENCES AT MARRIAGE

In his more recent work (1982), Hajnal has extended his description of the Western European marriage pattern, noting that marriage not only occurred relatively late but generally involved partners who were close to one another in age. Contemporary sociologists of marriage and the family place considerable importance on the age difference between spouses (Kephart and Jedlicka 1988, 290). A large gap often signals an unequal relationship in which the older party benefits from greater life experience, resources, and ultimately power within the marital relationship. The issue of marital power takes on special significance in the light of the ongoing debate on the Reformation's impact on the status of women and the nature of the family. A number of feminist historians have advanced the view that the Reformation brought new restrictions on women, confining them to the role of wife and mother under the domination of their husband (Roper 1989, 1994; Wiesner 1986). Luther, in particular, has been accused not only of misogyny but of laying the ideological groundwork for an increasingly authoritarian model of family life in which the husband and father exercised near total authority.

Related to marital power and dominance is the question of the emotional bonds that linked husband and wife (Flandrin 1979). Some scholars have suggested that age differences between spouses tell us something important about the affective character of marriage and the dominant motives governing mate selection: large age differences can be a sign that material interests, working perhaps through parental pressure, are influencing the selection of a spouse, while marriage patterns typified by small age differences may indicate the importance of affection and sexual attraction. Shorter has suggested that the declining age differences between spouses in many European populations in the eighteenth and nineteenth centuries show the rise of "companionate marriages" (1975).

Table 3.4 presents the average age difference between spouses separately by marital status as well as for the two religious groups. Overall, the age difference between spouses was modest. For primary marriages, the gap was 2.1 years for Catholics, 2.6 years among Protestants. These figures are remarkably similar to the gap found among spouses in many Western societies today. The largest difference, not surprisingly, occurred in marriages involving a previously married husband and a first-time bride. For Catholics, the gap was slightly less than ten years, for Protestants slightly over ten years. Interestingly, even when both partners had been widowed, the gap was significantly larger than in primary marriages. Again, though most remarriages today involve divorced rather than widowed persons, the age differences tend to be larger than in first marriages, with the male usually the older. Marriages involving a widow and a bachelor constituted only about 4% of marriages but are noteworthy nonetheless. In these cases, the woman was, on average, just over three years older than her new husband. Such marriages were sometimes seen as typifying unions based on money rather than love, and there is some evidence to suggest that practical considerations often played a role in these marriages. Several marriages in our villages involved not only a younger man but one who would seem to have gained economically

Table 3.4
Mean age difference between spouses by prior marital status, religion and
period of marriage

| Year | Prior Marital Status | | | | |
| | Bachelor/ Spinster | Bachelor/ Widow | Widower/ Spinster | Widower/ Widow | All Statuses |
| --- | --- | --- | --- | --- | --- |
| CATHOLICS | | | | | |
| 1750–89 | 1.69 | −5.11 | 8.32 | 4.60 | 1.78 |
| 1790–1815 | 1.96 | −0.44 | 10.09 | 8.46 | 3.14 |
| 1816–35 | 1.77 | −2.27 | 8.87 | 10.27 | 2.78 |
| 1836–50 | 2.53 | −1.15 | 10.37 | 5.39 | 3.54 |
| 1851–70 | 2.33 | −4.67 | 9.84 | 0.01 | 3.21 |
| Total | 2.10 | −3.01 | 9.63 | 5.95 | 2.98 |
| LUTHERANS | | | | | |
| 1750–89 | 2.43 | −6.70 | 11.38 | 3.76 | 3.25 |
| 1790–1815 | 2.66 | −1.46 | 12.88 | 10.50 | 4.17 |
| 1816–35 | 2.17 | −4.28 | 8.90 | 3.98 | 3.08 |
| 1836–50 | 2.81 | 0.67 | 6.93 | 7.57 | 3.33 |
| 1851–70 | 2.85 | 0.23 | 10.91 | 5.42 | 3.67 |
| Total | 2.59 | −3.69 | 10.60 | 6.38 | 3.53 |

by his marriage to a widow. Dominique Willmann, for example, was a blacksmith in the village of Eichoffen, some twenty kilometres from Mussig. He married Thérèse Schmitt, eight years his senior, in January 1825, just eleven months after her first husband, Georges Losser, also a blacksmith, had passed away (ADBR 4E 310 4). The couple took up residence in Mussig, and it seems probable he took over her late husband's trade. In a number of other cases, bachelor/widow marriages involved younger landless labourers or weavers marrying the widows of landholding farmers. We cannot say with any certainty that material considerations played a greater role in these marriages than others. Still, if emotion and affection grew in importance as the basis of marriage, the number of such marriages might be expected to decline over time. We will return to this issue later in the chapter when we consider remarriage.

Table 3.5 provides more detailed information on the gap in age between spouses, focusing exclusively on primary marriages. For neither Catholics nor Protestants is there evidence of any clear trend over time in the mean age difference. The age gap for both groups was larger after 1836 than in earlier periods but the difference is small, and reflects the somewhat greater increase in age at marriage for men in the middle decades of the nineteenth century. Knodel (1988) noted

Table 3.5
Mean age difference between spouses, standard deviation, and distribution of
marriages by age difference, religion and time period

| Years | Mean | sd | Wife Older 5+ | Wife Older 1–5 | Less than 1-Year Difference | Husband Older 1–5 | Husband Older 5–10 | Husband Older 10+ |
|---|---|---|---|---|---|---|---|---|
| | | | CATHOLICS | | | | | |
| 1750–89 | 1.7 | 5.7 | 11.2 | 18.0 | 15.5 | 26.1 | 23.0 | 6.2 |
| 1790–1815 | 2.0 | 5.5 | 7.1 | 19.2 | 19.2 | 33.1 | 14.3 | 7.1 |
| 1816–35 | 1.8 | 5.2 | 7.8 | 19.7 | 19.3 | 29.8 | 16.7 | 6.7 |
| 1836–50 | 2.5 | 4.9 | 4.8 | 15.4 | 18.5 | 33.9 | 20.7 | 6.6 |
| 1851–70 | 2.3 | 5.5 | 4.8 | 16.2 | 17.2 | 35.5 | 17.4 | 8.9 |
| Total | 2.1 | 5.3 | 6.8 | 17.9 | 17.1 | 32.8 | 18 | 7.3 |
| | | | LUTHERANS | | | | | |
| 1750–89 | 2.4 | 4.8 | 5.9 | 18.2 | 11.9 | 35.1 | 24.6 | 4.3 |
| 1790–1815 | 2.7 | 5.1 | 3.0 | 21.7 | 14.5 | 30.6 | 22.6 | 7.7 |
| 1816–35 | 2.2 | 5.0 | 6.3 | 18.4 | 16.7 | 36.8 | 16.1 | 5.7 |
| 1836–50 | 2.8 | 4.7 | 5.2 | 17.5 | 11.6 | 35.7 | 22.7 | 7.1 |
| 1851–70 | 2.9 | 4.6 | 3.4 | 12.8 | 17.4 | 39.1 | 21.7 | 5.5 |
| Total | 2.6 | 5.2 | 4.6 | 17.7 | 14.5 | 35.2 | 21.9 | 6.1 |

in his analysis of German data for the same time period that while the mean age difference remained constant, the standard deviation declined over time, reflecting a decrease in the proportion of marriages involving spouses who differed greatly in age. This, he speculated, was evidence for an increase in the importance of companionate marriage. In Alsace, there is little evidence of this occurring. Not only was the standard deviation relatively constant, but more detailed data on the distribution of marriages according to the age gap between spouses show no clear pattern of change. Knodel (1988), for instance, noted a steady decline in the proportion of marriages involving a husband at least ten years older than his wife. In Alsace, this occurred for neither Catholics nor Protestants. Indeed, for Catholics, the proportion of such marriages reached its high point over 1851–70. There is, on the other hand, some evidence of a shift toward a pattern of age differentials common in present-day European societies, one in which the husband is slightly older than the wife, with a significant decline over time in the proportion of marriages in which the wife was at least one year older than her husband. For Catholics, the figure fell from 29.2% in the pre-revolutionary era to just 21% in the years 1851–70, while for Protestants the corresponding decline was from 24.1% to 16.2%. Moreover, the proportion of marriages in which the husband was one to five years older than the wife rose somewhat. These changes were not huge but they do point to the growing popularity of marriages in which the husband was slightly older than the wife.

The meaning and importance of age differences between spouses takes a new turn, however, when we examine age differences by husband's occupation in figure 3.3. Bearing out the conclusions reached in the analysis of table 3.3, we can see a clear link between the status of the husband and the size of the age difference between the spouses. Although their numbers are small, professionals stand out clearly in this regard. The mean age difference for this group in the Catholic community was 6.6 years, while in the Protestant villages it was 5.9 years. Similarly, the gap in age between farmers and their wives was above average, while among lower-status groups such as *journaliers*, weavers and factory workers the age difference was typically smaller. It is possible that in marriages where the husband was of high status and the family economically more secure, the wife may have played a different role. Her contribution to the family's earning power may have been less important, or come more through her dowry and the status of her family. Her own contribution may have involved less tangible goods – youth, attractiveness, a spotless reputation.

What do these findings say about the ideas discussed at the beginning of this section? Certainly, the demographic data do not support the idea that a shift in the motivation leading to marriage occurred. Change in the pattern of age differences over time was modest. There was, it is true, a noticeable decline in the proportion of marriages in which the wife was significantly older than her husband. The greater prevalence of these marriages in the eighteenth century may suggest that more marriages occurred on a catch-as-catch-can basis, a man and a woman in need of a mate patched together with help from relatives and neighbours. The significance of the growth in popularity of marriages in which the husband was close in age but generally somewhat older than the wife, and the persistence of larger differentials among higher-status couples are harder to interpret. One could argue that from the perspective of women, the shift from a situation in which a goodly number of women married an available younger man (perhaps one with fewer resources to bring into the marriage than she did) to a pattern favouring unions in which the husband was older (and perhaps more dominant) did not herald a rise in the importance of sentiment in the choice of marriage partner. Much more qualitative research into the nature of marriage in this period will be necessary to explore these suggestions. It seems fair to conclude, though, that the modest changes in the age differences between husbands and wives

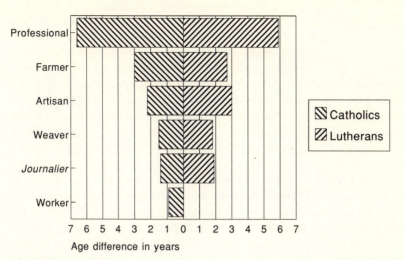

Figure 3.3
Mean age difference between spouses by religion and occupation of husband
*Note:* primary marriages only

do not, of themselves, suggest that a major change occurred in the nature of marriage during this period.

The absence of any marked difference between Catholics and Protestants on this dimension seems to undermine the contention that Lutheran teachings on the family helped create a more authoritarian family or strengthened the role of the husband and father. The mean age difference was slightly larger in the Lutheran communities and marriages in which the wife was significantly older than her husband were fewer. But the variation was small and does not support the argument that men played a more dominant role in Lutheran families than in the Catholic households of the region.

## PROPORTIONS NEVER MARRIED

Hajnal's original thesis concerning historical marriage patterns focused on two elements, the age at entry into marriage and the proportion of the population ultimately marrying. In Western Europe, he argued, the two were generally associated: a late age at marriage was normally accompanied by a lower proportion eventually marrying. While considerable research supports such an association, there is no necessary reason why they must go together. Moreover, recent research on England has indicated that the proportion never marrying was more sensitive to fluctuations in the economy and played a more critical role as a regulator of fertility and population growth (Weir 1984).

Unfortunately, in historical studies based on family reconstitution methods, analysis of marriage patterns is usually restricted to a consideration of age at marriage. The reason for this is that reconstitution data do not lend themselves to an accurate assessment of the proportion who ultimately marry. They can be used to produce an estimate of the proportion of the population remaining unmarried at the end of the childbearing period only for those who were born and died in the village. Since there may well be a link between the likelihood of marriage and migration, the resulting estimate will almost certainly be biased.

The importance of this issue suggests the use of other data to supplement what is available through family reconstitution. In this case, we have used manuscript census data for the region. Using only the five villages included in the reconstitution analysis would lead to results particularly subject to random fluctuations due to small numbers. Here, then, we have drawn on census data for the larger sample of twenty-six communities in the region. Figure 3.4 shows the proportion of never-married women aged 45–54 at three points in time for these communities. They point to a clear difference between the Lutheran and Catholic communities in the extent of permanent celibacy. For all three time points, the proportion never marrying in the Catholic villages was generally about double that in the Protestant communities. Only the overall figures for the two religious groups are presented, but more detailed analysis by area shows that the religious difference was apparent across different regions. Proportions never marrying were consistently higher in the Catholic communities regardless of whether they were predominantly agricultural or industrial.

The census figures also seem to point to a gradual tightening of marriage markets for both Catholics and Lutherans. The proportion who never married rose steadily from 1836 to 1866 for both Protestant and Catholic women. The rising age at marriage in the middle decades of the nineteenth century that we noted earlier appeared to translate into higher proportions never marrying among the cohorts of women who would have been at the normal ages of marriage during these years. For example, women aged 45–54 in 1866 would have been at the mean age at marriage twenty to thirty years earlier, that is during the period 1826–35. This, of course, was the period when age at marriage was increasing. Taken together, these two pieces of information suggest a marriage crisis during the middle years of the century. A shortage of land and falling rural incomes combined to restrict marriage opportunities for cohorts reaching marriage age during that period. Data from the latter part of the century suggest the crisis was resolved after 1870. Substantial out-migration from rural areas and new opportunities out-

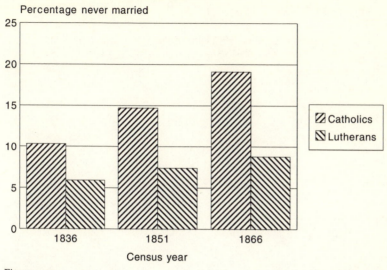

Figure 3.4
Percentage never married among women aged 45–54 by religion, selected years
*Source:* manuscript census

side the agricultural sector led to population decline in the countryside and allowed for a return to easier marriage for those who remained behind. What is especially striking for our concerns, however, is the similarity in the response of the two religious communities to this crisis. Although proportions never marrying were already significantly higher in the Catholic villages, the pressures leading to more restricted marriage had just as great an impact as they did in the Lutheran communities. As a consequence, the differential between the two communities was not significantly reduced as a result of the general upward movement in the proportion never marrying.

## SEASONALITY OF MARRIAGE

Studies of marriage patterns past and present have uncovered a variety of patterns of seasonality in the celebration of marriages. Both economic and cultural characteristics of societies influence decisions about the most appropriate times of the year to schedule wedding feasts (Van Poppel 1995a). In Western Europe, especially in rural areas, the timing of marriage was usually closely tied to the agricultural cycle. Although summer weddings are most popular in present-day Western societies, in the past summer and fall were times of intensive agricultural work that left little time to devote to the preparation and

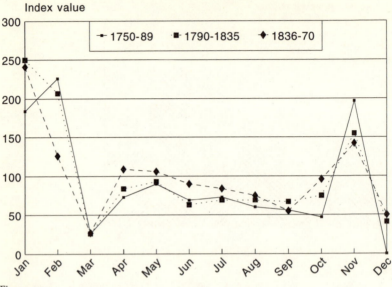

Figure 3.5
Seasonality of marriage by period of marriage, Catholics

proper celebration of a marriage. And the celebration could indeed be onerous for families. Feasts lasting several days were not uncommon and families required sufficient time to prepare, especially since the quality of the celebration reflected on their status within village society. Indeed, the scale of weddings became so elaborate that the authorities introduced regulations limiting the length and the number of guests who could attend the celebrations (Peter 1995, 131).

Religious considerations exerted an influence as well. In Alsace, both the Catholic and the Lutheran Church had long discouraged the celebration of marriage within the penitential seasons of Advent and Lent (Peter 1995). Dispensations from the ban were possible, though this might involve a cost to the parties involved, adding an economic as well as a spiritual constraint.

Figures 3.5 and 3.6 show the seasonal pattern of marriage for the Catholic and Lutheran villages for three time periods, and reveal large seasonal variations in both populations, especially in the eighteenth century. For both Catholics and Lutherans, the schedule of marriages followed a pattern typical of rural, agricultural populations. The most popular months to marry were in the winter, and in particular November, January, and February, when the demands of the agricultural cycle were least. The early spring (April and May) was reasonably popular

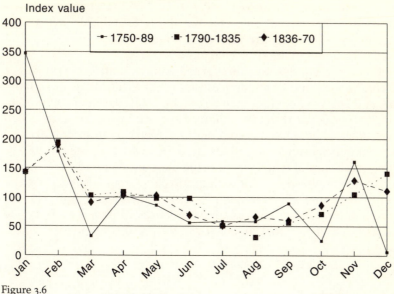

Figure 3.6
Seasonality of marriage by period of marriage, Lutherans

as well, while weddings were relatively rare through the summer and early autumn when the farming population spent long hours in the fields. This rather simple schedule was interrupted, however, by the influence of the ban on marriage in the seasons of Advent and Lent. Advent, beginning on the fourth Sunday before Christmas, covers much of the month of December. Lent, a forty-day period before Easter, is more variable but will normally encompass most, if not all, of the month of March. As the low index numbers for the months of March and December indicate, the ban was widely observed in the eighteenth century in both Catholic and Protestant communities.

The Revolution marked an important transition, however. Among Catholics, the absolute ban on marriage during Advent eroded somewhat in the nineteenth century, though the number of marriages in December was still less than half the average figure. No change in the index number for March is apparent across the three cohorts. Lutherans, by contrast, followed a different path. The religious proscription on marriage in Lent and Advent all but disappeared in the post-revolutionary period. After 1790, the proportion of marriages in both March and December reached average or above-average levels. If we consider the period 1790–1870 as a whole, the index for the month of March was ninety-four in the Protestant communities, and twenty-eight in the Catholic villages. As we shall see later, the changing seasonality of marriage was not the only indicator suggesting that the revolutionary era marked a fundamental turning point for the Lutheran population of the region.

A look at the index numbers for the winter months also suggests a declining influence of the agricultural cycle. While November, January, and February continued to be the most popular months throughout the period to 1870, the extent of seasonal variation diminished over time in both religious communities. One way to summarize this is to sum the absolute deviations from the average figure of 100. The greater the sum of the deviations, the more pronounced the seasonal differences in marriage. For both groups, this figure declined significantly over time. Changing employment patterns and, in the Lutheran community, changing religious practices combined to mute the extreme seasonality that characterized the pre-revolutionary period.

MATE SELECTION

All societies have structures that encourage marriage among members of certain social groups and discourage it among others. In Alsace, religion was of central importance. Marriages between Catholics and Protestants were actively discouraged, particularly by the Catholic Church. The archives of the diocese of Strasbourg contain numerous files dealing with the problem, particularly as it touched on the religious upbringing of the children born of these marriages (ADBR 1V 29). In the five reconstituted villages, mixed marriages were almost non-existent. Their absence is a testament to the power of social structures to regulate behaviour since, at least in the case of Mussig and Baldenheim, there was considerable daily contact between the Catholic and Lutheran residents of the two villages.

No formal rules regulated the social class suitability of prospective spouses, but it would not be surprising if family status played a significant role in the selection of a mate. While a full analysis of this problem requires more information than can be gleaned from marriage certificates, we can get some sense of the predominant mating patterns in the villages by examining the occupations of the fathers of the bride and groom. The occupations given on the marriage certificates have been grouped into five broad categories to facilitate the analysis. Two special cautions are necessary here, however. First, for the Catholic population, the data exclude the factory town of Husseren-Wesserling. The occupational structure for this community was so different that it made little sense to group it together with the rural, largely agricultural villages. Second, the number of marriages

Table 3.6a
Difference between actual and expected percentages of homogamous marriages
by religion, grooms

| Occupation of Bride's Father | Occupation of Groom's Father | | | | |
|---|---|---|---|---|---|
| | Farmer | Journalier | Artisan | Weaver | Other |
| CATHOLICS | | | | | |
| Farmer | +13.2 | −18.3 | −11.7 | −2.5 | −12.5 |
| Journalier | −9.0 | +18.9 | +4.0 | +3.9 | −6.5 |
| Artisan | −1.7 | −0.6 | +3.4 | −1.9 | +9.0 |
| Weaver | −2.4 | +2.9 | +2.5 | +3.5 | −7.0 |
| Other | −0.2 | −3.1 | +1.7 | −3.1 | +16.9 |
| N | 306 | 111 | 147 | 38 | 15 |
| LUTHERANS | | | | | |
| Farmer | +18.4 | −26.4 | −5.9 | −26.1 | +5.6 |
| Journalier | −6.3 | +13.1 | +2.3 | +5.1 | −0.7 |
| Artisan | −5.8 | +5.7 | +6.0 | +3.7 | −8.0 |
| Weaver | −5.3 | +7.1 | −3.1 | +17.3 | −9.2 |
| Other | −1.1 | +0.5 | +0.6 | −0.1 | +12.2 |
| N | 459 | 122 | 262 | 146 | 20 |

included in the analysis is limited by missing data. Priests, ministers and, later on, civic officials varied in the diligence with which they included information on occupation, especially for the fathers of the parties marrying. More importantly, occupational data for the fathers was often missing if the father had passed away before the marriage of his child. Thus, for the Catholic population only 58.5% of the marriages could be included in the analysis while among Protestants the figure is a more respectable 70%.

The results in table 3.6 are based on a comparison of the actual number of marriages between brides and grooms from given occupational categories and the number we would expect to see if marriages occurred at random with respect to occupation. For example, 52.3% of the women who married were the daughters of farmers. If the father's occupation played no role in the choice of marriage partner, we would expect that 52.3% of the grooms in each social category would choose the daughter of a farmer as his bride. When the figure is higher, it suggests that men in that group were more likely to marry a woman from that class. To make the results easy to read, we have subtracted the expected number from the number actually observed. Positive numbers thus indicate categories where marriages were more frequent than would be expected by chance and, of course, negative numbers suggest a smaller proportion of marriages than would be expected.

Table 3.6b
Difference between actual and expected percentages of homogamous marriages
by religion, brides

| Occupation of Groom's Father | Occupation of Bride's Father | | | | |
|---|---|---|---|---|---|
| | Farmer | Journalier | Artisan | Weaver | Other |
| CATHOLICS | | | | | |
| Farmer | +12.4 | −22.6 | −4.6 | −17.0 | −2.2 |
| Journalier | −6.3 | +17.2 | +0.6 | +7.6 | −18.0 |
| Artisan | −5.3 | −4.9 | +4.6 | +8.8 | +13.0 |
| Weaver | −0.3 | +1.2 | −0.7 | +3.1 | −6.2 |
| Other | −0.5 | −0.8 | +1.3 | −2.4 | +13.4 |
| N | 324 | 122 | 109 | 43 | 19 |
| LUTHERANS | | | | | |
| Farmer | +16.9 | −27.0 | −11.4 | −16.8 | −16.9 |
| Journalier | −6.5 | +14.8 | +3.1 | +6.1 | −2.2 |
| Artisan | −3.1 | +5.5 | +6.8 | −5.7 | +6.1 |
| Weaver | −7.7 | +6.8 | +2.3 | +17.7 | −0.2 |
| Other | +0.2 | −0.1 | −0.7 | −1.3 | +8.7 |
| N | 498 | 108 | 232 | 143 | 28 |

The first thing we note in the table is that the largest positive numbers are on the diagonals, indicating that people were more likely to choose a partner from their own social group. The children of farmers were especially likely to marry a partner whose father also owned land. Interestingly, there were fewer marriages than expected between farmers' children and the sons and daughters of fathers from all other occupational groups. While we have sometimes seen that artisans appeared along with farmers at the "top" of the village hierarchy, with *journaliers* and weavers forming the lower strata, the sons and daughters of farmers were no more likely to select a mate from the artisan category than from the other groups. Similarly, the children of artisans were more likely to "drop down" and select a mate from the families of the *journaliers* or weavers than to have married a son or daughter of a farmer. There was a significant exchange of partners between the families of *journaliers* and weavers, but what is especially striking are the very high negative figures for the cells showing the proportion of sons and daughters from these two groups that married a child of a farmer. While in some settings it was acceptable for a bright, attractive young woman from a lower social class to "marry up" with the son of a more privileged family, such marriages were relatively rare in these four villages. In the Lutheran villages, for example, the percentage of marriages involving the daughter of a *journalier* and the son of a farmer was 27 percentage points lower than would be expected if a pattern of random mating prevailed.[4]

The few differences between the Lutheran and Catholic communities indicate that class background had a similar influence on mate selection for both religious groups. The divisions were slightly larger in the Protestant communities, however. If there is a strong tendency to marry partners from some groups but not others, there will be large differences between the expected and observed percentages. By summing these differences without regard to sign, we can get a crude measure of the degree of selective mating. Following this procedure here, we find that the degree of homogamy was somewhat greater in the Lutheran communities. Among males, for example, the sum of the differences was 160 in the Catholic villages and 195 among Lutherans. For females, the differences were somewhat smaller, 175 among Catholics, 194 in the Lutheran villages.

It seems apparent, then, that marriage patterns reflected considerations of property and social position. In the four rural villages studied here, landowning families formed the upper crust of local society. Their children were most likely to choose a spouse from a family belonging to this same social class. *Journaliers* and weavers made up the bottom rung of the village hierarchy, though occasionally children from such families would marry a son or daughter from the landowning class. We cannot tell from these numbers, of course, how this process worked. Undoubtedly families strove in a number of ways to direct their children towards suitable partners, while at the same time, those in search of a spouse were not unaware of the importance of making a good match. The case of George Guntz and Veronique Frantz illustrates this in a particularly dramatic way (ADBR 3M 894). Frantz was a servant in the house of Guntz, a farmer in the wine-producing village of Nothalten. After the death of Guntz's wife, popular opinion held that Guntz and his servant began to live together as husband and wife. But before long Guntz made plans to marry another woman, apparently concluding that his servant was suitable as a temporary partner but not as a wife. Frantz would have none of it. "If the young wife enters this house, she won't stay for long," neighbours reported her saying. As it turned out, the marriage never took place. Guntz died after a brief illness and police concluded that Frantz had poisoned him and perhaps his first wife as well, who had died six months earlier. She was found guilty and executed in the nearby town of Barr before a crowd estimated at over 7000. She died, the commissioner of police reported, courageously and without saying a single word (ADBR 3M 404).

### ORIGIN OF SPOUSES

Historical research has discredited the notion of an immobile peasant population, in which people lived out their existence within the range

of the same church spire (Moch 1983). Migration in search of permanent or seasonal work, the practice of placing young people in
positions as domestic servants, and voluntary or obligatory military
service all created considerable mobility in predominantly rural, agricultural societies. Yet much of this movement was relatively short-
distance, and it is doubtful that many village-dwellers were drawn
into contact with people from different cultural backgrounds.

One of the most common ways of studying the degree of mobility
has been to record the place of birth listed for brides and grooms on
their marriage certificates. This approach has obvious limitations,
particularly when focusing on a village population, and cannot give
us any real sense of the proportion of the population that may have
migrated at some point in their lives. The question of interest here is
somewhat different, however, and touches once again on religion. The
strong opposition to mixed marriages imposed a particular dynamic
on the search for a spouse. If young men and women did not find
spouses in their own villages, the next obvious place to look would be
in the neighbouring communities. But for people in our Lutheran
villages, in particular, this was not so easy since they were located in
largely Catholic areas. How might this have affected the search for a
partner?

Table 3.7 shows the birthplaces of men and women marrying in
each of the villages studied. The first row of the table indicates the
percentage of brides and grooms born in the village, the second line
shows the percentage born in other communes of the canton to which
the village belonged, the third shows the percentage from other cantons in Alsace, while the remaining lines indicate the percentage orig-
inating in other regions of France, Germany, Switzerland or other
countries. It was more common for the marriage to be celebrated in
the village of the bride, and thus we would expect to find that a
higher proportion of brides were residents of the village where the
marriage occurred. This custom was not uniformly honoured, however, and in both Protestant and Catholic villages it was not unusual
to see weddings being celebrated in the parish church of the groom.
The majority of both brides and grooms were residents of the village
where the marriage occurred. There was, however, some significant
variation across villages. First, the factory town of Husseren-Wesserling clearly stands out as having the lowest percentage of marriages
involving natives of the commune. With the development of the
textile industry, the village drew residents of the surrounding countryside seeking employment. Not surprisingly, the factory, which
employed a large number of young adults, became a meeting place
for prospective spouses and thus a significantly higher percentage of

Table 3.7
Geographic origins of grooms and brides by village

| | Village of Marriage | | | | |
|---|---|---|---|---|---|
| Place of Birth | Baldenheim | Goxwiller | Mussig | Avolsheim | Husseren |
| GROOMS | | | | | |
| Commune | 72.0 | 71.0 | 60.5 | 62.7 | 40.4 |
| Canton | 10.6 | 3.7 | 19.3 | 15.3 | 32.3 |
| Alsace | 8.9 | 17.1 | 11.0 | 14.0 | 12.1 |
| France | 0.1 | 0.2 | 0.4 | 0.5 | 3.8 |
| Germany | 1.8 | 1.7 | 1.0 | 0.5 | 1.9 |
| Switzerland | 0.7 | 0.6 | 1.0 | 0.0 | 2.6 |
| Other | 0.0 | 0.0 | 0.0 | 0.0 | 0.9 |
| Unknown | 5.9 | 5.9 | 6.8 | 7.0 | 6.0 |
| BRIDES | | | | | |
| Commune | 77.2 | 80.7 | 77.5 | 69.7 | 57.4 |
| Canton | 11.3 | 1.9 | 10.9 | 12.4 | 25.2 |
| Alsace | 7.0 | 11.2 | 6.8 | 9.2 | 7.9 |
| France | 0.0 | 0.3 | 0.2 | 0.2 | 2.1 |
| Germany | 0.3 | 0.3 | 0.2 | 0.0 | 0.8 |
| Switzerland | 0.1 | 0.3 | 0.4 | 0.2 | 2.3 |
| Other | 0.0 | 0.0 | 0.2 | 0.0 | 0.7 |
| Unknown | 4.1 | 5.2 | 3.8 | 8.3 | 3.5 |

brides and grooms came from other villages in the canton. The data, it should be noted, refer to place of birth, not place of residence. No doubt many of those who married had moved previously from the surrounding area to take up residence closer to the factory. The factory also drew skilled personnel, managers, and technicians from a wider area, and this is reflected in the higher proportion of spouses born outside of Alsace. Among grooms, 9.2% were born outside the province, including men from Germany, Switzerland, Holland, and England.

When looking at the other four villages, the importance of the religious dimension is again clear. In the Lutheran villages, young people who did not find a mate in the village itself had to look farther afield. In Goxwiller, for example, 80.7% of brides and 71.0% of grooms were from the village. But few came from surrounding communities, most of which were Catholic, while a relatively large number (17.1% of grooms, 11.2% of brides) originated in other cantons of Alsace that were home to significant Protestant populations. For young people in the rural Catholic villages, on the other hand, the surrounding villages held a large number of potential spouses.

Overall, the data on place of origin suggest the marriage market was very much a local one. Indeed, marriage occurred within circles even more limited than suggested by considering place of birth alone. In many cases, when the bride or groom came from another village, there was already some connection between the two families involved. It was not uncommon for a woman to marry a man and move off to a nearby community and then see one of her children marry a man or woman from her native village. Sophie Ehlinger, for example, was born in Husseren and married there in 1845. After her marriage, she moved to the nearby town of Saint-Amarin. Her first child, Sophie, was born there in 1847 but married in Husseren in 1870. Data on birthplace alone thus tend to underestimate the connections among spouses marrying in these rural villages.

## MARRIAGE DISSOLUTION AND REMARRIAGE

In an era of high mortality, marriage was a fragile partnership. Although the family was in most respects the central institution in early modern societies, providing a livelihood to a couple and their children, controlling and transferring property, and seeing to much of the raising and training of the young, its institutional strength stood alongside its demographic weakness. The average length of marriages that ended in the death of a spouse was far shorter than today, and many men and women found themselves widowed at an early age. Death, of course, was not the only event that dissolved marriages. While divorce was rare in the villages of Alsace despite its tolerance by the Lutheran Church and legislation during the revolutionary period that opened the door to civil divorce, simple desertion was a more common route to ending a marriage that disappointed one or both of the partners. As always, the evidence to judge the extent of desertion is sketchy. It most often turns up as a by-product of other records, being mentioned in passing as other acts are recorded. Census-takers often noted the absence of a spouse, almost always a husband. Catherine Fritsch was recorded as married but living alone in the village of Goxwiller in the 1856 census, her husband having left for America (ADBR 7M 393). He may have intended to establish himself in his new country before sending for his wife and family but, as it happened, he never returned and his wife died alone in the village. In one of the rare police records of child abandonment involving a married woman, the mother reported she left the child in front of a neighbour's house in the village of Hochfelden because her husband had left for America and she could not support the child on her own

Table 3.8
Mean duration of marriage by age at marriage, sex, religion and period of marriage

| | Men | | | | Women | | | |
|---|---|---|---|---|---|---|---|---|
| | Catholics | | Lutherans | | Catholics | | Lutherans | |
| Age at Marriage | 1750–1789 | 1790–1830 | 1750–1789 | 1790–1830 | 1750–1789 | 1790–1830 | 1750–1789 | 1790–1830 |
| 15–19 | — | — | — | — | — | (23.6) | 29.1 | (33.3) |
| 20–24 | 26.4 | 26.1 | 28.2 | 31.2 | 22.3 | 26.6 | 26.7 | 29.1 |
| 25–29 | 24.8 | 25.9 | 25.0 | 29.7 | 25.8 | 24.9 | 23.3 | 26.4 |
| 30–34 | (17.8) | 24.0 | 23.8 | 23.4 | 18.8 | 20.8 | 20.2 | 20.4 |
| 35+ | (19.5) | 19.5 | 17.1 | 18.4 | (18.0) | (19.8) | (18.7) | (16.3) |
| Total | 22.2 | 24.5 | 24.6 | 26.9 | 22.2 | 24.5 | 24.6 | 26.9 |

Note: Results based on 26–50 cases are shown in parentheses; results based on 25 cases or less are omitted. Totals include a small number of cases for which age at marriage was unknown.

(ADBR 3M 892). In the police survey of cohabiting couples in Illkirch-Grafenstaden mentioned above, at least one of the men admitted to having abandoned a wife. To be sure, these cases hardly present a picture of widespread abandonment. The vast majority of couples no doubt stayed together until death. Yet they show that individuals found ways out of situations they found intolerable even when society worked hard to close off all the exits. In looking at quantitative evidence on the length of married life and the chances of remarriage we must remember that those who chose innovative ways to deal with life's problems are excluded from our calculations.

When we turn to the figures presented in tables 3.8 and 3.9, what is striking is not so much that "till death do us part" covered a far shorter period of time in the past than today, but that widowhood occurred at a very different stage of life than is the case in modern society. For the vast majority of people today, widowhood arrives after the major responsibilities of life have been discharged. Children have been raised, working life is nearing an end, and the consequences of a partner's death are more often emotional than material. Yet in the period being studied, widowhood occurred, on average, when men and women were in their early fifties and still in the prime of adult life. For the majority, young children were still in the house, and whether the survivor was male or female, pressing issues touching on economic survival and care for children had to be resolved.

As the figures in the two tables make clear, widowhood arrived at a similar time in life for members of both religious groups and, while the average length of married life increased by about two years over

Table 3.9
Mean age at widowhood by sex, religion and date of marriage

| Date of Marriage | Men | | | Women | | |
|---|---|---|---|---|---|---|
| | Catholics | Lutherans | Total | Catholics | Lutherans | Total |
| 1750–99 | 51.9 | 52.6 | 52.4 | 48.2 | 50.0 | 49.5 |
| 1800–30 | 52.5 | 54.0 | 53.2 | 51.8 | 53.7 | 52.7 |
| Total | 52.3 | 53.3 | 52.8 | 50.8 | 52.0 | 51.5 |
| N | 303 | 359 | 662 | 285 | 346 | 631 |

the period, this improvement was not dramatic. As we have seen, age at marriage rose slightly among Lutherans and was nearly constant for Catholics prior to 1830. The modest rise in the age at widowhood for both groups suggests an improvement in adult mortality levels, though it was probably too small to have affected people's thinking about the nature of widowhood and the advantages and disadvantages of remarriage.

Finding oneself widowed at age forty, with children to support and land to farm or a trade to be carried on, left people facing an important decision as to whether to remarry or go on alone. For some, help from relatives might be available and census records indicate that relatives often lived in the households of a man or woman who had been widowed. Others simply continued alone, sometimes moving in later life to stay with a child who had married or with a unmarried sibling. We would like to know, of course, just how many chose to remarry and how the decision might have been affected by the characteristics of the individuals involved.

A first look at the problem can be obtained by simply considering the proportion of marriages that involved a previously married partner. Table 3.10 shows these data for three time periods. The figures suggest several interesting points. First, as was true in all other European settings, remarriage was more common for men than women (Dupâquier et al 1981). The proportion of marriages involving a widower was much higher than that involving a previously married woman. Moreover, the difference increased over time. The proportion of marriages involving a widower and spinster remained fairly steady (though there was a noticeable decline in the Lutheran communities) while the percentage involving a widow declined sharply. Secondly, the tendency to remarry appears to have fallen off over time. Among both Lutherans and Catholics, the proportion of marriages that involved a man and woman marrying for the first time rose to its highest point in the period 1836–70. Finally, given the marked differences already observed between Protestants and Catholics, it is somewhat

Table 3.10
Distribution of marriages by marital status of partners, religion and period of marriage

| | Catholics | | | | Lutherans | | | |
|---|---|---|---|---|---|---|---|---|
| Period of Marriage | Bachelor/ Spinster | Widower/ Spinster | Bachelor/ Widow | Widower/ Widow | Bachelor/ Spinster | Widower/ Spinster | Bachelor/ Widow | Widower/ Widow |
| 1750–89 | 72.9 | 13.6 | 8.6 | 5.0 | 71.8 | 16.0 | 6.7 | 5.6 |
| 1790–1835 | 80.2 | 13.1 | 3.1 | 3.6 | 77.1 | 14.7 | 4.3 | 3.9 |
| 1836–70 | 81.1 | 13.5 | 3.4 | 2.0 | 86.0 | 11.0 | 2.1 | 0.9 |
| Total | 79.7 | 12.9 | 4.3 | 3.1 | 78.6 | 13.7 | 4.3 | 3.4 |

surprising to note that this did not carry over into remarriage patterns. The decline in marriages involving a widowed partner was somewhat sharper in the Lutheran villages, but the difference was modest. For both groups, the nineteenth century was marked by a rising proportion of primary marriages.

Data on the marital status of spouses do not directly address the issue of remarriage, nor do they allow us to see how the likelihood of remarriage varied among different groups in the population. Estimating the probability of remarriage is difficult with reconstitution data, however. It is important to insure that the widows and widowers included remain in observation until their own deaths. Practically speaking, this means limiting the analysis to couples who married in our villages and for whom the death dates of both partners are known. This is worrisome because the risk of remarriage may differ between those who stay in the village after the death of a spouse and those who leave. If the chance to remarry was an important reason that led people to leave the village, focusing only on those who stay may underestimate the likelihood of remarriage. Unfortunately, since we do not know the fate of those who left, we have no choice but to restrict the discussion to those who remained. Still, it is important to keep in mind the problems posed by focusing on this restricted group of widows and widowers.

Table 3.11 shows the proportion of widows and widowers who remarried by the amount of time elapsed since the death of their previous spouse. Since widows and widowers faced two competing "risks" – they can cease to be widowed by either remarrying or by dying themselves – the probabilities shown are based on what demographers call a multiple decrement technique, which takes account of these two possible events. The results point to significant differences in the likelihood of remarriage over time and among different groups. The first and most striking difference is between men and women. In

Table 3.11a
Cumulative probabilities of remarriage for widowers by selected characteristics

| Date of Dissolution | Proportion of Widowers Remarrying by | | | | | |
|---|---|---|---|---|---|---|
| | 3 months | 6 months | 12 months | 24 months | 60 months | 120 months |
| 1750–1815 | .073 | .181 | .310 | .396 | .486 | .523 |
| 1816–47 | .019 | .081 | .174 | .244 | .305 | .327 |
| RELIGION | | | | | | |
| Catholics | .034 | .110 | .238 | .313 | .388 | .417 |
| Lutherans | .060 | .157 | .258 | .342 | .421 | .452 |
| AGE AT WIDOWHOOD | | | | | | |
| < 35 | .147 | .333 | .493 | .679 | .827 | .910 |
| 35–49 | .063 | .232 | .445 | .576 | .667 | .684 |
| > 49 | .012 | .024 | .065 | .078 | .116 | .128 |
| Total | .049 | .137 | .250 | .330 | .407 | .437 |

most societies, men are more likely to remarry after either widowhood or divorce, but the differences in our villages were huge. If one assumes that virtually all remarriages would occur within ten years of the death of the previous spouse, the data suggest that men were more than twice as likely to remarry. Almost 44% of widowers had remarried within ten years compared to just over 21% of widows. The timing of remarriage was entirely different as well. For women, remarriage within ten months of a husband's death was considered taboo because the wife might be carrying a child from her dead husband. Thus, virtually no remarriages occurred among still fertile women in the ten months following the death of a husband, and only about 3% married before the first anniversary of the husband's death. The peak period for remarriages, especially among younger women, was in the second year following the death. For widows less than thirty-five years of age, the proportion remarried jumped from about 10% after one year to 44% at the end of two years. Men, on the other hand, remarried with stunning speed. Almost 14% married within six months and one-quarter had done so within twelve months. The chances of remarrying were also greatly influenced by the age at which widowhood occurred. Not surprisingly, younger widows and widowers were far more likely to remarry.[5] Interestingly, though, male remarriage rates remained much higher in all age categories. While one in ten widows under the age of 35 remarried within a year, a half of all widowers of the same age range did so. As the information on the changing marital status of partners suggested, there is convincing evidence that remarriage rates

Table 3.11b
Cumulative probabilities of remarriage for widows by selected characteristics

| Date of Dissolution | Proportion of Widows Remarrying by | | | | | |
|---|---|---|---|---|---|---|
| | 3 months | 6 months | 12 months | 24 months | 60 months | 120 months |
| 1750–1815 | .000 | .008 | .036 | .188 | .276 | .307 |
| 1816–47 | .000 | .000 | .028 | .057 | .094 | .100 |
| RELIGION | | | | | | |
| Catholics | .000 | .000 | .034 | .132 | .197 | .210 |
| Lutherans | .000 | .008 | .032 | .124 | .189 | .215 |
| AGE AT WIDOWHOOD | | | | | | |
| < 35 | .000 | .000 | .098 | .439 | .641 | .696 |
| 35–49 | .000 | .012 | .042 | .123 | .181 | .201 |
| > 49 | .000 | .000 | .000 | .005 | .016 | .016 |
| Total | .000 | .004 | .032 | .128 | .192 | .212 |

declined over time, and that the decrease was sharper for women than men. The probability of a widow remarrying with five years declined by almost two-thirds between our two time periods, while for men the drop was just over one-third. For men, however, the declines were especially large at short durations. Thus while the probability of remarrying within ten years fell by about 40%, the likelihood of remarrying within six months declined by more than half.

Although remarriage had a long history of theological controversy, at least in the Catholic tradition (Ariès 1981), these debates appear to have had little impact on the behaviour of ordinary people in Alsace. Large numbers of both Catholics and Lutherans remarried, often very rapidly, after the death of a spouse, particularly if the surviving partner was still young at the time of the death. It is significant, however, that the tendency to remarry seemed to weaken during the nineteenth century. Along with a declining age difference between spouses, declining remarriage rates and a longer interval between death and remarriage has been seen by some as evidence of the growing importance of sentiment in married life with the emergence of urban, industrial societies. To say that love replaced financial and status considerations as the basis of marriage would overstate the case, but the decline in remarriage rates and the sharp drop in remarriages occurring shortly after the death of a spouse do point to an important change in the behaviour of widowers and widows and may signal a shift in the sentiments about the nature of the marital bond.

## SUMMARY AND CONCLUSION

In the villages of Alsace during the eighteenth and nineteenth centuries, success or failure, abject poverty or relative comfort relied to a large extent on the economic status of one's family. A growing literature on the family in the past has shown us the importance of marital alliances in such a setting and their far-reaching consequences for the couple and their families (Sabean 1990). Not surprisingly, the marital choices of the young were carefully watched and, no doubt, widely discussed even if the young were granted a reasonable amount of discretion in their choice of partner.

The demographic data presented here confirm the importance of material considerations in the operation of the marriage market. There was a high degree of homogamy in the selection of mates, with the children of landowners occupying a privileged position in the local market. Although some theorists have argued that the landless stood to profit from earlier marriage, the data suggest they were usually the last to marry, reflecting, I would argue, both their weaker bargaining position in the local marriage market, and the greater time it took them to amass the means to establish their own household.

Similar considerations undoubtedly shaped marriage patterns in most European rural communities in this period but, in Alsace, a further factor came into play. The Reformation created two distinct religious communities which developed over time different beliefs and practices concerning marriage. While both communities fit within the broad European marriage pattern described by Hajnal, marriage consistently occurred later and in a more restrictive way in the Catholic communities of Alsace. Interestingly, the differences were maintained even though both communities were buffeted by the changing economic and political circumstances of the times. The crisis of the rural world that intensified in the region in the middle decades of the nineteenth century led to later marriage for both groups, but the gap between Lutherans and Catholics was still maintained. By 1870, the end of the period studied in this work, differences in marriage patterns between the two religious groups were still clearly identifiable. Indeed, on some dimensions, notably in the seasonal character of marriage, the contrast grew sharper. Some of these differences, especially those involving age at marriage and the proportion never marrying, had implications for population growth in the two communities. Other things being equal, the more universal character of marriage among Lutherans would have led to a higher rate of population increase. As it happened, however, other things were not equal. In the next two chapters, we examine differences in fertility, which had the effect of partially offsetting the higher rate of nuptiality in the Lutheran communities.

# CHAPTER FOUR

# *Illegitimacy and Bridal Pregnancy*

Sexual relations outside marriage, and the births that might be expected to follow in a setting where contraception was limited, were far from rare in Alsace, particularly in the aftermath of the French Revolution. According to the Princeton studies of the decline of fertility in Europe, Alsatian rates of non-marital fertility were similar to those found among the states of southern Germany (Coale and Treadway 1986). When compared to other regions of France, however, Alsace stood near the top, leading LeBras and Todd (1981) to identify the area, along with the Nord and the Basque country, as the leading centres of rural illegitimacy. This fact would have come as a surprise, and certainly a disappointment, to the leaders of the Reformation in Alsace. One of their major goals was to restore the moral character of the population, which they saw as having been corrupted by pre-Reformation Catholicism (Abray 1985). Extramarital sexual relations were a prime target of their campaign, and they passed a series of harsh measures designed to eradicate the scourge of illegitimacy. That goal was never achieved, though, and by the nineteenth century, illegitimacy and bridal pregnancy were common not only in the cities but in the villages as well. What lay behind these relatively high levels? What role did religious affiliation play in the evolution of these trends? What consequences did the women who bore these children face? Answering these questions requires the use of both traditional sources of demographic data and a variety of other historical materials, which can cast an indirect light on the topic.

## CONCEPTUALIZING NON-MARITAL CHILDBEARING

Historical demography has established a set of clear rules for addressing the issues of illegitimacy and bridal pregnancy. By using information in civil or parish registers on the dates of marriages and births (or baptisms), we can classify births as illegitimate if occurring outside of marriage, premaritally conceived but legitimate if the bride was pregnant on her wedding day, or post-maritally conceived and born. The social reality that underlies these categories was a good deal more complex, however. Some conceptions occurred so close to the marriage date that the couple themselves probably were unaware that a child was on the way. Often, though, the bride was well along in her pregnancy. In these cases, the difference between bridal pregnancy and an illegitimate birth that was followed by marriage was a fine one. To cite an extreme case, Anne Marie Fritsch married Laurent Walter in the village of Goxwiller on the day after Christmas in 1836 (ADBR 4E 163 4) and gave birth to their first child on New Year's Day 1837 (ADBR 4E 163 2). They lived together for thirty years before Laurent's death and had four more children. Their situation would seem to have differed little from that of Marie Anne Spiess, who gave birth to an illegitimate daughter in Mussig in February 1856 (ADBR 4E 310 3). The child was acknowledged by Francois Antoine Ottenwelter who married her on 2 April of the same year (ADBR 4E 310 5). They too had a long and fruitful married life together, producing seven more legitimate children. Although the first births to these two couples will be classified differently, the community's perception of the couples and their children was likely much the same.

On the other hand, women who shared the same official status might face very different fates. Mothers who did not marry the fathers of their illegitimate children faced a situation that was usually difficult and occasionally disastrous. Ostracism or a marginal status within the village community often awaited those left alone with their child. For some, abandoning the child or suffocating the infant at birth seemed the only solution. Madeleine Kammerer was a servant in the town of Molsheim, some six kilometres from her home in the village of Dangolsheim. In April 1868 police stopped to question her by the side of the road just outside the town (ADBR 3M 894). She told them she was on her way to visit her family but that she had begun her menstrual period and was too tired to walk further. But when the police found the dead body of a baby boy in a basket with her, she admitted that she had given birth in a field during the night and claimed that the child had died shortly after birth. However, the police determined the child had been suffocated, and the frightened young woman was arrested and consigned to the hospice in Molsheim to await her trial. No details surfaced concerning the conception of the child. No man stepped forward to acknowledge involvement and none faced any official sanction. The young mother, however, was convicted of infanticide and sentenced to six years of hard labour (ADBR U 78).

Like the birth to Marie Anne Spiess, this event will be classed as another illegitimate birth, though the consequences of this birth for mother and child were radically different. Seldom can we uncover such detail surrounding a given case, but this and other examples are enough to remind us that the categories we use cover a wide range of human experience.

## DATA AND METHODS

Family reconstitution is a powerful tool for studying populations in the past, but it is not a method ideally suited for analyzing non-marital fertility (Knodel 1988). A significant proportion of out-of-wedlock births occurred to women who resided in the village only briefly, and relying on records from a single community limits what can be discovered about the experiences of these transient mothers. At the same time, a significant number of rural women left the villages to give birth to their babies in the city. These problems cannot be entirely overcome, but it is possible to push the analysis of this topic further than is usually done in reconstitution studies by making use of census data as well. This allows us to do two things. First, non-marital fertility rates can be computed for the larger sample of communities, comparing rates by religion and economic characteristics. And second, by merging census data with the family reconstitution materials, a fuller analysis of the careers of women who bore a child outside of marriage can be undertaken.

Studying non-marital childbearing in the Alsatian context, however, becomes more complex given the religious division of the population. As we have seen, the extension of French rule in Alsace during the seventeenth century brought with it various efforts to strengthen the position of Catholicism in the province (Châtellier 1981), including a 1682 act that made all illegitimate children wards of the king and required that they be baptized in the Catholic religion of the sovereign (Denis 1977).[1] This requirement undoubtedly created a strong incentive for Lutheran parents of illegitimate children to evade registration. When baptism in the Catholic faith (and registration) did take place, it might occur in a variety of different locations. The Catholic registers for the parish of Mussig, for example, contain baptisms of children of Lutheran parents who never resided in the village. Conversely, for the Protestant villages, the illegitimate births that occurred may have been registered in a variety of Catholic parishes.

For the pre-revolutionary period, then, estimates of the extent of illegitimate fertility are rather fragile, and this should be kept in mind when interpreting the findings.[2]

## ILLEGITIMACY AND BRIDAL PREGNANCY IN ALSACE

It is impossible to know how widespread the "immorality" of which early reformers complained really was in sixteenth-century Alsace. Nonetheless, as Abray (1985) has pointed out, the new Lutheran clergy were convinced a problem existed and were determined to improve the situation. One aspect of this moral campaign centred on the punishment of those found guilty of engaging in non-marital sexual relations. Kintz (1984), in his classic study of Strasbourg society in the sixteenth and seventeenth centuries, described the harsh treatment meted out to mothers of illegitimate or premaritally conceived children. Mothers were sometimes taken to prison along with their child immediately after giving birth, and they might remain there for up to four weeks. Unwed mothers were often referred to, even in official documents, by derogatory names such as *hure* (whore), and *vettel* (slut). Foreigners who gave birth in the city could expect even harsher treatment including public exposition, perhaps accompanied by their child (Kintz 1984, 210–17).

As the sin was seen to reside in the sexual act rather than the birth of the illegitimate child, it is perhaps not surprising that no clear distinction was made between a premarital conception and a birth outside marriage. Kintz (1984, 211) noted that the pastor of the Lutheran parish of St-Pierre-le-Jeune classified as illegitimate any child born less than thirty-five weeks after the wedding. Couples were supposed to acknowledge their sinfulness before marrying. Some who did were imprisoned and brought directly from their cells to be married before the altar. In these cases, the marriage ceremony was altered to reflect their fallen state. Hiding one's situation was no solution either. Couples who saw their first child born in the early months of their marriage might also face a brief jail sentence and the civic and religious condemnation that went with it.

What Dreyer-Roos (1969) has called the "austere Lutheran morality" of the city of Strasbourg in this era may well have served to keep the level of illegitimacy low in comparison to other urban centres. Kintz's figures show that only about 1% of births occurred outside marriage while perhaps 5% of all births were premaritally conceived. Dreyer-Roos suggests the illegitimacy ratio remained low until after the integration of Strasbourg into the kingdom of France in 1681, but rose dramatically during the eighteenth century. The influx of French administrative officials and, in particular, the establishment of a military garrison changed the character of the city. Rapid population growth was fuelled by immigration to Strasbourg from the countryside as well as from parts of Germany and Switzerland. These newcomers (including some who came for the purpose of giving birth in the city) played a disproportionate role in the growth of illegitimacy and helped increase the illegitimacy ratio to more than 15% on the eve of the Revolution (Dreyer-Roos 1969, 187). The nineteenth century saw a virtual explosion of illegitimacy in the urban areas generally, and in Strasbourg in particular. By 1868, more than one-quarter of all births occurred outside of marriage (Migneret 1871, 237).

In Alsace, as elsewhere, illegitimacy was far less common in the rural areas than in the cities. This was, in part, a reflection of the fact that some mothers would leave the villages and give birth to their children in the towns, thereby increasing the illegitimacy ratios of the cities and decreasing those of the rural areas. Data from Strasbourg for the mid-nineteenth century, for example, show that two-thirds of the illegitimate births that occurred in the city were to women who were born elsewhere (Migneret 1871, 237). Still, it seems clear that illegitimacy ratios were significantly lower in rural areas. Most studies of rural communities in the seventeenth and eighteenth centuries point to illegitimacy ratios of less than 2% (Denis 1977; Boehler 1995; Peter 1995). Yet, authorities in the rural areas, like their counterparts in Strasbourg, took the issue very seriously, and their actions may have helped to keep the rates low. Sanctions both formal and informal were commonly employed. Fines, often hefty, were the most common outcome of disciplinary procedures invoked against both parents of the illegitimate child. When the fines could not be met, other penalties, including imprisonment, might be handed out (Gerst 1975; Peter 1995). As in the cities, strangers or women who bore a second illegitimate child received the most severe punishment. Public exposition or a similar form of public humiliation such as pulling a cart of manure through the village was sometimes prescribed. Beyond the legal penalties, village communities developed a range of informal sanctions that might be directed at those who violated the moral standards of the community in a public way. Sarg (1977), in his study of rural customs, noted that mothers of children born out of wedlock were frequently relegated to a special place in the church, designated by such names as *Huchebänkel* (the whore's pew) or *Schandbänkele* (the pew of shame). They were prohibited from participating in traditional ceremonies such as the *relevailles*, a religious

Table 4.1
Illegitimacy ratios for the five reconstituted villages

| Village | 1750–1789 | 1790–1815 | 1816–1835 | 1836–1850 | 1851–1870 | 1750–1870 |
|---|---|---|---|---|---|---|
| Avolsheim | — | 1.0 | 3.0 | 7.7 | 6.2 | 3.9 |
| Husseren | 2.1 | 3.6 | 3.8 | 4.0 | 3.1 | 3.3 |
| Mussig | 2.6 | 1.4 | 2.1 | 4.0 | 5.0 | 3.1 |
| Baldenheim | 2.8 | 1.7 | 3.8 | 6.0 | 5.9 | 3.7 |
| Goxwiller | 0.9 | 2.7 | 5.3 | 4.9 | 4.6 | 3.0 |
| Total | 2.1 | 2.0 | 3.5 | 4.9 | 4.9 | 3.4 |

service designed to welcome the mother back into the community after her confinement (Gélis 1984, 292), and their children were baptized after rather than during Sunday services.[3] It is impossible to know how commonly local people observed such practices; it seems likely penalties may have been applied with more force to some than to others. Sarg (1977, 64) suggested that the pastor in Lutheran parishes could use his discretion in applying the prescribed sanctions. A birth acknowledged by the father and followed in short order by marriage likely brought a different reaction than a birth to a young servant with no family in the village and no marriage prospects. Nevertheless, it is clear that Alsatian communities, at least in the pre-revolutionary period, responded with considerable concern to violations of norms surrounding sexual relations and childbearing.

Despite the religious and social condemnation of non-marital sexuality, such behaviour was never absent and grew more common over time. Table 4.1 shows the illegitimacy ratio for the five villages included in the reconstitution study for five time periods. In comparison with other areas of Europe, the illegitimacy ratio was high even in the eighteenth century and, though the figures for the early period probably underestimate the true rate, there seems little doubt that illegitimacy became more common in the nineteenth century. In no village did the ratio reach 3% in the pre-revolutionary period, while after 1836 it stood above 3% in all five communities. Interestingly, the ratios for the Lutheran and Catholic villages were generally similar. Both religious communities experienced an increase during the nineteenth century and, looking over the period as a whole, the ratio was between 3% and 4% for all the villages.

Surprisingly, the industrial village of Husseren-Wesserling does not stand out as a centre of non-marital childbearing. Although the ratio reached a higher level earlier in time, it remained relatively constant

Table 4.2
Illegitimacy ratios for the twenty-six communes by economic type and dominant
religious affiliation

| Village Type | 1811– 1820 | 1821– 1830 | 1831– 1840 | 1841– 1850 | 1851– 1860 | 1861– 1870 | 1811– 1870 |
|---|---|---|---|---|---|---|---|
| Catholic Agricultural | 4.4 | 5.2 | 7.0 | 7.3 | 6.9 | 6.0 | 6.1 |
| Catholic Rural-Industrial | 3.4 | 4.1 | 5.8 | 6.1 | 6.3 | 10.6 | 6.0 |
| Catholic Industrial | 8.9 | 9.1 | 8.2 | 6.8 | 7.9 | 8.5 | 8.2 |
| TOTAL CATHOLIC | 4.9 | 6.1 | 7.0 | 6.8 | 7.1 | 7.9 | 6.7 |
| Lutheran Agricultural | 4.5 | 6.3 | 7.3 | 6.1 | 8.1 | 7.2 | 6.6 |
| Lutheran Rural-Industrial | 3.6 | 3.7 | 6.0 | 4.2 | 5.1 | 5.3 | 4.6 |
| TOTAL LUTHERAN | 4.0 | 4.8 | 6.5 | 4.9 | 6.3 | 6.6 | 5.4 |

throughout the nineteenth century. The growth of factory production may have been associated with a rise in the ratio in the late eighteenth century, but the ratio did not continue to increase, and by the middle years of the nineteenth century, it was actually lower than in the agricultural villages.

It is dangerous to make too much of trends involving particular villages, where the ratios are based on relatively small numbers of births. Data from the larger sample of villages show the evolution of illegitimacy in the nineteenth century in more detail. Table 4.2 presents the ratios for twenty-six communes grouped together by economic characteristics and religious identity. The data for this larger group of communities confirm the existence of a trend towards greater illegitimacy as the nineteenth century wore on. The figures also underscore the modest (and inconsistent) differences among communities that differed in religion and economic character. As was the case with the reconstituted villages, illegitimacy reached a higher level earlier in time in the industrialized area but then remained relatively stable in the decades that followed. While the trends are similar, overall, the ratios presented here are noticeably higher than when dealing with the five villages included in the reconstitution. This almost certainly reflects an urban effect in that the aggregate sample contains a number of larger communities. In the case of the industrial communities in particular, the inclusion of Masevaux, a town of some 3000 inhabitants that had a high level of illegitimacy, boosted the average for this group of communities.

Table 4.3
Coale index of non-marital fertility ($I_h$) by economic type and
dominant religious affiliation

| Village Type | Year | | | |
|---|---|---|---|---|
| | 1836 | 1851 | 1861 | 1875 |
| Catholic Agricultural | .037 | .040 | .037 | .039 |
| Catholic Rural-Industrial | .042 | .039 | .058 | .056 |
| Catholic Industrial | .057 | .035 | .045 | .028 |
| TOTAL CATHOLIC | .044 | .038 | .045 | .040 |
| Lutheran Agricultural | .046 | .026 | .045 | .033 |
| Lutheran Rural-Industrial | .037 | .032 | .032 | .041 |
| TOTAL LUTHERAN | .041 | .029 | .037 | .037 |

The illegitimacy ratio is a weak tool for analyzing trends in non-marital fertility (Van De Walle 1980). The proportion of births that occurs outside marriage can be influenced by a wide variety of demographic factors. For example, if married women reduce the size of their families, the illegitimacy ratio will increase even though no change occurred in the behaviour of unmarried women. It is preferable to examine rates of non-marital fertility which relate the number of illegitimate births to the number of unmarried women of childbearing age. To do so requires a count of the population by age, sex, and marital status, something that is not available until 1836. Even though this limits the analysis to the later stages of the period, it does permit a closer look at variations in non-marital childbearing. Table 4.3 shows Coale's standardized measure of illegitimate fertility ($I_h$) by religion and economic structure for the twenty-six communes in the larger sample.[4] The findings suggest that the rate of non-marital fertility was remarkably stable during this period. It declined slightly for both religious groups between 1836 and 1851, a period when age at marriage was rising. This suggests that the larger number of young unmarried women in the villages was not accompanied by a corresponding increase in out-of-wedlock births.[5] Differences by religion or type of economic activity were both modest and inconsistent. As was true when looking at the illegitimacy ratio, there is no evidence to suggest that industrialization, at least in a rural context, was associated with higher levels of non-marital fertility. Overall, one is led to conclude that while non-marital childbearing was more common in Alsace than in many other regions of Europe during this era, this high level was shared in by all major sectors of the population.

## THE SOCIAL CONTEXT OF ILLEGITIMACY

The aggregate data presented above indicate the incidence of illegitimacy in Alsace, but reveal nothing about the context in which this form of childbearing occurred. They give no information about the characteristics of the women who gave birth to these children nor any sense of the consequences of the event for the mother and her child. In particular, they do not distinguish between illegitimate births that were followed by the marriage of the parents and births to women who were left on their own to raise their child.

To explore these issues it is essential to make use of the individual-level data that form the basis of the family reconstitution study. Even here, though, formidable obstacles exist. For women who marry and live out their days in the community, a good deal of information about the context and consequences of non-marital childbearing is available. But many who bore an illegitimate child left little trace in the records. Servants, in particular, often came from elsewhere, lived in the village for only a short time, and vanished after giving birth to their child. All we know about their lives comes from the details listed on the birth certificate, and these are often few. Sometimes local officials did no more than record the mother's name and the name given to her child.

The first question one would like to answer concerns the proportion of women who married the father of their illegitimate child.[6] Any answer to this question depends, however, on the reliability of the information touching on acknowledgment of paternity. This is a complex and interesting issue that needs some discussion. Acknowledgment of paternity was affected in the first place by changing legislation. Prior to the French Revolution, midwives were required to attempt to ascertain the name of the father *in doloribus parta*, in the pain of labour. Thus, the parish registers almost always listed the name of a father supplied by a desperate and harassed mother. Not surprisingly, such claims were sometimes disputed by the man so named. The parish register of Goxwiller for 1746 lists a birth to Madeleine Pfleger, who named Jean Michel Eberstein from the nearby village of Bernardswiller as the father (ADBR 3E 163 1). On the following page, the pastor noted that Eberstein denied being the father of the child and his denial was supported by three witnesses. The denial was then crossed out, however, and a new version of the baptismal certificate was created listing him as father. Whether he recanted or his denial was rejected by the pastor cannot be determined.

With the new legislation introduced during the Revolution and the promulgation of the Napoleonic code in 1804, the situation changed dramatically (Brinton 1936; Van De Walle 1980). The father's name could be mentioned only if he voluntarily acknowledged his involvement. In this case, identifications would seem well founded, but the fact that the man had to make some positive step in order to be recognized as the father leads to a variety of practical problems. In many cases where an acknowledgment occurred, the father came forward at the time of the birth and his name was registered on the birth certificate. Often, though, this was not the case. Acknowledgment may have come about at a later time, and detecting it is not always easy. Moreover, the need to officially register acknowledgment may not have appeared great to many a couple. Having accepted the child as a full member of the family, going through official procedures to acknowledge paternity may have seemed an unnecessary burden. There are a number of cases where illegitimate children who eventually married did so under the name of their mother's husband, though no statement of acknowledgment can be found in the local records. Did no acknowledgment take place or has the record been lost? Finally, the survival status of the child undoubtedly played a role. Children who died shortly after birth were seldom the object of an acknowledgment. In at least some of these cases, it would seem likely that the future husband of the mother was indeed the father. Having not acknowledged paternity at the time of the birth, however, couples would have seen no point in doing so on their wedding day. And yet in the absence of any *acte de reconnaissance* it would be dangerous to assume the future groom was the father and that he would have acknowledged the child had he or she survived.

Given the problems involved in identifying couples who began their childbearing experience with a premarital birth, it is essential to be cautious in interpreting the figures presented in the following set of tables. Table 4.4 provides a breakdown of the destiny of mothers of illegitimate children insofar as the vital registers and manuscript census allow us to follow them. As is evident, the fate of many mothers remains unknown. This was particularly the case in the eighteenth century when, as was described above, the need for Lutheran mothers to have their children baptized in a Catholic parish led to the inclusion of baptisms of children who probably never resided in the village. The Revolution introduced civil registration and regular censuses, and this made it easier to track the mothers of out-of-wedlock births. Still, one-third of mothers disappeared from view after their child was born. While it is impossible to say what proportion of these

Table 4.4
Destiny of mothers of illegitimate children

| Destiny | 1750–89 | 1790–1835 | 1836–60 | 1750–1860 |
|---|---|---|---|---|
| Married father | 16.7 | 22.3 | 27.1 | 23.6 |
| Married other man | 8.3 | 28.5 | 27.1 | 24.8 |
| Never married | 14.6 | 15.4 | 12.5 | 14.0 |
| Unknown | 60.4 | 33.8 | 33.3 | 37.6 |
| Total | 100.0 | 100.0 | 100.0 | 100.0 |
| N | 48 | 130 | 144 | 322 |

mothers eventually married, it does seem likely that few would have married the father of their child. Among those whose fate is known, more than one in five remained single, significantly above the level for the general population. Census records show that most of these women lived, at least for a time, with other family members, usually a parent, before establishing a household of their own.

Of those who remained in the village and married, about half did so with the father of their illegitimate child. As explained above, this is probably an underestimate. In several cases, the child died shortly after birth and the mother married not long after. In at least some of these cases, it seems likely that the woman married the father of the child and that no acknowledgment was recorded in light of the child's death. Yet, it suggests a significant number of women went on to marry a man other than the father of their out-of-wedlock child, and it raises a question as to how the fate of these two groups of women differed and, indeed, how they fared in comparison to women without a premarital birth.

Table 4.5 compares three groups of women based on their childbearing experience prior to marriage. The first group comprises women who bore no children before marrying, the second, mothers of illegitimate children who married the father of the child, and, finally, those women with an out-of-wedlock birth who married a man other than the father of their child. Again, it is worth noting that some of those women listed as marrying a man other than the father of their illegitimate child may be improperly classified, especially in cases where the child in question died at or shortly after birth. Given the already small number of cases in the two categories, however, it was not possible to further subdivide mothers according to the survival status of their child.

The information in table 4.5 suggests that the conditions surrounding a woman's first birth had important implications for her future.

Table 4.5
Selected characteristics of women and their spouses by legitimacy status of first birth

|  | No Premarital Birth | Premarital Birth | | |
|  |  | Acknowledged | Not Acknowledged | Total |
|---|---|---|---|---|
| Age at first marriage | 25.4 | 27.0 | 29.3 | 28.1 |
| Age difference from spouse | 3.5 | 1.1 | 3.3 | 2.2 |
| % where wife older | 27.5 | 45.6 | 39.7 | 42.6 |
| % where husband 5+ years older | 33.3 | 20.6 | 32.9 | 27.1 |
| % widower | 15.5 | 3.9 | 32.5 | 18.6 |
| % from out of town | 38.1 | 52.6 | 60.0 | 56.4 |
| Months from illegitimate birth to marriage | — | 40.5 | 58.2 | 49.5 |
| Number of cases | 2292 | 76 | 80 | 156 |

Note: The category "No Premarital Birth" includes all marriages occurring before 1861 without a birth prior to the marriage date. Age data refer only to first marriages of women who had not had a premarital birth.

Marriage occurred at a later age for mothers of out-of-wedlock children, especially for those women who did not marry the father of their child. These women were, on average, close to thirty years of age at the time of their marriage. The men they married also differed in important ways from the husbands of women without a premarital birth. In almost half of the cases involving a premarital birth to a couple that eventually married, the wife was older than her husband. The average age difference between the spouses in these cases was just over one year.[7] The situation among women who married a man other than the father was quite different. The average age difference of 3.3 years masks two quite different marriage patterns. On the one hand, a significant number of these women (39.7%) married a younger man, often with a lower-status occupation such as a weaver. On the other hand, many married a man who was significantly older. This, in turn, was partly a function of the fact that almost one-third of these women married a widower compared to only 15.5% of those without a premarital birth, and only 3.9% of the mothers who married the father of their illegitimate child. It is striking to note as well that women who married a man other than the father of their child were far more likely to have a husband who came from outside the village.

These data suggest that a premarital birth that was followed by marriage to the father of the child did not necessarily lead to serious problems for the women involved. Their fate was not so different from that of women who began their childbearing after marriage. Indeed, the fact that many were older than their husbands may have strengthened their position within the marriage. By contrast, women who were abandoned by their lover and left to care for a child on their own were at a great disadvantage when they married. Their chances of making a "good match" were limited. Frequently, it seemed, they were married off to a man in desperate need of a mate and, as in the case of Marguerithe Schneider, assumed the responsibility of raising another's children. She married Jean Jacques Offerlé, five years her senior, six months after the death of his second wife, and became mother to his nine surviving children, including an eight-month-old baby (ADBR 7M 240).

To this point, the analysis has grouped together all mothers of illegitimate children regardless of the number of children they bore outside of marriage. But, as Laslett (1980) has suggested, women who gave birth to more than one illegitimate child often accounted for a significant proportion of non-marital childbearing. Among these women, illegitimate childbearing was not only repetitive but often transmitted across generations and shared among kin. There is some evidence that a core of unwed mothers who never married did fall into what Laslett has termed "a bastardy-prone subsociety." In the village of Husseren, for example, two sisters, Marie Eve and Marie Anne Spony, each gave birth to two illegitimate children. Neither sister ever married, and the 1836 census lists them as living together with their children (ADHR 6M 21). One of their daughters, Catherine, later became the mother of an illegitimate child as well. Such cases were relatively rare, however. It is true that 17% of unwed mothers did give birth to more than one illegitimate child, and these mothers accounted for almost one-third of all such births. But these figures are inflated by the cases of mothers who were living in cohabiting relationships and eventually married. In several instances, the father of the children was from Germany or Switzerland, and there may have been legal impediments which delayed the marriage. Overall, in these rural communities of Alsace, repetitive childbearing outside of marriage or cohabiting relationships was a relatively rare event.

Marriage, sought after or not, or life in a bastardy-prone subsociety were not the only outcomes for unwed mothers, however, as the case of Catherine Marguerithe Nickel demonstrates. She gave birth to a daughter at age twenty-eight whom she named after herself (ADBR 4E 163 2). Following the birth, she and her daughter lived with her mother. After her mother's death, she and the child kept house together until the daughter married at age twenty-six. She then lived with her unmarried sister (who bore no children), and, finally, by herself until her death at age seventy-six. She never married nor did she give birth to other illegitimate children. Her daughter bore no illegitimate children nor was she pregnant on her wedding day in 1863 when she married a local glazier. We cannot know why life unfolded as it did for her, whether she wished to marry but could find no one who viewed her as a suitable partner. We do know she lived her life in the company of family members and raised a daughter who, on appearances, became a member of respectable society. Although she never married, neither she nor her daughter joined the ranks of the bastardy-prone subsociety.

## PATTERNS OF BRIDAL PREGNANCY

As was noted above, the line between illegitimacy and bridal pregnancy was not always clear. The conditions leading to such births were often more similar than different. A couple may have entered into sexual relations in the context of a promise (formal or informal) to marry, but whether these relations led to a conception and subsequent birth before or after their marriage depended on many things. How quickly the woman conceived after the beginning of sexual relations and the flexibility of the wedding date would determine the couple's status on their wedding day. Unforeseen circumstances – the death of a suitor or a parental veto of the planned marriage – might lead to a different destiny than that imagined by the couple.

In looking at bridal pregnancy, then, it makes sense to examine the process of family formation as a whole, and classify marriages according to the circumstances surrounding the beginning of childbearing. Table 4.6 examines the experience of couples with regard to pregnancy and childbearing at the time of their marriage. The focus here is on couples for whom both the beginning and end of marriage occurred locally. The results show an increasing tendency over time for couples to either conceive or bear a child before marriage. Among both Catholic and Lutheran couples married before 1790, almost 90% came to the altar with the bride not having conceived their first child. It is, of course, possible that some percentage of these couples had begun to have sex, but the initiation of relations in these cases most likely occurred fairly close to the wedding date. This figure declined among later cohorts as both the proportion of couples with a premarital birth, and especially those with a premarital conception, increased sharply. While this pattern holds true for both religious groups, the increase was sharper among Lutherans. For the early cohorts, bridal pregnancy was somewhat more common among

Table 4.6
Distribution of marriages (per 1000) by childbearing experience at the time of
marriage, religion and period of marriage

| Period of Marriage | Illegitimate | Illegitimate & Premarital | Premarital | Neither |
|---|---|---|---|---|
| | | CATHOLICS | | |
| 1750–89 | 16 | 0 | 90 | 894 |
| 1790–1815 | 13 | 0 | 145 | 842 |
| 1816–35 | 36 | 12 | 182 | 769 |
| 1836–50 | 26 | 15 | 189 | 770 |
| Total | 23 | 7 | 154 | 816 |
| | | LUTHERANS | | |
| 1750–89 | 3 | 0 | 83 | 914 |
| 1790–1815 | 12 | 0 | 100 | 888 |
| 1816–35 | 29 | 6 | 171 | 794 |
| 1836–50 | 21 | 21 | 261 | 697 |
| Total | 13 | 4 | 132 | 851 |

Note: Only marriages that occurred and ended locally are included.

Catholics but, as was true on other dimensions, the behaviour of
Lutheran couples changed markedly during the nineteenth century.
The proportion of Lutheran brides pregnant on their wedding day
rose to over 25% among those marrying in the period 1836–50, more
than triple the proportion among the cohort marrying prior to the
Revolution.

Premarital conceptions that took place close to a planned wedding
date may have caused little concern. The woman herself might not
have known she was pregnant, and certainly other members of the
community, including the wedding guests, would have had nothing
to discuss as the celebration proceeded. Where a long gap occurred
between conception and marriage, circumstances might have been
different. The couple would almost certainly have become aware of
their situation, and might even have changed their plans in the face of
it. Family members and curious village residents, as well as the priest
or minister, would have known a child was on the way. It is important, then, to examine the distribution of premarital conceptions
according to the elapsed time between the marriage date and the
birth of the premaritally conceived child. The figures in table 4.7 indicate that the majority of conceptions took place long enough prior to
the wedding such that the woman herself was probably aware of
being pregnant. Among both Lutherans and Catholics, only about
one in eight such pregnancies resulted in a birth in the seventh or

Table 4.7
Elapsed time from marriage to first birth for brides with premarital conception by religion and period of marriage

| Interval in Months Since Marriage | Period of Marriage | | |
|---|---|---|---|
| | 1750–1815 | 1816–56 | 1750–1856 |
| CATHOLICS | | | |
| < 3 | 19.6 | 26.2 | 24.0 |
| 3–6 | 64.7 | 63.1 | 63.6 |
| 7–8 | 15.7 | 10.7 | 12.3 |
| Mean | 5.0 | 4.6 | 4.7 |
| N | 51 | 103 | 154 |
| LUTHERANS | | | |
| < 3 | 29.6 | 23.8 | 26.1 |
| 3–6 | 55.6 | 63.1 | 60.1 |
| 7–8 | 14.8 | 13.1 | 13.8 |
| Mean | 4.2 | 4.9 | 4.6 |
| N | 54 | 84 | 138 |

eighth month of the couple's married life. The majority of births occurred three to six months after the wedding, and it is possible that some of these marriages were brought about by the pregnancy or the date of the wedding was advanced because of the approaching birth.[8] Yet the rather large number of births that occurred shortly after the ceremony would seem to suggest that being pregnant on one's wedding day was not necessarily a sign of great shame. In both religious communities, approximately one-quarter of pregnant brides gave birth less than three months after their wedding.

It is striking too that despite the rise in bridal pregnancy that occurred during the nineteenth century, the timing of births in relation to marriage changed very little. One might have thought that the increasing frequency of premarital conceptions would have weakened the pressure on couples to marry quickly, leading to an increase in the proportion of births soon after the wedding. Knodel (1988) found just such a pattern in his study of German villages. In the case of Alsace, however, there is no evidence of such a development. The average interval between marriage and first birth was virtually unchanged as was the distribution of births across the three time categories.

A second way to examine this issue is to compare the seasonality of marriages for those with and without a premarital conception. If news of an impending pregnancy convinced a couple to move up their wedding date, a larger percentage of marriages might take place in the less favoured times of the year. Although harvest time was generally too busy for wedding celebrations, a couple facing the birth of a child might decide to marry then rather than wait for a planned date in a more favourable time such as November or January. There is evidence that a premarital pregnancy did have a modest effect on the timing of marriage. As we have seen, the winter months were the most popular time to marry, and this was true for both pregnant and non-pregnant brides in both religious communities. The extent of seasonality was less among couples where the bride was pregnant, however, indicating marriages were more evenly spread out over the year.[9] Among Catholic couples, the average monthly deviation was 42 for pregnant brides, and 58 for brides who were not pregnant; among Lutheran women, the figures were 32 and 49 respectively. The more even distribution of marriages throughout the year in situations where the woman was pregnant suggests some couples may have set or moved up a wedding date in order to marry before the child was born or the woman was too obviously pregnant.[10]

To this point, the analysis has focused on the overall incidence of bridal pregnancy in the two religious communities. We can gain more insight into the circumstances surrounding these births by looking at the influence of selected characteristics of marrying couples on the likelihood of a premarital conception. Table 4.8 uses the occupation of the groom as an indicator of the couple's social position and shows the distribution of couples by their childbearing status at the time of marriage. For both Catholics and Lutherans, clear differences in the prevalence of bridal pregnancy existed along social class lines. Both illegitimacy and bridal pregnancy were significantly more common among couples where the husband held a lower-status occupation. The brides of *journaliers* and weavers were particularly likely to have either conceived or given birth prior to marriage. With fewer resources, contracting marriage for women and men in these groups may have been more difficult. A longer period of saving, both to fund the wedding itself and to set up a household, may have meant longer courtship periods and a greater risk of a premarital conception. And, of course, the social stigma attached to a premarital conception among the disadvantaged classes may simply have been less. Wealthier families, more sensitive to any hint of dishonour and often more tied to the church, may have worked harder to prevent behaviour that would have brought shame upon the family name. Interestingly, the patterns by social status were strikingly similar in the two religious groups. Premarital sexual activity was by no means confined to the lower orders, but couples from less advantaged groups were significantly more likely to conceive their first child prior to their passing before the minister or priest.

Table 4.8
Distribution of marriages (per 1000) by childbearing experience at the time of
marriage, religion and husband's occupation

| Husband's Occupation | Illegitimate | Illegitimate & Premarital | Premarital | Neither |
|---|---|---|---|---|
| | | CATHOLICS | | |
| Farmer | 10 | 5 | 121 | 864 |
| Artisan | 33 | 0 | 143 | 825 |
| Journalier | 34 | 6 | 201 | 759 |
| Weaver | 37 | 24 | 213 | 726 |
| | | LUTHERANS | | |
| Farmer | 6 | 6 | 89 | 900 |
| Artisan | 13 | 0 | 130 | 857 |
| Journalier | 13 | 13 | 158 | 816 |
| Weaver | 41 | 7 | 207 | 745 |

Figure 4.1 shows the percentage of brides pregnant by their age at the time of marriage. If premarital conceptions were largely the result of unguarded moments of passion among the young and impetuous, one would expect to find that younger brides were more likely to approach the altar with a child on the way. Indeed the pregnancy might have led to marriages that otherwise would have occurred at a later date. This does not seem to have been the case, however. Except for older brides, where the incidence of bridal pregnancy was lowest, variation by the age of the bride was modest among both Catholics and Lutherans.[11] As we saw in the tables of chapter 3, the vast majority of marriages occurred to women between the ages of twenty and thirty-four, and, in these age categories given in figure 4.1, the proportion of brides who were pregnant was quite similar. It seems clear, then, that premarital sexual relations were not limited to any one age group and may have been common for a significant and growing proportion of couples during courtship.

Data on the proportion pregnant by the marital status of the spouses are shown in figure 4.2. They reveal that, among both Lutherans and Catholics, the likelihood of premarital conception varied significantly by marital status. For Catholics, the likelihood was greatest for widows marrying bachelors and in situations where both partners were marrying for the first time; for Lutheran women, the highest proportion occurred among first-time brides marrying bachelors. The chances of a bridal pregnancy were greatly reduced among Lutherans and Catholics when the groom was a widower.

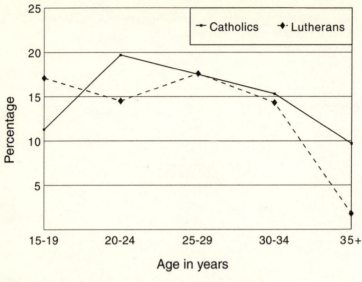

Figure 4.1
Percentage of brides pregnant by age at marriage and religion

The relatively high probability that widows who married bachelors would be pregnant on their wedding day may, at first, seem surprising. It might suggest a strategy of entrapment whereby a widow
in difficult circumstances tried to catch a new husband by initiating
sexual relations in order to become pregnant. Equally, it may suggest
that emotionally and financially vulnerable widows were seen as
easy prey by ambitious bachelors. It would be wrong to arrive at
such conclusions too quickly, however. For one thing, a number of
these marriages followed a rather distinctive path. Some involved
marriage to a relative of the woman's late husband; others appear to
have involved marriage to a man who served as an apprentice or
hired hand to the family. In these cases, the pregnancy and marriage
may have developed out of a form of cohabiting relationship. It is
possible as well that norms regarding sexual behaviour differed for
"experienced" women such as widows. In this case, the decision to
begin sexual relations would have seemed less momentous. The very
low rates of bridal pregnancy observed among marriages involving
widowers may also reflect the special conditions surrounding these
marriages. As was shown in chapter 3, many of these marriages
occurred very quickly after the death of the man's previous wife.
This suggests two factors could have been operating: first, the time
in which to begin sexual relations and conceive was very short;

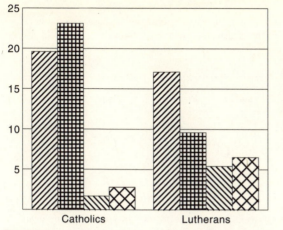

Figure 4.2
Percentage of brides pregnant by marital status of partners and religion

secondly, a number of these marriages appear to have had an "arranged" character. In the absence of spontaneous mutual attraction, it is perhaps not surprising that sexual relations did not begin until after the wedding took place.

Before we draw together the findings about premarital sex and childbearing, it is worth looking at how the pregnancy status of the bride affected the couple's future. The data in table 4.9 compare the experiences of brides who were pregnant with those of women who conceived for the first time only after marriage. The results reveal that marriage occurred only slightly earlier for women with a premarital conception. Combined with the fact that these women were already pregnant, and thus experienced their first birth within eight months of their marriage, childbearing obviously began earlier among those women who premaritally conceived. The difference was not huge, but it does amount to a "head start" of just over one year. As a result, the average number of children born to women pregnant at the time of their marriage was slightly greater than among those who began childbearing later. The difference was quite small, however, and suggests that, as far as we can tell, bridal pregnancy had few long-term consequences for couples.

### SUMMARY AND CONCLUSION

The evidence presented in this chapter points to the existence of relatively high levels of both illegitimacy and bridal pregnancy in Alsace. Even in the eighteenth century, premarital births and conceptions

Table 4.9
Mean age at first marriage and first birth, age difference with spouse, and mean number of children ever born by religion and pregnancy status

|  | Catholics | | Lutherans | |
|---|---|---|---|---|
|  | Pregnant | Not Pregnant | Pregnant | Not Pregnant |
| Age at marriage | 25.7 | 26.0 | 23.7 | 23.9 |
| Age at first birth | 26.1 | 27.2 | 24.2 | 25.3 |
| Age difference with spouse | 0.9 | 2.2 | 2.7 | 2.6 |
| Mean number of children ever born | 7.1 | 6.6 | 5.5 | 5.1 |
| N | 137 | 554 | 121 | 585 |

Note: Includes only primary marriages for women whose marriage occurred prior to 1856 and ended locally. For those not pregnant at marriage, only women who had at least one post-marital birth are included. Mean number of children ever born is based on families where the wife survived to age 45.

were not rare, and rates of both types of behaviour increased significantly in the nineteenth century. The Alsatian situation was not out of line with the experiences of neighbouring German states, but looked at in the context of France, Alsace stood out as one of the regions with the highest levels of rural illegitimacy and bridal pregnancy (Van De Walle 1980; Knodel and Hochstadt 1980).

Knodel (1988) and others have pointed to the problems that arise in attempting to make any easy link between rates of illegitimacy and bridal pregnancy and the prevalence of premarital or extramarital sexual relations. Variations in marriage patterns, abortion and infanticide, and contraception all influence the likelihood of premarital relations resulting in conception or birth. Nevertheless, it seems safe to conclude that a significant minority of couples began having sex before marriage, and that this proportion likely increased over the time period considered here. Understanding why this was so, given the limited information available, presents a greater challenge.

Most discussions of bridal pregnancy and illegitimacy in this period point to the role played by norms regarding sexual relations during courtship. In Alsace, as in many Germanic regions, there was widespread toleration, if not necessarily approval, of sexual relations commencing once a promise to marry had been made (Gerst 1975; Boehler 1995; Peter 1995; Sabean 1990).[12] An ensuing pregnancy, even one where the birth preceded the marriage ceremony, was not perceived as a serious offence against community standards so long as the marriage indeed took place and the child was accepted into the family. It also seems clear that the destiny of couples expecting a child at the time of their marriage did not differ radically from those who conceived after their wedding day.

Where non-marital relations led to pregnancy but not marriage, the situation was quite different. As we have seen, those who married someone other than the father of the child often made matches that would appear to have been less than ideal. Many others left the village and we have no information on their fate. We do know from other sources, however, that unmarried mothers faced a difficult situation. Alsace never used the system of towers, common in other parts of France, that allowed women to give up their children anonymously to the care of the foundling homes, and abandonment of infants and children seems to have been relatively rare (Migneret 1868, 947). Still, some who left their villages for the city sought to remedy their situation before the child arrived by procuring an abortion, while others, alone or with help, decided to do away with their new-born children. The problem was particularly acute in Strasbourg, leading the mayor to complain of the involvement of midwives in the practice: "Some midwives, moved by distress, material interest or moral failing, offer their services to unmarried girls in particular, among whom the mortality of newborns whether as stillbirths or due to deaths from convulsions, (a common term used to cover the deaths of entire generations dying due to lack of care or perhaps as a result of more concrete actions), is such that it leads to the inevitable suspicion that the desire of many unmarried mothers to be free of their worrisome burden is all too often seconded by the connivance of midwives of little conscience" (ADBR 5M 8).

Police and court records also suggest that, while infanticide was not a common practice, it was certainly not unknown and seems usually to have involved unmarried women.[13] For the many more who did not resort to such drastic actions, life was hard for them and their children. Infant death rates were significantly higher among illegitimate children,[14] and even when the children survived, a life of dire poverty was a likely outcome (Fuchs 1992).

Although their position may have been marginal, this did not necessarily imply membership in Laslett's "bastardy-prone subsociety." Laslett himself admits the boundaries of this group were fluid and ill-defined, but he uses the term to refer to those for whom bastardy was not an isolated event. Membership could result from repetitive bastard-bearing, but also from kin or marriage connections to others who bore children outside of marriage. There were certainly some women in these villages who appear to have been candidates for membership in such a group. On the whole, though, repetitive non-marital childbearing was relatively rare in rural Alsace.

A significant rise in illegitimacy and bridal pregnancy has been observed in a number of European regions during the nineteenth century (Shorter et al 1971). Opinion is divided concerning the sources of this increase (Blaikie 1993, 14–17). Shorter (1975) has argued in favour of a change in the emotional character of male-female relationships, suggesting that the rise of sentiment was associated with more frequent premarital sexuality and a consequent increase in illegitimacy and bridal pregnancy. Laslett (1977), however, has remarked that a rising illegitimacy ratio was generally accompanied by a rise in the proportion of births attributable to "repetitive bastard-bearers," a fact that does not sit well with Shorter's interpretation. Others have linked rising illegitimacy to the changing economic situation of the rural population, though the nature of the economic effect is hard to specify. Lee (1981), for example, sees rising wages for servants and day-workers as conferring greater freedom on young people in nineteenth-century Bavaria, allowing them to satisfy their sexual desires and still be in a position to support the children born of their liaisons. Sabean (1990, 333), by contrast, suggests the penalty attached to a *mésalliance* rose between the eighteenth and nineteenth centuries, leading landowners, at least, to conclude that the shame of a pregnant, unmarried daughter was more easily supported than the economic penalty that might result from a poor marriage.

These are hard propositions to evaluate on the basis of the demographic evidence alone. In the villages examined here, it appears that the rising illegitimacy ratio was linked to an increase in births among couples who eventually married as well as to an increase in the number of women who bore more than one illegitimate child. The proportion of couples who had experienced a premarital birth rose from 1.4% among those marrying between 1790 and 1815 to 4.2% for the marriage cohort 1836–50. At the same time, the proportion of unwed mothers who experienced more than one out-of-wedlock birth rose from 8.5% among those who gave birth 1800–35, to 26.1% among those who bore children between 1836 and 1860.[15] Thus, there was an apparent increase in out-of-wedlock childbearing among various groups in the rural population.

The connection of illegitimacy to economic considerations has been emphasized, particularly in the case of England, but for other parts of Europe as well (Levine 1977; Lee 1981; Viazzo 1986). As the data on occupational differences make clear, the rate of non-marital childbearing did vary by social class. Yet, it is hard to see economic factors as primarily responsible for either regional differences or trends over time. Urban areas in Alsace did experience markedly higher rates of illegitimacy, in part as a function of the migration of pregnant women from the rural areas. But no clear connection can be made between the economic characteristics of villages and overall rates of illegitimacy or bridal pregnancy. Despite our expectations, Husseren-Wesserling, site of a large textile factory and a magnet for young men and women in search of work, did not experience especially high rates of either illegitimacy or premarital conceptions. It would appear that in the case of Alsace, at least, there is no simple explanation for the apparent increase in premarital sexuality during the nineteenth century.

Central to the theme of this book are the differences between Alsace's two major religious communities. At first glance, the differences in this area seem small. Both illegitimacy and bridal pregnancy were common in the two religious communities, and for both, rates increased over time. The trend upward was sharper among Lutherans, however, particularly in bridal pregnancy. Taken together with evidence on other demographic trends in this period, the difference is worth remarking. The Lutheran community experienced important changes between 1750 and 1850, changes which will be explored in more detail in the concluding section of the book. Rising rates of illegitimacy and bridal pregnancy were, I believe, one part of the new demographic regime that came to characterize the Lutheran community of Alsace in the nineteenth century.

CHAPTER FIVE

# Marital Fertility

Placed in a European context, Alsace appears as both a region of high fertility and a participant in the widespread decline in fertility that touched much of the continent in the last decades of the nineteenth century. The Princeton studies of European fertility decline (Coale and Treadway 1986) locate the onset of a sustained drop in marital fertility in Alsace in the decade 1880–90, similar to the experience of most of southern Germany and northern Switzerland, but making Alsace a latecomer among the regions of France.

This characterization of fertility change in Alsace is based, however, on aggregate population data. As such, it is not possible to detect variation in fertility patterns among groups within the population. Moreover, as recent research has shown, there is reason to doubt our ability to accurately identify the onset of fertility decline on the basis of rather simple summary measures of fertility (Guinnane et al 1994; Okun 1994). The Princeton studies used as a rule of thumb a 10% decline in their standardized indicator of marital fertility ($I_g$). But both Knodel's 1988 work on Germany and more recent simulation approaches have shown convincingly that contraceptive practice can make inroads in a population without producing a noticeable decline in aggregate measures of marital fertility.

These findings provide a backdrop against which to reexamine the course of marital fertility in Alsace. Had fertility control spread to parts of the population before the date suggested by aggregate data as marking the onset of fertility decline? Did fertility patterns differ in the two religious communities? More broadly, what can the Alsatian experience tell us about the role of culture in shaping the fertility patterns of a society?

## STUDYING MARITAL FERTILITY

It would not be unfair to say that historical demography has been dominated by concern with the issue of fertility decline. Indeed, one of the major rationales for historical research has been to extract "lessons from the past" (Knodel and Van De Walle 1979) in order to hasten fertility decline in developing societies. As a result, considerable progress has been achieved, both substantively and methodologically, in understanding fertility change. At the same time, continued research has raised new issues that make it harder rather than easier to arrive at a convincing theory of fertility change. Some attention to these questions is essential before looking at what happened in Alsace.

The central goal of much historical demographic research has been to pinpoint the date at which conscious control of fertility within marriage originated, and to identify the social and economic factors that brought about this change. However, dating the onset of fertility decline, once a seemingly straightforward task, has come to be viewed as increasingly complex. In studies of the developing world, demographers can gather direct information on fertility intentions and contraceptive use. While the difficulties involved in obtaining this information should not be underestimated, a growing sophistication in survey research has led to a deeper understanding of the dynamics of fertility even if it has not yet produced an acceptable theory of fertility change.

In the historical context, however, knowledge of behaviour is often obtained indirectly. Seldom, if ever, do we have direct information on such determinants of fertility as the duration of breastfeeding, frequency and timing of sexual relations, or efforts at contraception. Moreover, most of these factors are themselves interrelated, making it harder to measure them through various processes of triangulation. As a result, fairly simple indicators of fertility decline that focus on an overall decrease may be misleading. As Knodel (1988) has found, a rising level of underlying natural fertility can offset increases in the use of fertility control and leave the impression that little has changed.

The problem is not simply a technical one, however. The search for a method that could identify the onset of fertility transition resulted from a particular set of assumptions about demographic behaviour in the past. The most critical of these assumptions was that conscious efforts to limit fertility did not appear until relatively recently, and they manifested themselves in attempts to stop childbearing before the natural end of a woman's reproductive life. Louis Henry (1953, 1979) first staked out this position with his concept of natural fertility. For Henry, this meant the absence of parity-specific actions intended to restrict the number of children ever born. The effect of Henry's approach was to focus the investigation on what is called "stopping behaviour"; that is, conscious efforts to stop childbearing after a given number of births (or surviving children) had been achieved. By the same token, this approach led analysts to discount the significance of variation in "pre-transition" levels of fertility, variation amply documented in historical studies. Such variability was assumed to result from differences in breastfeeding patterns or cultural norms which regulated the resumption of sexual relations after a birth. Since these factors were not thought to be consciously linked to issues of family size by the actors themselves, they were viewed as theoretically unimportant. In the terms of the Coale-Trussell model (Coale and Trussell 1974), variation in the level of fertility was unimportant, while variation in the age pattern of fertility was critical, since it was the latter that would indicate the presence of conscious control over fertility.

As research in both historical and contemporary settings accumulates, the clarity of the distinction between stopping and spacing behaviour has tarnished. It is probably true that efforts to stop childbearing usually indicate a conscious attempt to limit family size.[1] But it is not so clear that spacing behaviour always reflects an absence of motivation to limit the number of births. There is no doubt that some of the variation in birth intervals, and hence in completed fertility, among historical populations resulted from differences in the duration of breastfeeding, for example. Yet it is certainly possible that couples, and perhaps women in particular, had more than one motive for prolonged breastfeeding or for abstaining from intercourse during lactation. Even if their minds were not fixed on reducing the final size of their family, women may well have sought a respite from repeated pregnancies. They could have believed that abstaining from sex while breastfeeding was good for their child's health while also being quite conscious of (and thankful for) the fertility-reducing effect of this behaviour. Moreover, some analysts have come to question whether variation in breastfeeding time alone was, indeed, the source of the substantial variation in birth spacing that has been recorded in European populations of the past. Perhaps couples, wanting to limit the number of children they would have and aware of the limited effectiveness of the methods of contraception available, combined efforts to space births in the early years of their marriage and, at a later date,

Table 5.1
Age-specific marital fertility rates and modified Coale index of marital fertility ($I_g'$)
by religion and period of marriage

| Period of Marriage | 20–24 | 25–29 | 30–34 | 35–39 | 40–44 | 45–49 | $I_g'$ |
|---|---|---|---|---|---|---|---|
| | | | CATHOLICS | | | | |
| 1750–89 | 461 | 475 | 392 | 343 | 201 | 14 | .897 |
| 1790–1815 | 489 | 472 | 405 | 328 | 182 | 15 | .887 |
| 1816–35 | 513 | 452 | 399 | 304 | 162 | 19 | .855 |
| 1836–60 | 458 | 455 | 414 | 316 | 160 | 19 | .861 |
| % Change | −0.7 | −4.2 | +5.6 | −7.9 | −20.4 | +35.7 | −4.0 |
| | | | LUTHERANS | | | | |
| 1750–89 | 422 | 355 | 305 | 232 | 111 | 12 | .656 |
| 1790–1815 | 381 | 343 | 284 | 210 | 94 | 10 | .606 |
| 1816–35 | 346 | 323 | 253 | 189 | 71 | 7 | .543 |
| 1836–60 | 450 | 326 | 242 | 155 | 67 | 7 | .535 |
| % Change | +6.6 | −8.2 | −20.7 | −33.2 | −39.6 | −41.7 | −18.4 |

to stop childbearing altogether. Santow (1995), in particular, makes a powerful claim that *coitus interruptus* was known and practised in many populations in the past, and that the demographic data for these communities are consistent with a model in which spacing was deliberately practised through the use of *coitus interruptus*.

Santow's argument concerning the deliberate use of birth spacing and her rejection of a "great divide" approach to fertility, which contrasts uncontrolled fertility in the past with the controlled childbearing of populations using parity-specific contraception, have important consequences for this study; as we shall see, Catholic and Lutheran fertility patterns differed in important ways at a time when conventional measures of fertility control do not provide convincing evidence of its use in either group. Her argument forces us to consider ways in which cultural practices may have regulated fertility other than through the use of parity-specific control designed to stop childbearing. We will return to this issue after examining the data on marital fertility from the villages in our study.

TRENDS IN MARITAL FERTILITY

The analysis of marital fertility in Alsace begins with a series of basic indicators that chart the levels and trends of marital fertility in the Catholic and Lutheran communities. Table 5.1 and figures 5.1 and 5.2

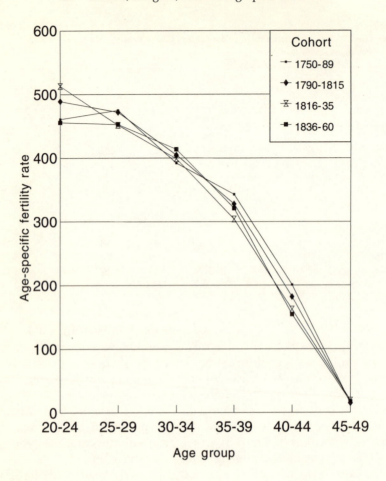

Figure 5.1
Age-specific marital fertility rates, Catholics

show the age-specific marital fertility rates by religion and period of marriage.[2]

The graph for the Catholic population suggests a pattern of fertility close to what one would expect to find in a "natural fertility" population. The curves are convex and change very little across marriage cohorts. The figures in table 5.1 indicate no clear pattern of change over time among Catholics, except in the case of the 40–44 age group, where the rate declined steadily over time. The decline in this group could be the first indicator of a tentative attempt at family limitation,

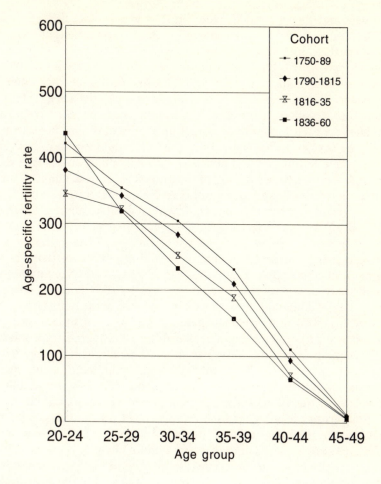

Figure 5.2
Age-specific marital fertility rates, Lutherans

but the evidence is far too slight to warrant any firm conclusion on this point. The stable character of Catholic fertility extends not only to the age pattern but to the level as well. The Coale index of marital fertility $(I_g')^3$ was high (85–90% of the Hutterite standard) and declined by only 4% between the cohort married in the years 1750–89 and that of 1836–60.

In the Lutheran community, fertility rates were lower than those observed among Catholics and declined over time. For all age groups and all cohorts, Catholic rates exceeded those found among Lutheran women, and the differences were greatest in the older age groups. Thus, even in the eighteenth century, marital fertility was significantly lower in the Lutheran community. The $I_g'$ measure for the Lutheran cohort 1750–89 was only 73% of the Catholic rate. Yet, even from this lower starting point, Lutheran fertility rates moved steadily down. $I_g'$ declined by just over 20% from the earliest to the latest cohort. With the exception of the 20–24 age group, age-specific rates also declined for each successive cohort. This pattern of decline across virtually all age categories is not quite what we would expect to find in cases where fertility control aimed at stopping childbearing spreads through a population. Looking at the graphical representation of the Lutheran rates in figure 5.2, we note that for the first three cohorts the curves retain a convex shape. Only with the final cohort does the curve begin to take on the concave shape more characteristic of populations in which fertility control is well established. This raises interesting questions about the nature of the fertility decline experienced by the Lutheran population. In the next sections, we explore in more detail the components of fertility change in the two religious communities. Before doing this, however, let us first look at the trends in marital fertility in the individual villages used for the reconstitution study, as well as the limited information available for the aggregate sample.

Table 5.2 presents the same measures of fertility for the five villages but, given the smaller number of cases, separated into only two cohorts. Despite the variations in the economic and geographic characteristics of the villages, the religious difference stands out clearly. Marital fertility was higher in all three of the Catholic villages than was the case in either of the Lutheran communities. Still, interesting differences are apparent among the individual villages. While the relatively small number of cases suggests caution in interpretation, it is interesting to note that a drop in fertility is indicated in the industrial community of Husseren, while in the other two Catholic villages fertility remained high. Indeed, in Mussig, age-specific marital fertility rates rose across the board. For Husseren, however, $I_g'$ declined by 19% and, of special note, the largest declines occurred in the older age categories. It is possible, then, that Husseren may have moved toward the practice of fertility control before the other (less industrialized) Catholic communities.

The two Lutheran communities also followed somewhat different paths. $I_g'$, for example, was higher in Baldenheim for the later cohort than was the case for the cohort in Goxwiller who married prior to 1816. And while fertility declined in both villages, the decline was sharper in the case of Goxwiller. Indeed, the sharp decline in marital fertility rates among those past age thirty suggests that fertility con-

Table 5.2
Age-specific marital fertility rates and modified Coale index of marital fertility ($I_g'$)
by village and period of marriage

| Period of Marriage | 20–24 | 25–29 | 30–34 | 35–39 | 40–44 | 45–49 | $I_g'$ |
|---|---|---|---|---|---|---|---|
| AVOLSHEIM | | | | | | | |
| 1792–1815 | 492 | 508 | 428 | 358 | 215 | 17 | .959 |
| 1816–60 | 490 | 465 | 406 | 323 | 268 | 17 | .876 |
| HUSSEREN | | | | | | | |
| 1750–1815 | 474 | 473 | 435 | 343 | 200 | 19 | .925 |
| 1816–60 | 462 | 412 | 354 | 269 | 109 | 23 | .750 |
| MUSSIG | | | | | | | |
| 1750–1815 | 472 | 456 | 362 | 315 | 170 | 10 | .835 |
| 1816–60 | 478 | 483 | 456 | 346 | 197 | 15 | .943 |
| BALDENHEIM | | | | | | | |
| 1750–1815 | 436 | 360 | 317 | 237 | 112 | 13 | .672 |
| 1816–60 | 402 | 348 | 291 | 195 | 86 | 7 | .600 |
| GOXWILLER | | | | | | | |
| 1750–1815 | 375 | 338 | 270 | 206 | 93 | 9 | .590 |
| 1816–60 | 383 | 274 | 172 | 136 | 44 | 5 | .429 |

trol was becoming well established in the village among couples who married in the nineteenth century. When we look at those who married near the mid-century, we find many couples like Georges Denni and Anne Marie Meyer who married in 1853, had two sons in 1854 and 1858, the latter born when his mother was just twenty-nine, and no more thereafter. We obviously cannot know whether any given case resulted from the deliberate use of fertility control, but the increasing popularity of this form of family building hints at the spread of family limitation in the village.

While aggregate data from the larger sample of villages are of limited help in understanding fertility patterns, they do confirm that marital fertility was significantly higher in the Catholic villages of Alsace. Table 5.3 provides the Coale index of fertility for four points in time, based on the censuses of 1836, 1851, 1861 and 1875. The age-sex-marital status distribution from the manuscript censuses was used in the computation along with the average annual number of marital births in the ten-year period bracketing each census. For both communities, the measures are remarkably stable – not surprising, perhaps, given the relatively short time frame – but they also point to significantly higher marital fertility among Catholics. Although these additional data tell us nothing about the sources of this difference, the

Table 5.3
Coale index of marital fertility ($I_g$) for aggregate sample of twenty-six
communes by dominant religious affiliation

| Census Year | Catholics | Lutherans |
| --- | --- | --- |
| 1836 | .870 | .633 |
| 1851 | .847 | .554 |
| 1861 | .868 | .612 |
| 1875 | .872 | .675 |

fact that the results are quite similar to those for the villages in the reconstitution sample gives us greater confidence in the representative character of the villages chosen, and thus in the significance of the more detailed analysis that follows.

## NATURAL FERTILITY AND FERTILITY CHANGE

Recent research in historical demography has drawn attention to physiological aspects of fertility that demographers have often ignored (Knodel 1988). In studying change in historical populations, it was often assumed that physiological determinants of fertility levels remained essentially constant over time. One could then conclude that a rise or fall in fertility levels was attributable to some form of behavioural change, though, to be sure, not necessarily change consciously intended to alter family size. Knodel (1988), however, has uncovered evidence of an increase in the underlying level of natural fertility in his study of fourteen German villages. Interpretation of such changes centres on improvement in environmental factors that influence fecundity or intrauterine mortality, as well as behavioural changes that might affect infant feeding patterns. Earlier weaning or increased use of other forms of infant feeding might lead to shorter birth intervals and higher fertility. Yet, change in volitional factors related to birth spacing, such as abstinence or *coitus interruptus*, might also affect conventional measures of the underlying level of natural fertility. Thus, before addressing the issues of stopping and spacing directly, it is essential to look at the issue of natural fertility, especially as it relates to religious differences in overall patterns of fertility.

Examining these questions in a historical context is particularly difficult given the absence of direct information on many critical components of fertility. Fortunately, the development of indirect methods of estimation allows us to use reconstitution data to touch on at least some of these issues. Table 5.4 presents data on the interval between

Table 5.4
Interval from marriage to first birth by religion and period of marriage

| Period of Marriage | Catholics | | | Lutherans | | |
|---|---|---|---|---|---|---|
| | % 8–11 months | Mean Interval* | Mean Interval | % 8–11 months | Mean Interval* | Mean Interval |
| 1750–89 | 52.0 | 14.73 | 16.06 | 39.2 | 16.16 | 16.97 |
| 1790–1815 | 42.8 | 14.71 | 15.38 | 37.1 | 15.73 | 16.44 |
| 1816–35 | 48.2 | 13.97 | 13.97 | 30.9 | 18.13 | 19.80 |
| 1836–60 | 57.2 | 13.72 | 14.27 | 53.4 | 15.14 | 16.90 |
| Total | 50.1 | 14.25 | 14.86 | 39.7 | 16.20 | 17.32 |

Note: Includes only women in first marriages. Column marked with asterisk shows the mean excluding intervals of greater than sixty months.

marriage and first birth, as usual by religion and period of marriage. These data are of interest because it is assumed that if no deliberate effort is made to delay the first conception then variation in the speed with which the first child is conceived will reflect underlying differences in fecundity.[4] Again, the most striking feature of the table is the difference between the two religious groups. Regardless of the measure used (and, of course, they are strongly related), the Catholic population appears to begin childbearing earlier. Looking at all marriage cohorts together, approximately half of first births to Catholic women occurred before the end of the first year of marriage, whilst only two of five Lutheran wives became pregnant at the same rate. The average interval between marriage and first birth is presented for all women not pregnant at the time of their marriage, and separately for those who bear their first child within sixty months of marriage. This second measure both controls for the distorting effect of the small number of very long intervals on the mean and guards against the possibility of cases where the first birth may not have been registered. In either case, however, the Catholic average was approximately two months shorter than the mean for Lutheran mothers.[5]

A proper analysis of this problem requires more care, however. The average length of time from marriage to first birth varies by age at marriage, for instance, undoubtedly because of changes in fecundity that occur with age. In table 5.5, we control for this by standardizing using the marriage distribution for the combined sample of villages. We also present two other indicators: Bongaarts' indicator of fecundability and the Coale-Trussell measure of the underlying level of marital fertility (commonly designated by M).[6] Carrying out these adjustments muddies the waters somewhat. There is no full agreement among the various measures about the direction of change over

Table 5.5
Indicators of fecundability by religion and period of marriage

| Period of Marriage | Catholics | | | Lutherans | | |
|---|---|---|---|---|---|---|
| | Mean Interval | Bongaarts' Index | Coale-Trussell M | Mean Interval | Bongaarts' Index | Coale-Trussell M |
| 1750–89 | 15.31 | .331 | 1.03 | 17.03 | .216 | 0.90 |
| 1790–1815 | 15.96 | .247 | 1.08 | 15.95 | .188 | 0.85 |
| 1816–35 | 13.98 | .290 | 1.09 | 19.46 | .157 | 0.81 |
| 1836–60 | 14.74 | .390 | 1.08 | 17.55 | .340 | 0.91 |
| Total | 14.94 | .310 | 1.07 | 17.48 | .215 | 0.87 |

Note: Mean interval is based on all marriages and standardized using the distribution of all marriages in all villages for period 1750–1860. For Bongaarts' index, see Bongaarts, 1975.

time for either religious group. Indeed, there is no clear evidence of any time trend, either positive or negative, in terms of fecundability. On the other hand, fairly clear evidence emerges pointing to a higher level of natural fertility in the Catholic population, across all cohorts and regardless of the measure used. We will return to the implications of these findings shortly but first it is worth examining one other indicator of natural fertility, the proportion of women remaining childless.

The most extreme form of subfecundity involves the inability to have children. In the Alsatian villages we are studying, it seems likely that very few if any couples sought to remain permanently childless. Thus, by examining the proportion of couples who remained together until the end of the wife's childbearing years yet bore no children, the degree of primary sterility can be estimated. Figure 5.3 presents this estimate for the two religious groups. Given the restricted number of cases, it is not possible to subdivide the analysis by period of marriage. However, the data presented above, which point to the absence of clear time trends in the level of fecundity, suggest grouping marriage cohorts together should not entail serious problems. The first striking aspect of the graphs is the low level of sterility among those married before age thirty-five. For those who married before age thirty, childlessness was very rare: across both religious groups, less than 4% of such couples remained childless. Even among those marrying in the age group 30–34, over 90% went on to have at least one child. It is only after this point that the curve begins to rise steeply, reaching close to 100% for those marrying past age forty-five.

Comparing the two religious communities is made difficult by the small numbers marrying before age twenty or after age thirty-five. Two measures we can compute suggest that while differences were

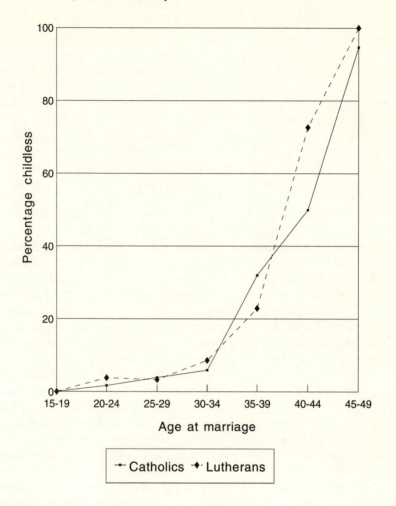

Figure 5.3
Childlessness among married women by age at marriage

small, childlessness was slightly more common in the Lutheran population. Among those married between ages 20–29, for instance, 3.0% of Catholic couples remained childless versus 3.6% of Lutheran couples. Alternatively, standardizing for age at marriage using the overall distribution of marriages for the combined sample, the rate of childlessness in the Catholic population was 8.8%, while in the Lutheran community 10.0% of couples remained permanently childless.

As we have noted, Knodel's study of German villages, which stretches over a longer period of time, found clear evidence of rising levels of natural fertility, particularly for cohorts marrying in the latter half of the nineteenth century. While the sources of this change were not clear, Knodel emphasized the importance of this trend for understanding the evolution of fertility in the villages he studied. No such trend is evident for our five Alsatian villages. Most of the indicators fluctuate over time rather than move steadily upward. There is some evidence of a decline in underlying fertility during the revolutionary and Napoleonic period, followed by an increase which results in the highest levels of fecundity being obtained by those marrying after 1835. Were data available for subsequent cohorts, it might have been possible to establish a claim for rising fecundity in the nineteenth century. As it is, the evidence is too limited to establish any clear trend, and it seems unlikely that changes in underlying natural fertility were of importance for the period studied.

However, a difference between the two religious communities is suggested. The average interval between marriage and first birth, for instance, was consistently shorter among Catholic couples, and the Coale-Trussell indicator ($m$) was higher among Catholics in all marriage cohorts. It is hard to speculate on possible reasons for this difference, if indeed it is a real one. Certainly the Lutheran population was, if anything, more prosperous than the Catholic population, and evidence on the height of army recruits indicates Lutheran men were slightly taller than their Catholic counterparts, suggesting that nutrition levels in the Lutheran community would have been at least the equal of those enjoyed by Catholics.[7] Thus, we should not be too quick to attribute the differences, admittedly small ones, to physiological factors. Variation in behaviour, including efforts to extend the time between births, could also have played a role. In any case, even if a difference in the underlying level of natural fertility existed, it was certainly rather small and does not, of itself, account for much of the difference between the two religious communities.

## FAMILY LIMITATION

As was noted above, traditional interpretations of fertility decline have focused on "stopping" behaviour as an indicator of the spread of fertility control. While no foolproof technique has been developed for estimating the proportion of couples engaging in this form of family limitation, a number of measures do give us a sense of the likelihood that couples were attempting to control the size of their families in this way. This section examines some of these measures, with a

Table 5.6
Indicators of stopping behaviour by religion and period of marriage

| Period of Marriage | Coale-Trussell m | $\dfrac{TMFR\,30+}{TMFR\,20+}$ | Age of Mother at Last Birth |
|---|---|---|---|
| | | CATHOLICS | |
| 1750–89 | −.04 | .50 | 41.3 |
| 1790–1815 | .05 | .49 | 40.8 |
| 1816–35 | .12 | .48 | 40.6 |
| 1836–60 | .08 | .50 | 40.3 |
| Total | .05 | .49 | 40.7 |
| | | LUTHERANS | |
| 1750–89 | .22 | .46 | 38.9 |
| 1790–1815 | .27 | .45 | 37.6 |
| 1816–35 | .37 | .44 | 36.7 |
| 1836–60 | .62 | .38 | 36.3 |
| Total | .34 | .44 | 37.6 |

particular eye to the differences between the two religious groups. Tables 5.6 and 5.7 present three commonly used indicators of fertility control, first for the two religious groups, and second for individual villages. The first indicator, the Coale-Trussell index 'm,' measures deviations from the age pattern of natural fertility. Coefficients close to zero indicate little variation from an age pattern of natural fertility as defined by Henry. As fertility at older ages begins to fall below the levels one would expect to find in the absence of deliberate fertility control, the m index begins to rise. Recent research has undermined the view that a given index value can be taken as "proof" of the existence of family limitation. However, a rising index value, if consistent with other indicators, seems to suggest the spread of fertility control. For Catholics, m hovered near zero for all marriage cohorts. By contrast, among Lutheran couples, the index rose from a modest level of .22 for those married in the eighteenth century, to a high of .62 for the cohort 1836–55.

The m values are consistent with the trends in the two other indicators of marital fertility control provided in table 5.6. Since the spread of efforts to halt childbearing should produce relatively larger declines in the fertility of women past age thirty, one would expect that fertility past age thirty would form a progressively smaller share of total fertility as the proportion of couples controlling increased. Similarly, efforts to prevent further births before the end of the childbearing period would be expected to lower the average age at which women bear their last child. Historical studies of natural fertility

Table 5.7
Indicators of stopping behaviour by village and period of marriage

| Village | Coale-Trussell m | | TMFR 30+ / TMFR 20+ | | Age of Mother at Last Birth | |
| | 1750– 1815 | 1816– 1860 | 1750– 1815 | 1816– 1860 | 1750– 1815 | 1816– 1860 |
| --- | --- | --- | --- | --- | --- | --- |
| Avolsheim | −.03 | .08 | .50 | .49 | 41.3 | 40.6 |
| Husseren | −.03 | .22 | .51 | .46 | 41.3 | 40.0 |
| Mussig | .07 | .00 | .48 | .51 | 40.6 | 40.9 |
| Baldenheim | .23 | .38 | .46 | .44 | 38.7 | 36.9 |
| Goxwiller | .28 | .73 | .45 | .35 | 37.9 | 35.7 |

populations have often found that the average age of mothers at their last birth was approximately forty years. As the data in table 5.5 make clear, the value of both these indicators was falling in the Lutheran population. Average age of mothers at last birth declined from 38.9 years for the oldest cohort to just 36.3 for the last cohort to marry.[8] By contrast, among Catholic women, the average decreased slightly over time, but even for the cohort 1836–60, women gave birth to their last child, on average, at age 40.3. Similarly, fertility past age thirty accounted for approximately 50% of Catholic fertility for all four cohorts. Among Lutherans, however, its share fell to just 38% for the last cohort to marry.

The data for individual villages confirm the importance of the religious division, while again pointing to smaller differences among communities that shared the same faith. For the three Catholic villages, virtually all indicators point to the persistence of fertility patterns reflecting little or no deliberate control. Only in the case of Husseren is there even a hint that fertility control might have been taking root in the nineteenth century.

For the two Lutheran villages, the results are harder to interpret. Fertility was certainly lower in the late eighteenth and early nineteenth centuries than was the case in the Catholic villages. Data on age at last birth and the m index hint at the possibility that some Lutheran women from this older cohort, especially in the village of Goxwiller, may have been practising birth control but the evidence is far from conclusive. On the other hand, for couples married after the Napoleonic era, the evidence is stronger, again, particularly in the case of Goxwiller. m rose from .28 to .73 for the later marriage cohort, while average age of mother at last birth fell to 35.8. In Baldenheim, the indices move in the same direction, though the increase was smaller. Before drawing conclusions about the spread of family limi-

Table 5.8
Mean age at last birth by religion, age at marriage and period of marriage

| | Catholics | | Lutherans | |
|---|---|---|---|---|
| Age at Marriage | 1750–1815 | 1816–60 | 1750–1815 | 1816–60 |
| 15–19 | 39.0* | 41.4* | 35.4 | 34.4* |
| 20–24 | 40.6 | 39.9 | 38.0 | 34.4 |
| 25–29 | 41.2 | 40.5 | 39.3 | 38.3 |
| 30–34 | 41.1 | 40.9 | 39.8 | 39.9 |
| 35–49 | 43.0* | 41.4 | 42.7* | 41.2* |
| Total | 41.0 | 40.5 | 38.3 | 36.5 |

Note: Complete families only. Cells marked by an asterisk are based on less than 20 families.

tation, however, it is worth pressing the analysis further in an effort to clarify the trends in fertility in the two religious communities.

The data in table 5.8 consider average age at last birth once again, but now according to women's age at marriage. The desire to stop childbearing would likely be greater among those married longer, as they would have had more time to achieve an intended number of children. Other factors undoubtedly enter into the equation as well. Declining frequency of intercourse with longer marriage duration and perhaps a greater chance of secondary sterility among those who have given birth more frequently will tend to obscure this relationship. Still, at least with respect to the religious comparison, the results are quite clear. Among Catholics, the differences by age at marriage were modest. Even among those marrying early, the last birth occurred when the wife was almost forty years of age. For Lutheran women, however, there was a clear relationship between age at marriage and age at last birth, one that grew stronger among successive cohorts. While not in itself definitive, it is consistent with a gradual spread of family limitation in the Lutheran community.[9]

The last tool to be used in examining the issue of stopping behaviour is the parity progression ratio. Parity progression ratios allow us to look at the childbearing process as a series of transitions from one parity to the next. In each case we look at the proportion of women who, having borne a given number of children, go on to have another. Since the likelihood of having an additional child is clearly affected by the amount of childbearing time available to a woman, the ratios are presented for a restricted group of women. First, in figure 5.4, parity progression ratios are shown for all women who survive in an intact union until their forty-fifth birthday. Second, in figure 5.5, the focus is restricted to women who married before age twenty-five and remained in that union until the end of their childbearing years. This

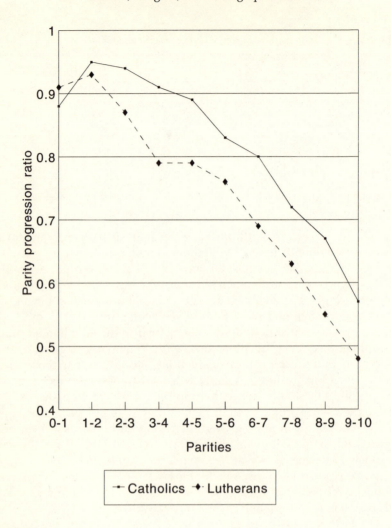

Figure 5.4
Parity progression ratios

has the unfortunate consequence of reducing the number of cases on which the ratios are based, but it does allow for a more careful comparison of the behaviour of Lutheran and Catholic women.

Both figures show a similar pattern, though, as would be expected, the contrast is sharper in the second graph which focuses on women who have long reproductive careers. The Catholic pattern shows a smooth decline in the ratios from the lower to higher parities. From

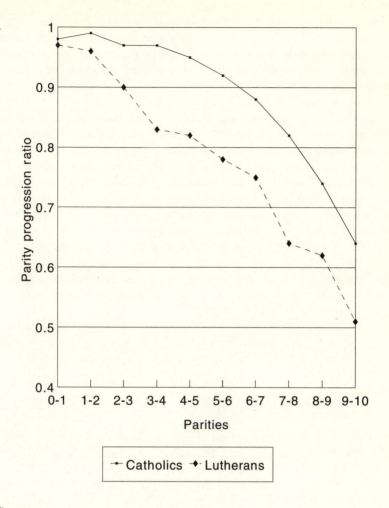

Figure 5.5
Parity progression ratios for women marrying before age 25

very high levels at lower parities (it is only with the transition from four to five births that the ratio falls below .9), the ratios drift downward with rising parity. In the case of early marryers, the ratios were extremely high; more than 60% of those with nine births went on to have a tenth child.

The ratios for Lutheran mothers were uniformly lower. However, the path they trace was not as smooth as that for their Catholic counterparts. Especially interesting is the growing divergence between the ratios at parities three and four. As a result, while over 70% of Catholic women had five or more births, less than half of Lutheran mothers experienced a fifth birth. After this point, the ratios follow a more similar line, declining gradually as women moved to higher parities, though with the probability of transition being consistently higher for Catholic women.

As with the other measures examined, the parity progression ratios give no definitive proof that fertility control was adopted by Lutheran women but not by Catholics. The ratios for the Catholic mothers, along with the data presented above, do, however, conform to the pattern we would anticipate in a population in which little or no effort at family limitation was present. The Lutheran picture is less clear. The sharp declines in the ratios at middle parities could point to the efforts of a core of "stoppers" within the Lutheran community. The data for early marryers are particularly striking here. Only 57% of Lutheran women who married before age twenty-five and remained in their marriage until the end of their childbearing period had five or more births. This is consistent with what we might expect to observe in a population in which a significant group of couples were attempting to limit the size of their families. Drawing firm conclusions about the fertility patterns of these two populations would be premature, however, without a consideration of the issue of birth spacing.

BIRTH SPACING

Analyzing birth intervals from family reconstitution data is complicated by the wide variety of factors that can affect the length of time between births. Factors such as fecundity and intrauterine mortality have a direct physiological effect on the average length of time between births, but these, in turn, are influenced by the age of the woman, nutrition levels, exposure to disease, and a number of other variables. Other variables, such as coital frequency, are influenced by social factors such as marital duration and social norms regarding sexual behaviour. Similarly, breastfeeding exerts a physiological influence on the likelihood of conception but is also a function of behavioural norms regarding the appropriate length and style of feeding. Moreover, in some settings, ideas about breastfeeding are intertwined with conventions about the appropriateness of sexual relations in the period when breastfeeding occurs. If relations are prohibited and the ban is observed, it is not the physiological effect of breastfeeding that matters but the social custom which prescribes abstinence.

Table 5.9
Mean first-birth intervals by religion and period of marriage

| | Catholics | | | Lutherans | | |
|---|---|---|---|---|---|---|
| Period of Marriage | Marriage to First Birth | First to Second Birth | N | Marriage to First Birth | First to Second Birth | N |
| 1750–89 | 14.25 | 23.85 | 126 | 16.37 | 31.39 | 232 |
| 1790–1815 | 14.88 | 24.29 | 144 | 15.79 | 31.87 | 166 |
| 1816–35 | 13.79 | 23.12 | 145 | 18.90 | 31.59 | 100 |
| 1836–60 | 13.86 | 23.79 | 132 | 15.31 | 34.96 | 97 |
| Total | 14.20 | 23.76 | 547 | 16.46 | 32.14 | 595 |

Note: Women in first marriages only. Excludes those with premarital conception.

In addition to attempting to quantify the effects of these variables, demographers have also been concerned with the motivation that lies behind the behaviour. Do couples deliberately attempt to shorten or prolong the length of time between births, and, if so, why? Is the motivation related to such issues as the health and well-being of mother and child, or is spacing an effort to limit the number of births?

The lack of information on many of these issues makes it difficult to interpret data on birth intervals. Nevertheless, careful consideration of these data is essential for a proper understanding of the fertility patterns of a population. The analysis that follows presents data on various aspects of spacing, and assesses the significance of these findings for the overall fertility patterns of the two religious groups.

Table 5.9 presents data on the interval between the first and second birth for Catholic and Lutheran women by marriage cohort. It seems unlikely that women from either group would have attempted to stop childbearing after the first birth. Thus, examining the length of the first birth interval may help shed light on behaviour affecting the timing of births in a situation in which deliberate efforts to prevent further births were absent. The findings show a clear difference between the two religious groups that remained remarkably stable over time. For Catholic couples, the second child typically arrived about two years after the birth of the first. This figure is similar to that uncovered in a number of other historical populations thought to be characterized by natural fertility.[10] Among Lutheran couples, however, the waiting time until the birth of the second child was longer, averaging over thirty-two months throughout the period as a whole, and reaching almost thirty-five months for the last cohort. For Catholics, the interval between the first and second births was nine months longer than the interval from marriage to the first birth; for Lutherans, the difference was sixteen months.

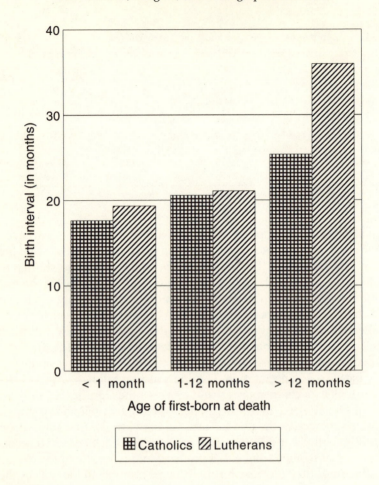

Figure 5.6
Mean first birth interval by age at death of first-born

These figures make no distinction according to the survival status of the first-born child, however. It is well known that intervals following a birth that results in an early death tend to be significantly shorter than is the case when the child survives infancy. To explore this issue further, figure 5.6 presents average birth intervals according to the destiny of the first-born. The difference between Catholics and Lutherans was quite small when the first birth resulted in an infant

Table 5.10
Mean inter-birth intervals by religion and parity

| Number of Children Ever Born | 1-2 | 2-3 | 3-4 | 4-5 | Last | N |
|---|---|---|---|---|---|---|
| | | | CATHOLICS | | | |
| 4 | 27.51 | 29.49 | — | — | 44.25 | 105 |
| 5 | 24.85 | 29.91 | 30.45 | — | 41.01 | 116 |
| 6 | 22.31 | 25.59 | 28.51 | 31.39 | 43.82 | 104 |
| 7+ | 21.19 | 23.07 | 25.22 | 26.27 | 35.38 | 308 |
| 4+ | 23.09 | 25.80 | 27.01 | 27.28 | 38.51 | 633 |
| | | | LUTHERANS | | | |
| 4 | 32.05 | 40.77 | — | — | 55.34 | 117 |
| 5 | 27.71 | 32.31 | 34.87 | — | 53.75 | 110 |
| 6 | 27.46 | 31.18 | 31.92 | 36.98 | 43.69 | 95 |
| 7+ | 23.13 | 27.08 | 28.71 | 29.31 | 38.64 | 200 |
| 4+ | 26.88 | 32.00 | 31.14 | 31.78 | 45.96 | 522 |

Note: Where an inter-birth interval was also the last interval for a family, these intervals were excluded. The calculation of the last interval is based on complete families only.

death. On the other hand, when the child survived the first year of life, Lutheran women waited almost three years to give birth to their second child. For Catholic women, the second child arrived in just over two years. Catholic and Lutheran behaviour patterns thus differed significantly in the light of a successful outcome of the first pregnancy.

The slower pace of childbearing in the Lutheran community is further illustrated by data on subsequent birth intervals. Table 5.10 shows the average length of the first four inter-birth intervals as well as the average interval between the penultimate and the last-born child. The results reflect the experiences of families with at least four children, and are broken down by religion and by the number of children ever born. It should be noted that excluding families with less than four births makes the Lutheran families studied here less representative of their communities. Just over one-third of Lutheran families were excluded by this provision as opposed to slightly less than one-quarter of Catholic families.

Given these restrictions, it is not surprising that the differences between the two religious communities were less marked. Even so, Lutheran intervals were consistently longer.[11] Among the largest families, with seven or more births, Lutheran intervals ranged from two to four months longer. Overall, the differences were even larger as a greater proportion of Lutheran families were concentrated in the lower parities.

There is special interest in examining the last birth interval. The final birth interval tends to be significantly longer than preceding intervals for physiological reasons and perhaps due to factors such as declining frequency of sexual relations with marital duration. But unusually long final intervals may also reflect efforts to stop childbearing. Imperfect forms of contraception may prevent an additional birth for some time before being "interrupted" by an unwanted pregnancy. The final interval for Lutheran couples averaged almost four years, longer than is typical of most natural fertility populations. Not surprisingly, the average length of the last interval declined with parity. Again, however, the very long intervals for Lutheran mothers of four or five children may reflect efforts on the part of some proportion of these couples to halt childbearing.

The shortage of cases makes it difficult to extend this analysis to include all the factors that might bear on the issue of birth spacing. Nevertheless, in table 5.11 we reexamine the same set of birth intervals, this time differentiating among couples according to marriage cohort and age at marriage, as well as religion. For Catholics in the oldest cohort, birth intervals were relatively short and only weakly related to age at marriage. Only for the final interval was there a noticeable difference and even this was quite modest, amounting to barely three months. For the later cohort, however, differences by age at marriage, though not huge, were more pronounced. Intervals were consistently longer among early marryers (the first interval being the only exception), and there was a marked difference in the length of the last interval. For those married before age twenty-five, the last interval extended to over forty-five months, eleven months longer than for late marryers, and over four months longer than was true for early marryers in the older cohort.

Among Lutheran couples, a different pattern was evident. For the older cohort, intervals were consistently longer for those married before age twenty-five. The final interval was more than eleven months longer among early marryers, much as was the case for Catholics married after 1815. However, for the later cohort, the differences by age at marriage were smaller. No clear pattern can be observed for the first four inter-birth intervals.[12] The average of the first four intervals was less than one month longer among those married before age twenty-five. And the difference in the last interval, while still significant, declined from eleven months to just over five months.

It seems clear from these results that throughout the period studied, the tempo of childbearing was slower among Lutheran women than among Catholic women. This is so even after controlling for differences in fertility levels and marriage patterns. Especially intrigu-

Table 5.11
Mean inter-birth intervals by religion, age at marriage and period of marriage

| Period of Marriage | Age at Marriage | 1–2 | 2–3 | 3–4 | 4–5 | Last | N |
|---|---|---|---|---|---|---|---|
| | | CATHOLICS | | | | | |
| 1750– | < 25 | 23.24 | 25.12 | 26.90 | 28.89 | 40.73 | 151 |
| 1815 | 25+ | 23.32 | 26.94 | 28.43 | 27.49 | 37.78 | 136 |
| 1816–60 | < 25 | 22.66 | 27.10 | 28.70 | 28.24 | 45.30 | 143 |
| | 25+ | 23.21 | 24.70 | 24.82 | 25.39 | 34.07 | 200 |
| | | LUTHERANS | | | | | |
| 1750– | < 25 | 27.15 | 33.46 | 31.56 | 33.71 | 50.59 | 253 |
| 1815 | 25+ | 26.60 | 30.31 | 30.78 | 29.61 | 39.13 | 93 |
| 1816–60 | < 25 | 24.68 | 33.27 | 31.18 | 29.94 | 46.91 | 94 |
| | 25+ | 29.68 | 27.60 | 29.52 | 29.12 | 41.25 | 74 |

Note: Only couples with four or more children are included. Where an inter-birth interval was also the last interval for a family, these intervals were excluded. The calculation of the last interval is based on complete families only.

ing are the changes that occur in the length of the last birth interval. For Lutheran women married before 1816, the last interval was remarkably long, especially for those who married at an early age. Somewhat surprisingly, the average length of the last interval for these early marryers actually declined over time. This trend hints at the possibility that Lutheran women were gradually shifting away from a strategy based on spacing to one designed to stop childbearing. Alternatively, it could suggest greater mastery of contraceptive practice among women in the later cohort. Among Catholic women, on the other hand, the gap between early and late marryers increased over time, pointing perhaps to the first signs of family limitation in the Catholic community. To be sure, the evidence is far from clear and open to several interpretations. Nevertheless, these findings merit further discussion and we will return to them, following a brief detour to examine occupational differentials in fertility patterns in the two religious communities.

## OCCUPATIONAL DIFFERENTIALS

Powerful arguments have been made about the effect of different economic circumstances on fertility patterns (Tilly 1984; Medick 1981; Schneider and Schneider 1995). In earlier chapters, significant differentials in age at marriage and premarital childbearing by the occupational status of the husband were recorded. The question to be addressed here is whether this variability extended to marital fertility patterns as well, and whether the effect of occupation differed in the two religious communities.

The measure of occupational status is, unfortunately, crude. Just three occupational categories are included: farmers, artisans and professionals, and wage-workers. The final category includes day-labourers or *journaliers* in agriculture as well as workers in both rural and large-scale industry, the last group comprising the employees of the factory in Husseren. A finer division by occupational categories is not possible given the small number of cases available for analysis.

Table 5.12 presents summary measures of fertility for the three occupational categories subdivided by religion and period of marriage. Differences in marital fertility by occupational status appear modest and are overshadowed by the much larger differences by religion which have already been noted. Among Catholics, marital fertility was very high in all three occupational categories, with the Coale index ($I_g'$) above 0.8 for all categories in both cohorts. The somewhat lower figure for Catholic wage-workers married prior to 1815 may have reflected slightly lower natural fertility. The Coale-Trussell indicator of underlying natural fertility (M) was lowest for wage-workers and increased for the cohort married after 1815. The index of fertility control (m) rose for all three categories, but the increase was small. Overall, there is no clear evidence that would point to significant change in marital fertility in any occupational category of the Catholic population. Deliberate fertility control, if practised at all, must have been typical of only a small minority of the population even among those who married in the nineteenth century.

The situation in the Lutheran community was, as often, somewhat more complex. For the older cohort, all three occupational categories were characterized by a moderate level of marital fertility, one significantly below that experienced by Catholics who shared the same occupation. For both farmers and artisans, however, fertility levels declined, the index of fertility control (m) increased sharply, and the age of mothers at the time of their last birth dropped to 35.8 in the case of farmers' wives and 36.4 for the wives of artisans. Among Lutheran wage-workers, on the other hand, fertility decline was modest. $I_g'$ declined by only 8% while m remained virtually unchanged. Age of mother at last birth did decline from 38.9 to 37.2 but remained above the average for the other two occupational categories. At the same time, wage-workers in the Lutheran communities did not conform to what might be called a "Catholic" fertility pattern either. Marital fertility rates for these women were lower and child-bearing ended earlier than was true for any of the Catholic groups.

Table 5.12
Index of marital fertility, index of fertility control, and age of mother at last birth by religion, occupation of husband and period of marriage

| Occupation | $I_g'$ | | | Coale-Trussell m | | | Age of Mother at Last Birth | | |
|---|---|---|---|---|---|---|---|---|---|
|  | 1750– 1815 | 1816– 1860 | Change | 1750– 1815 | 1816– 1860 | Change | 1750– 1815 | 1816– 1860 | Change |
| | | | | CATHOLICS | | | | | |
| Farmer | .94 | .91 | −.03 | −.01 | +.11 | +.12 | 41.4 | 40.8 | −0.6 |
| Artisan | .96 | .83 | −.13 | −.06 | −.01 | +.05 | 40.9 | 40.5 | −0.4 |
| Worker | .80 | .82 | +.02 | +.07 | +.18 | +.11 | 40.3 | 40.3 | 0.0 |
| | | | | LUTHERANS | | | | | |
| Farmer | .61 | .49 | −.11 | +.26 | +.66 | +.40 | 37.9 | 35.8 | −2.1 |
| Artisan | .67 | .54 | −.13 | +.28 | +.64 | +.36 | 37.9 | 36.4 | −1.5 |
| Worker | .68 | .62 | −.06 | +.24 | +.26 | +.02 | 38.9 | 37.2 | −1.7 |

Still, it appears that Lutheran wage-workers and their wives adapted more slowly to the new regime of controlled fertility which seems to have spread its roots among the more prosperous classes of the Lutheran community during the nineteenth century. These findings, along with the difference noted at the village level between Baldenheim and Goxwiller, suggest that while fertility control may have appeared earlier in the Lutheran community, it did not necessarily touch all parts of the population at the same time.

## SUMMARY AND CONCLUSION

This chapter has presented a great deal of detailed information on marital fertility patterns in Alsace. Before discussing the implications of these patterns, it is useful to summarize the major findings. All of the analysis points to the fact that the marital fertility rates of the Catholic population consistently exceeded those experienced by Lutheran women. For the earliest cohort, married between 1750 and 1789, the modified Coale index of marital fertility ($I_g'$) for the Catholic population was 37% higher than that of the Protestant community. Standardizing for differences in age at marriage, the marital fertility schedule of the Catholic population implied a completed family size of 6.6 children while the average Lutheran woman of this marriage cohort would have given birth to only 5.0 children.[13]

From this lower starting point, fertility declined significantly in the Lutheran community, and, as a consequence, the differential between the two populations widened. For the last cohort analyzed, those married between 1836 and 1860, $I_g'$ was 64% higher in the Catholic community. Completed family size declined modestly among Catholics to 6.0 children per woman, but for Lutheran mothers it fell to just 3.9 children. These findings raise two obvious questions: first, why was marital fertility lower among Lutherans, and second, why did fertility decline more rapidly in the Lutheran community? ·

The lower fertility of Lutheran women in the eighteenth century was primarily the result of a slower pace of childbearing. Although a somewhat earlier end to childbearing also played a part, the longer intervals between births for Lutheran mothers led to significantly lower marital fertility rates in all age groups. In the nineteenth century longer spacing of births as well as a significantly lower age at last birth combined to increase the gap between the two communities. A comparison of the age-specific marital fertility rates for cohorts married after 1815 shows that the largest differences occurred among women past age thirty. Rates for Catholic women in their thirties remained near the levels recorded in the eighteenth century, but among Lutheran women they had declined sharply, by 24% in the 30–34 age group, and by 33% among women 35–39. Not surprisingly, then, the Coale-Trussell index of fertility control (m) for the Lutheran population rose from 0.22 to 0.62, while average age at last birth fell from 38.9 to 36.3.

While longer intervals between births contributed to the lower overall fertility of the Lutheran population, the sources of this difference in birth spacing between the two populations remain unclear. Were the longer birth intervals in the Lutheran community the unintended result of different infant-feeding patterns or did they reflect conscious efforts to lengthen the time between births? And, if Lutheran couples did attempt to increase the time between pregnancies, did this pave the way for the adoption in the nineteenth century of other forms of fertility control aimed specifically at limiting family size? The data in figure 5.6, which revealed a similarity in the length of the first birth interval following an infant death but a difference of about ten months when a child survived infancy, could be seen as supporting an interpretation linked to differences in breastfeeding. Earlier weaning among Catholics would have allowed for shorter birth intervals and higher completed fertility. In the absence of direct information on lactation in the two communities, however, it would be imprudent to accept this conclusion too easily.[14] Santow's 1987 analysis of the relationship between breastfeeding and post-partum amenorrhoea in Java revealed the complicated association between these phenomena. While breastfeeding delays the resumption of ovulation and lengthens the time between births (Pinto Aguirre et al

1998), the onset of pregnancy may, in turn, lead to the termination of lactation. This fact points to the importance of learning not only about infant-feeding patterns but also about the conditions under which sexual relations resume after a birth, since this may be the key factor that determines both the timing of a new pregnancy and the cessation of breastfeeding.

Understanding this process requires paying attention to the norms surrounding both infant-feeding patterns and sexual behaviour. Until recently, such issues have been seen by historical demographers as simple disturbances in a system of natural fertility. The variation in such behaviours is treated as random and their origins thought to be inexplicable. Yet, these practices may reflect important differences in cultural views about the relations between mothers and their children, and between husbands and wives. Breastfeeding involves a close bond between mother and infant, and demands that the two remain in close proximity throughout much of the day. A commitment to a longer period of breastfeeding may have signalled a greater concern for the health of mother and child. Similarly, norms governing sexual practices in the post-partum period may reveal something significant about the nature of the marital bond. Seccombe (1993) has highlighted the importance of this issue and provided compelling testimony taken from both letters of and retrospective interviews with working-class women in England about their beliefs and behaviour in this area. In their comments, women emphasized their desire for a respite from the constant pressure of childbearing, citing both economic and health concerns for doing so. Their ability to achieve this rested, of course, on the degree of cooperation they received from their husbands. Abstinence or *coitus interruptus* were the most likely mechanisms available to couples to extend the time between births, and, in both cases, the husband's participation would have been critical. If husbands were unwilling to cooperate by either abstaining from sex or practising withdrawal, their wives were faced with a difficult choice – bearing unwanted children or using such traditional "female-only" forms of control as abortion or infanticide.

The lack of direct evidence about the practices of women and men in the past is frustrating for historical demographers. We are not completely ignorant regarding sexual behaviour and the use of birth control in the past, however. The problem we face is in the interpretation of the scattered sources that make reference to such intimate forms of behaviour. In Alsace, as is often the case elsewhere, direct observations of such behaviour tend to occur in the context of official investigations of one form or another, or to come from sources such as the diaries of prominent persons who are not representative of the population as a whole. Such investigations were likely to occur, of course, only when authorities perceived a need to enter into the private lives of ordinary people, and this they did only when people's behaviour constituted a threat to the social order. Thus, for example, the only direct reference to the practice of *coitus interruptus* we have found involved adulterous relationships: "the said Peter [the adulterer] arranged to ejaculate outside the vessel of the woman in question" (quoted in Boehler 1995, 1494).[15] The dilemma facing the historical demographer is to determine what interpretation we can place on such testimony. Does the rather matter-of-fact recording of the behaviour suggest that the practice was well known and perhaps widely used? Or is the truth closer to the view put forward by Van De Walle and Musham (1995), who suggest that the lack of evidence about the use of *coitus interruptus* among married couples indicates that the technique was considered appropriate only outside the marital relationship?[16] Similar questions may be raised concerning the use of abortion and infanticide. There is no question that virtually all police and court records dealing with these acts involved unmarried women. Yet, that alone should not lead us to assume that these practices were unknown among married couples.[17]

Fertility regulation becomes even more significant as we move forward in time. Our analysis has shown that the use of some form of fertility control was spreading through the Lutheran population of Alsace in the nineteenth century. By mid-century, contemporary observers in both the Lutheran and Catholic communities recognized the growth of family limitation among Lutheran couples. Again, we lack direct information on the mechanics of fertility decline, but evidence of a precocious adoption of family limitation among Lutherans fits with the findings of other studies of Protestant populations in this area of Europe (Perrenoud 1988; Head 1988; Zschunke 1984; Pfister 1985). Interestingly, the earlier decline of fertility following upon the pre-decline pattern of "controlled" fertility through spacing suggests a possible link between the two. Referring to the early decline of fertility among the Calvinist population of Geneva and the surrounding countryside, Perrenoud remarked: "the concept of natural fertility runs the risk of misleading, because it begins from the assumption that a radical change in behaviour occurs over time when there might have been a progressive shift from one type of behaviour to another" (1988, 74).[18] The question that remains is why the Lutheran population adopted these strategies well before they penetrated the Catholic community. This question is explored at length in the conclusion of this book.

# CHAPTER SIX

# Infant and Child Mortality

The death of a young child, now a rare event in affluent societies, was tragically common in the lives of the families we have been studying. About one of every five children born would not survive their first year of life, and almost one in three would die before turning ten. Here, more than ever, averages give us only a partial view of the problem. For some families, the tragedy was complete. Jean George Klein and Anne Marie Schaeffer married in Baldenheim in April 1801 and saw their first child, a boy, born on 3 February 1802.[1] The child survived for only fifteen hours, however. In November 1805, another boy was born, but he too lived for only a few hours. Four more pregnancies followed, one resulting in twins, but all five infants were still-born. The couple themselves lived a long life, Jean George dying in 1856 at the age of eighty-six, and Anne Marie a few months later at the age of seventy-eight. But their fifty-five years of married life together left no surviving heir.

For others, precarious conditions had little direct impact on their children. At the same time and in the same village where the Kleins suffered through six pregnancies that resulted in no surviving children, Jean Jacques Frantz and his wife Anne Marie gave birth to seven children, five boys and two girls, all of whom survived to adulthood. Fourteen grandchildren and twelve great-grandchildren were born in Baldenheim and perhaps many more elsewhere.

In an era when rates of infant and child mortality were high, one would expect to find considerable variability in the experiences of families. Physiological factors alone might be expected to influence the survival chances of infants and children. Our main interest, however, is in the effect of economic and cultural factors on mortality. Given the high level of mortality that prevailed in pre-transition populations, were there significant differences among social groups in the risk of death? In particular, did the differences in demographic behaviour we have observed between Catholics and Lutherans extend to the issue of mortality?

## APPROACHES TO THE STUDY OF MORTALITY IN THE PAST

In seeking to understand the course of mortality in societies of the past, many historians and demographers have left little scope for the influence of social and cultural variables, emphasizing instead the autonomous character of mortality trends. Classical models of transition theory, for example, assume that death rates in the pre-transition era were uniformly high and fluctuated in response to environmental factors beyond the control of individuals and societies (Notestein 1945; Coale 1973).

Crisis theories of historical mortality trends have also downplayed the significance of social and cultural factors. Stemming from the work of Meuvret (1946), and developed in the analyses of Dupâquier (1979b), crisis theories point to the volatile nature of mortality in the past and argue that population patterns in these societies were driven by the movement between periods of "normal" mortality and periods marked by huge increases to crisis levels of mortality. Such crises were the result of famine, disease, war, and other extraordinary events that pushed death rates to catastrophic levels for short periods of time. So great was the impact of such crises, they might eliminate the growth of population that occurred over a generation or more marked by "normal" rates of fertility and mortality.

Crisis theory has deepened our understanding of mortality patterns in early modern societies. There is no doubt that most, if not all, European societies before the mid-eighteenth century experienced periodic bursts of crisis mortality that had devastating demographic and social consequences. Yet crisis theorists have generally viewed these bursts as resulting almost exclusively from forces beyond the control of social institutions. Their work has focused on how changes in climate or in the virulence of disease have affected death rates, with little attention paid to the ways in which societal responses exacerbated or mitigated the consequences of these events.[2]

A third important contribution to the study of historical mortality is contained in the work of Thomas McKeown. The early writings of McKeown and his collaborators (1955, 1962), which questioned the efficacy of medical intervention in lowering death rates prior to the development of drug therapies in the 1930s, was a useful corrective to naive beliefs about the impact of scientific progress on mortality. In his later work, however, McKeown developed a more radical model of population change that laid overwhelming emphasis on the role of improved nutrition in the decline of mortality and the modern rise of population. In doing so, McKeown opened wider the door to the influence of social and economic variables. He recognized that social and economic changes taking place in late eighteenth- and nineteenth-century societies allowed for a larger and more varied supply of food, and ultimately produced a better-nourished population. Yet, he directed very little attention to the mechanisms that would have allowed an improved food supply to produce lower levels of mortality. His work leaves the impression that a more abundant and varied food supply led, more or less automatically, to a better-nourished and more disease-resistant population.

More recent historical studies have begun to question the validity of explanations that identify mortality change as largely the product of such "exogenous" factors as climate change or variation in the virulence of disease agents. Post (1985, 1990), in his careful studies of famine in eighteenth-century Europe, has found that the severity of crises was a function both of the environmental trigger and the societal reaction to the problem. While it is true that the malnutrition that results in times of famine can make people less resistant to disease, it is also true that the changes in patterns of social interaction that often accompany such times can contribute to mortality rates. Residential overcrowding, for example, or changes in migration can increase the spread of infectious diseases. Thus, how social institutions respond to famine is just as important as the biological consequences of malnutrition.

Much recent work has also challenged McKeown's nutrition-based theory. Kunitz and Engerman (1992), for example, point out that empirical evidence suggests only a weak relationship between economic indicators and mortality decline. Indeed, most analysts now seem sceptical that any "one variable" approach can do justice to the great diversity of paths that societies have followed to lower mortality levels. What is needed, they argue, is a multifaceted approach to the study of mortality change, one that takes account of economic and environmental variables while also acknowledging the significance of human agency and social organization.

It is, of course, fine to argue in general terms for greater attention to be paid to social and cultural variables. But which factors might one expect to influence death rates, particularly in a pre-industrial setting? I would suggest three areas that might be productively explored: societal efforts to improve public health; the health practices of individuals and families, especially in relation to food preparation and personal hygiene; and changing values and attitudes, particularly concerning children.

Although McKeown (1976, 127) himself acknowledged that public health efforts aided in reducing mortality, he placed such efforts in the later part of the nineteenth century, after considerable progress had already been made. More recent work gives public health initiatives more credit, and argues that their impact was felt much earlier (Szreter 1988, 1997; Preston and Haines 1991a; Rollet-Echalier 1990; Caldwell 1986). These initiatives included technological approaches, changing such things as sewage treatment and water supply, as well as legislation regulating food supply and housing patterns.

The everyday practices of families and households have also been studied for their consequences on health. Some cultures, using a kind of commonsense reasoning, worked out solutions to such problems of daily living as food preparation and personal hygiene that anticipated modern scientific approaches, even though, as Landers (1992, 24) states, this may have involved doing "entirely the right thing for completely the wrong reasons." Others, by contrast, followed customs that had disastrous consequences for survival prospects, particularly for infants. This seems to have been especially true in the case of infant-feeding practices. While the exact nature of the mechanisms linking breastfeeding, the length of birth intervals, reduced fertility, and the risk of infant mortality is a subject of considerable debate, there is ample evidence that the duration and intensity of breastfeeding influence the risk of infant mortality (Fildes 1986; Knodel and Kintner 1977; Palloni 1989; Forste 1994; LeGrand and Phillips 1996). An outstanding historical example involved much of Bavaria and the Alpine regions of Austria where an early end to breastfeeding and the introduction of supplementary feeding were associated with exceptionally high levels of infant mortality (Knodel 1988; Viazzo 1989). As Knodel's study of fourteen German villages has shown, infant-feeding practices varied considerably, even within the same region, and undoubtedly reflected local custom and tradition. Young mothers probably looked to their own mothers or other relatives or neighbours for advice on feeding their babies, providing an important avenue by which custom and tradition could shape childcare practices and children's chances of survival.

More generally, Preston and his associates (Ewbank and Preston 1990; Condran and Preston 1994; Preston and Haines 1991b), have emphasized the interaction between public health initiatives and private behaviour in determining the mortality risks faced by young children.

Improved scientific understanding of the nature of disease and better public health initiatives may have paved the way for improvement in the health of populations, but a significant decline in mortality rates did not occur until new methods of dealing with illness penetrated the popular mind and changed parent behaviour. This occurred slowly, however, as traditional practices regarding the care and feeding of infants and young children proved remarkably resistant to the new gospel of childcare that began to emerge in the late nineteenth century, despite the efforts of both governments and professional associations to bring about change. In the United States, it was only in the period 1900–30 that these efforts began to bear substantial fruit in the form of significantly lower rates of infant and child mortality (Ewbank and Preston 1990).

Finally, and more controversially, is the question of the attitudes and motivations of individuals, and their consequences for the life-chances of children. Knodel and Van De Walle (1979) and Shorter (1975) have argued that the inability of couples to control their fertility led families to have more children than they desired, and weakened their motivation to do what was necessary to protect their lives and health. As a result, the premature deaths of some of these children might have been seen as a blessing – not something to be actively pursued, perhaps, but also not an outcome to be lamented when a surplus mouth was taken by accident or disease. In such circumstances, childcare may have been characterized by neglect and an unwillingness to expend resources to insure the health of children. Determination to do whatever was necessary to safeguard the lives of children would have to await the spread of effective means of fertility control.

To be sure, theories that make assumptions about human motivation concerning intimate and emotion-laden behaviour in the past necessarily rest on rather sketchy evidence. Observations of doctors, officials and clergymen, or the sayings contained in popular proverbs hardly provide a compelling argument, and, in any case, each one found can usually be countered with another that points in the opposite direction. Nevertheless, the controversy has helped to direct attention to the customs and practices of parents in caring for their children. While we may never know how parents in the past viewed the loss of a child, greater knowledge of what they actually did in the face of illness may help us understand why mortality rates of infants and children varied among social groups.

The stumbling block for historical demographers in coming to terms with these issues is, of course, the shortage of evidence. The difficulty in assembling information should not deflect us from a

Table 6.1
Summary measures of infant and child mortality by religion and period of birth

| | Catholics | | | | Lutherans | | | |
|---|---|---|---|---|---|---|---|---|
| Measure | 1750–1789 | 1790–1815 | 1816–1835 | 1836–1870 | 1750–1789 | 1790–1815 | 1816–1835 | 1836–1870 |
| $_1q_0$ | .191 | .185 | .190 | .212 | .157 | .187 | .155 | .178 |
| $_4q_1$ | .118 | .125 | .118 | .125 | .165 | .117 | .103 | .075 |
| $_5q_0$ | .287 | .287 | .285 | .310 | .297 | .282 | .242 | .240 |
| $_5q_5$ | .037 | .052 | .050 | .039 | .074 | .048 | .039 | .028 |
| $_{10}q_0$ | .313 | .324 | .321 | .337 | .349 | .317 | .272 | .261 |
| % Neonatal | 62.5 | 58.4 | 48.1 | 44.1 | 49.5 | 53.2 | 52.4 | 53.5 |
| N | 418 | 963 | 1260 | 1862 | 1178 | 1006 | 677 | 1051 |

careful consideration of these topics, however. Moreover, research on the social history of medicine has located new sources of information that cast a useful light on the problems to be raised here.

## TRENDS IN INFANT AND CHILD MORTALITY

Despite the high quality of the registers of vital events for our villages, mortality records present a number of problems that limit our investigation. A full discussion of the problems encountered and the solutions adopted is available in the appendix, but several points need to be noted here in order to place the results in context. First, there are serious gaps in the parish registers for the Catholic villages. Thus the figures for the Catholic population prior to 1785 are based on the village of Mussig alone, and even here there is evidence of under-registration of infant deaths. Second, all the analysis is based on the experiences of children born to couples who married and lived out their lives in one of the villages. This obviously limits the focus to the most stable families in the villages. Finally, because of inconsistency in the classification of early infant deaths as either stillbirths or deaths of live-born babies, we have included stillbirths in the count of infant deaths. This has the effect of inflating the infant mortality rates for the villages being studied.

With these caveats in mind, we can turn to the results presented in tables 6.1 through 6.3, which provide basic estimates of infant and child mortality rates for both the reconstitution and aggregate samples. The first general finding is that there is no clear evidence of a decline in rates of infant mortality over time. As was noted above, data for the five villages over the period 1750–89 are flawed for the

Table 6.2
Infant mortality rates for aggregate sample of twenty-six communes by dominant
religious affiliation

|            | 1811–20 | 1821–30 | 1831–40 | 1841–50 | 1851–60 | 1861–70 | Total |
|------------|---------|---------|---------|---------|---------|---------|-------|
| Catholics  |         |         |         |         |         |         |       |
| IMR        | .211    | .200    | .226    | .214    | .225    | .236    | .219  |
| % Neonatal | 51.7    | 49.6    | 48.3    | 49.4    | 47.5    | 46.1    | 48.9  |
| Lutherans  |         |         |         |         |         |         |       |
| IMR        | .189    | .183    | .170    | .144    | .186    | .195    | .178  |
| % Neonatal | 57.0    | 56.9    | 57.4    | 62.6    | 60.9    | 51.7    | 57.0  |

Catholic population, and probably slightly underestimate the risk of infant death even for the Lutheran communities. Even allowing for this, infant death rates in the decades preceding the Franco-Prussian War were no lower than in any of the previous time periods. This conclusion is confirmed by the data for the larger sample of twenty-six villages. For both the Lutheran and Catholic communities, the infant mortality rate moves up and down over the course of the nineteenth century, showing no definite progress towards lower mortality. The proportion of infant deaths that occurred in the first month of life (neonatal deaths) was higher in the Lutheran villages, as we would expect in the light of their lower overall rate; yet there is no clear upward trend in either religious community that would indicate the kind of decline in the post-neonatal death rate that normally accompanies declining infant mortality.

A second, though more qualified, finding is that rates of infant mortality were generally lower in the Lutheran communities. Data from the larger sample indicate that the infant mortality rate was, on average, about forty points higher in the Catholic communities. The data from the five reconstituted villages generally support this conclusion, though the picture is less clear; the religious differential appears smaller, particularly in the period before 1815. It is apparent that something more than the religious factor was involved: the ranking of villages with respect to the risk of infant death does not fit neatly with a simple Catholic/Lutheran dichotomy. Taken together, the two villages close to the Rhine, Baldenheim and Mussig, did better than the two agricultural villages of the interior, Avolsheim and Goxwiller, which hints at the possibility of a regional effect as well as a religious influence. Environmental factors may have created a natural setting within which the religious variable operated. In each of these two geographic pairings (which also shared important economic characteristics), the

Table 6.3
Infant mortality and child mortality by village and period of birth

| Village 1q0 | 1750–89 | 1790–1815 | 1816–35 | 1836–70 |
|---|---|---|---|---|
| Avolsheim | — | .250 | .202 | .221 |
| Husseren | — | .154 | .160 | .189 |
| Mussig | .196 | .146 | .201 | .220 |
| Baldenheim | .132 | .159 | .138 | .179 |
| Goxwiller | .188 | .224 | .190 | .177 |
| 4q1 | 1750–89 | 1790–1815 | 1816–35 | 1836–70 |
| Avolsheim | — | .169 | .141 | .162 |
| Husseren | — | .091 | .075 | .134 |
| Mussig | .117 | .114 | .132 | .089 |
| Baldenheim | .154 | .106 | .125 | .056 |
| Goxwiller | .180 | .137 | .073 | .104 |

risk of dying in infancy was about four percentage points lower in the Lutheran community than in the Catholic village.

The industrial commune of Husseren provides further evidence of a regional effect, perhaps linked to geographic factors. In the period 1790–1835, Husseren had the second lowest infant mortality rate, higher only than the rate for Baldenheim. Imperfect registration likely depressed the rate slightly, but the true figure was probably close to the calculated rate and certainly below the level of mortality in the villages of the Plaine d'Alsace. The mountainous setting of the village, with its abundant fresh water supply from the Vosges, may have contributed to this relatively favourable experience, offsetting whatever negative effects early industrialization produced. Viazzo (1989, 1994) found that the Alpine regions of Switzerland had below average levels of both general and infant mortality, which he attributed, in part, to cleaner water than in low-lying regions, a factor that helped reduce the incidence of gastrointestinal disease (1989, 217).[3]

Equally intriguing is the apparent increase in the infant death rate in Husseren in the years after 1836. There is evidence of rising mortality generally; the rate increased after 1836 in four of the five villages.[4] The situation in Husseren may have been further aggravated by difficult times for the textile factory. Wholesale layoffs were frequent during this period as the factory suffered through the vagaries of the international textile trade (Schmitt 1980). The curé of the local parish wrote to the bishop of Strasbourg in 1854, pleading for assistance to the many poor thrown out of work at the factory. There is also evidence of substantial emigration in these years, with a number of families listed as leaving for America (Schrader-Muggenthaler 1989; Kintz 1993). A deteriorating economy combined with greater mechanization (and perhaps environmental damage) may have overcome some of the natural advantages that the community initially held.

The data from the five reconstituted villages also allow us to examine trends in child mortality. Here, the religious differential appears fairly clear. Among Lutheran families, the probability of death in early childhood (between ages one and five) declined from .165 in the pre-revolutionary era to .075 in the years leading up to the Franco-Prussian War. Similarly, for children between the ages of five and ten ($_5q_5$), the likelihood of death fell sharply during the nineteenth century. As a result, though there was no progress made against infant mortality, the chances of a child born in a Lutheran community surviving to age ten improved significantly if not dramatically between the beginning and end of the period studied here. Prior to 1789, approximately 35% of children died before their tenth birthday; the corresponding figure for the years 1836–70 was 26%.

Trends in the Catholic population are more difficult to chart, though overall there seems little evidence of significant improvement. The data for the years 1750–89 are, as noted above, flawed, and in any case refer only to the village of Mussig. The figures in tables 6.1 and 6.3 show no indication of a decline in the risk of childhood mortality. If we assume the figures for the early years underestimate the mortality level in Mussig prior to the Revolution, it is possible that some improvement in survival prospects did occur in the period following the Revolution. If so, the progress was slight and did not continue into the nineteenth century. Taking the three Catholic villages together, the probability of dying between ages one and five remained stable in the period from 1790 to 1870. The risk of death in the later childhood ages declined slightly, but not enough to have any significant impact on the overall probability of dying by age ten, which actually reached its highest point in the last time period examined. Again, even assuming that figures for the early years underestimate infant and childhood mortality risks, it is hard to see how any significant improvement in the survival rates of Catholic children could have occurred prior to 1870.

### ENDOGENOUS AND EXOGENOUS SOURCES OF INFANT MORTALITY

It is unfortunate that neither parish nor civil registers of deaths recorded information on cause of death. Occasional notations were made beside particular entries and other sources provide some information about the outbreak of particular epidemics, but no analysis of cause of death structure is possible with these data. There is, however, an indirect way of examining broad differences in the sources of infant mortality. Demographers and medical specialists often distinguish between infant deaths that result from congenital or other prenatal factors as well as trauma connected to the birth itself, and those that are the consequence of factors in the child's environment. The former are referred to as endogenous causes of mortality, the latter as exogenous causes. If social factors influenced mortality rates, we would expect their effects to be felt most clearly when examining the exogenous element of infant mortality.

In the absence of direct information on cause of death, demographers have developed several techniques for quantifying the contribution of each set of factors. A simple method is to compute a neonatal death rate, which measures the probability of dying in the first month of life, and a post-neonatal death rate, which indicates the probability of dying between one month and one year of age for those children who survive the first month. To be sure, some infant deaths in the first month will be the result of environmental factors (infanticide being one obvious example), and it is possible that some deaths after one month could be the result of endogenous factors, though such is more likely in a modern setting than in eighteenth- and nineteenth-century societies.

Table 6.4 provides neonatal and post-neonatal death rates for the Lutheran and Catholic populations for the years 1785–1870, that is, the period when we believe registration to have been virtually complete. The data indicate that almost all the difference in infant mortality between the two groups was attributable to differences in the risk of dying after the first month of life. The neonatal death rate for Catholic infants was only 3.2% higher than for Lutheran children, while the post-neonatal rate in the Catholic communities was more than 25% higher. This points to an important role for exogenous or environmental factors in producing the higher infant mortality in the Catholic population.

A somewhat more sophisticated way to approach this problem is to use a "biometric" graphic technique developed by the French demographer Jean Bourgeois-Pichat (1951), to distinguish between infant deaths due to endogenous and exogenous sources. His method consists of cumulating infant deaths from one month of age to one year and plotting the result against a logarithmic transformation of age measured in days. The resulting line indicating the cumulative number of deaths at given ages should be close to a straight line. By extending the line back to the origin, Bourgeois-Pichat argued, the

Table 6.4
Summary measures of infant and child mortality by religion
(period of complete death registration)

| Mortality Measure | Catholics | Lutherans |
|---|---|---|
| Neonatal | .096 | .093 |
| Post-neonatal | .113 | .090 |
| % Neonatal | 48.6 | 53.2 |
| $_1q_0$ | .198 | .175 |
| $_4q_1$ | .122 | .100 |
| $_5q_5$ | .045 | .039 |
| $_0q_{10}$ | .328 | .286 |
| N | 4178 | 2882 |

rate of endogenous mortality can be estimated. This technique was followed here, though with a regression equation to estimate the point at which the graph would meet the intercept. The method works remarkably well for both the Lutheran and Catholic populations. In both cases, the plots result in almost perfect straight lines ($R^2$ equals .996 for Catholics, .997 for Lutherans) and produce an estimated endogenous mortality rate of 71 per 1000 for the Lutheran population and 77 per 1000 for the Catholic group.

As was the case with the neonatal and post-neonatal rates, these findings suggest that the experience of the two religious groups differed most with respect to environmental influences on the life chances of their children. In the circumstances, this is not surprising. Endogenous sources of mortality were largely beyond the control of mothers and midwives, and we might expect to find important differences between two populations in the same setting only if there were substantial variation in such demographic factors as the distribution of mothers by age. This is not the case here, though more Catholic women did continue childbearing into their forties, and this may have contributed to the slightly higher level of endogenous mortality. More intriguing, however, is the significantly higher exogenous mortality in the Catholic population. We explore this question more fully after first examining the seasonal dimension of infant mortality.

SEASONALITY OF INFANT MORTALITY

The data from the five reconstituted villages give us an exact date of death for each infant that died, and this allows us to look at the seasonality of infant deaths. Seasonal fluctuations in infant mortality have received considerable attention, in part because they provide indirect evidence on the likely causes of death. Infant death rates might vary over the year for a number of reasons. Variations in climate could lead to elevated risks in certain seasons. Hot summers can increase the numbers of deaths due to such causes as dysentery and diarrhoea via food contamination. Harsh winters, on the other hand, may increase the risk of death due to respiratory problems. In colder climates, the winter months generally hold the greatest risk for infants, while in hotter locations, the peak usually occurs during the summer. Alsace is marked by a continental climate, with relatively harsh winters and moderate to warm summers, which leads us to expect moderate peaks in both summer and winter.

Examining seasonality in infant mortality is not a straightforward task, however. Simply examining the frequency of infant deaths by month of occurrence can produce results that are seriously flawed, due to the pronounced seasonality in births. The greatest risk of infant death occurs in the first month of life, and thus months with above-average numbers of births are also likely to see unusually large numbers of infant deaths. But what we are really interested in uncovering is whether certain periods of the year are more dangerous for the health of newborn children. To get at this problem requires looking at monthly variation in mortality rates that are unaffected by fluctuations in the number of births.

The method used here, developed by Knodel (1988) in his study of German villages, constructs a matrix of mortality risks by month of birth and month of death. Thus, for example, we can examine the probability of a child born in January dying in the first thirty days of life (covering part of January and February), in the second thirty days (covering part of February and March) and so on for the first twelve months of life.[5] Calculations can be repeated for each month of birth and the resulting probabilities combined to produce an estimate of the risk of infant death during each calendar month.[6] In this way we can examine monthly fluctuations in infant mortality that are free of the distorting effect produced by seasonal variations in births.

The importance of following this procedure is well illustrated in figure 6.1. The dotted line, which shows the unadjusted mortality risk, points to a seasonal peak during the winter months with the greatest risk occurring in February. Aside from the excess mortality in the period from December to March, infant mortality rates were below average in all other months, except for a slight excess in September. By contrast, the adjusted data indicate the greatest risk of infant death occurred in late summer. Mortality rates were above average in the winter months but not to the extent suggested by the unadjusted data. The moderate excess of the winter was followed by a declining risk

Index number of deaths

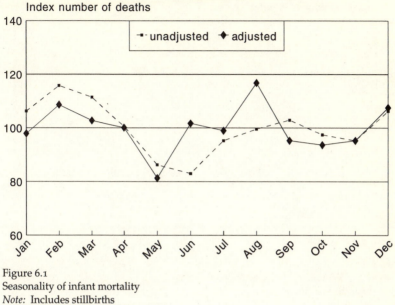

Figure 6.1
Seasonality of infant mortality
*Note:* Includes stillbirths
For definition of adjustment, see text.

through spring before rising back to normal and then above normal levels in the early summer and late summer months respectively. This pattern is more in line with what we might expect to find in a climate with relatively extreme conditions in both winter and summer, but we would miss it in the unadjusted data because the relatively low fertility rates in spring and early summer mean a smaller number of newborn infants are at risk during the summer months.

It would be interesting to push the analysis further so as to examine differentials in the seasonal patterns of infant mortality. Unfortunately, the relatively small number of infant deaths we are dealing with leads to large random fluctuations in monthly probabilities as we begin to subdivide the sample. This is apparent in figure 6.2, which presents monthly probabilities of infant death by religion. The peaks and valleys in the curves are sharper here and exaggerate monthly fluctuations. Still, it is interesting to note that August remains the most dangerous month for both religious groups. In other seasons, the patterns diverge somewhat. The Catholic communities show the expected excess mortality in the winter months, but the Lutheran rates are above average only in December. By contrast, rates are above normal throughout the summer months in the two Lutheran villages. A better understanding of these differences

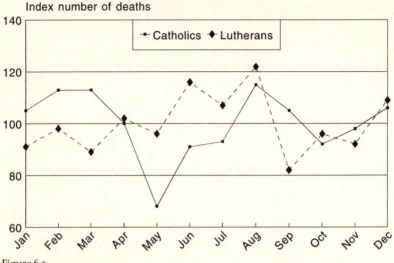

Figure 6.2
Seasonality of infant mortality by religion
*Note:* Includes stillbirths

would require a closer look at regional variations in climatic and economic factors, but this would necessitate a much larger sample than we have here.

## DEMOGRAPHIC FACTORS AND MORTALITY

The preliminary data on trends in infant and child mortality suggest that rates differed between the Catholic and Lutheran communities. Locating the sources of these differences is a complex task, however. The risk of infant death, in particular, is often influenced by a variety of other demographic factors such as the age of the mother, the length of time between births, and the number of births a woman has had. And, as is clear from the previous chapter, Catholic and Lutheran women differed on a number of dimensions of childbearing. To understand the religious differential, then, it is essential to take account of the different childbearing regimes of the two religious groups.

However, unravelling the influence of demographic factors on infant mortality is further complicated by the interrelationships among these variables. For instance, if the chance of infant death increases with the age of the mother, is the greater risk a function of physiological change in the mother as she ages, or is it linked to the fact that most children born of older mothers will have a number of older siblings? Or, to take another instance, in large families the intervals between births will be shorter. Is it the shorter length of time between confinements or the strain of the greater number of births that increases the risk of infant death? These are not easy issues to resolve, and it is helpful to look first at the influence of some of the immediate demographic variables, and then to move toward a multivariate analysis of differentials in infant and child mortality.

It would not be surprising to find an association between the age of a mother and the risk of death for her offspring. Young mothers who have not yet fully matured physically may experience higher-risk births, while mothers nearing the end of the childbearing years may also have higher-risk births due to deteriorating health. However, since most young women are just beginning childbearing while older mothers are coming to the end of their childbearing years, having already given birth to a number of children, it is important to try to separate the effect of age from that of repeated childbearing. One way to do this is to examine the risk by age of mother while holding constant parity; that is, to look at the risk of death for children of a given birth order by the age of the mother at the time of the birth. This is not as simple at it seems. First of all, few women past age thirty-five are giving birth to their first children while virtually no women in their early twenties have reached higher parities. Moreover, those women who do begin having their children at later ages (or who are already having a fifth or sixth child by their mid-twenties) are a select group that may differ from other women in important ways.

Nevertheless, in figure 6.3, we examine this issue by showing the risk of infant death[7] by age of mother for all births, and separately for parities two through four. When considering births of all orders, age of mother had little effect on the risk of infant death up until age thirty-five.[8] However, the risk of death increased noticeably among mothers thirty-five years of age or older. Most of these mothers, of course, would already have given birth to a number of children. Yet, when we restrict the focus to the risk of death for second-, third- and fourth-born children, older mothers still faced an increased risk. On the other hand, the children of young mothers (aged twenty to twenty-four) faced a significantly lower risk. A large proportion of the births to these younger mothers were first-borns, which, as we shall see, faced a higher risk of early death. When we remove these births from the analysis, the babies of younger mothers appear to have experienced a substantially lower risk of death during infancy. Parity, of course, is not the only factor that influences the relationship between age and the risk of infant death, and we will have more to say on this issue when we present the results of the multivariate analysis.

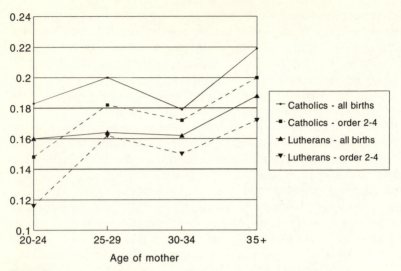

Figure 6.3
Infant mortality ($_1q_0$) by age of mother, religion and birth order

The association just noted between birth order and survival prospects has led some observers to wonder whether this relationship may indicate variation in the treatment of children by their parents (Knodel 1988; Imhof 1981). Later-born children may have received poorer care for a variety of reasons. A shortage of family resources leading to malnutrition might have had particular impact on infants and young children. It is also possible that a greater proportion of higher-order births were "unwanted," leading parents to provide less in the way of care and resources to these children. The data presented in this section cannot specifically test these hypotheses, but they will help us to establish whether mortality rates did, indeed, vary by birth order after controlling for differences in family size.

Figure 6.4 shows the probability of dying in infancy and early childhood by birth order for both Catholics and Lutherans. For both groups, there was a curvilinear relationship between birth order and the risk of infant death. The probability was higher for first-borns, declined and remained relatively constant for the middle parities, and then turned upward for the fifth and subsequent births (sixth in the case of Catholics). In the case of child mortality, on the other hand, there was no clear relationship between birth order and survival prospects for either Catholics or Lutherans.

The link between birth order and mortality prospects is complicated, of course, by the effect of family size. All families contribute a

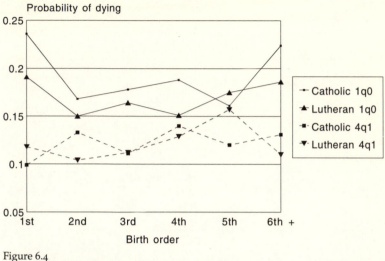

Figure 6.4
Infant and child mortality by birth order and religion
*Note:* Includes stillbirths

first-born child to the analysis, but only the relatively prolific families contribute children to the analysis of mortality among higher-order children. If these more fertile families were, for some reason, at greater risk of experiencing infant and child deaths, what appears to be a birth order effect may really be the result of other factors that led these families to bear a large number of children and suffer many deaths. To get a clearer picture of this situation, it makes sense to look at the joint effect of birth order and family size.

Table 6.5 presents these findings for the whole sample, while table 6.6 separates the results for Lutherans and Catholics. For the whole sample, there is evidence that both birth order and family size affected the risk of infant death. Leaving aside the small number of one-child families, the risk of infant death rose with the size of family. At the same time, when we focus on the larger families, we again see evidence of a curvilinear relationship between birth order and the risk of dying. In families with six to nine children, the risk of death was greatest for the first-born, declined for the middle children, and then increased to .195 for the last-born children. In families of ten or more, the last born infants faced the greatest risk of infant death, while those at parities two through nine fared best. With respect to early childhood mortality, there is still some evidence of a family size influence, but no apparent relationship between birth order and the probability of dying in any of the family size categories.

Table 6.5
Infant and child mortality by birth order and size of family

| Birth Order | | Family Size | | | |
|---|---|---|---|---|---|
| $_1q_0$ | 1 | 2–5 | 6–9 | 10+ | Total |
| 1 | .259 | .179 | .246 | .241 | .214 |
| 2–5 | | .152 | .170 | .213 | .166 |
| 6–9 | | | .195 | .211 | .199 |
| 10+ | | | | .279 | .279 |
| Total | .259 | .160 | .188 | .226 | .185 |
| $_4q_1$ | | | | | |
| 1 | .068 | .106 | .109 | .146 | .106 |
| 2–5 | | .101 | .136 | .168 | .123 |
| 6–9 | | | .118 | .123 | .119 |
| 10+ | | | | .157 | .157 |
| Total | .068 | .103 | .127 | .147 | .122 |

It is important here to look at the two religious communities separately since a disproportionate number of the higher-order births occurred to Catholic women. Doing so necessitates using slightly different categories so as to avoid problems of small numbers of cases. Again, however, for both Catholics and Lutherans, the risk of infant death was related to family size and, among the largest families, a link to birth order is apparent as well. Among Catholics with eight or more children, the probability of dying in the first year of life rose from .184 for birth orders two through four to .260 for parities eight and higher. Similarly, among Lutherans, the increase was from .158 to .211, a jump of 33%. In the case of early childhood mortality, on the other hand, there is little evidence that either birth order or sibsize played a very significant role. It appears that part of the effect attributed to sibsize when considering the whole sample was in fact a result of the rising proportion of Catholic children among those in the largest sibsize categories. Since, as we have seen, child mortality rates were higher among Catholics, this served to inflate the mortality risk for children in these categories.

These findings are open to several interpretations. The lack of any clear relationship between either birth order or family size and the risk of early childhood mortality seems to cast serious doubt on the hypothesis that parents provided poorer quality care to some of their children. On the other hand, the positive relationship between birth order and infant mortality in larger families is consistent with the hypothesis of differential treatment. Such an interpretation seems less plausible, however, than an alternative view that focuses on the impact of physiological factors such as the strain of repeated child-

Table 6.6
Infant and child mortality by birth order, family size and religion

|  | Family Size | | | |
| Birth Order | Catholics | | Lutherans | |
| $_1q_0$ | 5–7 | 8+ | 5–7 | 8+ |
| --- | --- | --- | --- | --- |
| 2–4 | .174 | .184 | .162 | .158 |
| 5–7 | .161 | .197 | .162 | .194 |
| 8+ |  | .260 |  | .211 |
| $_4q_1$ |  |  |  |  |
| 2–4 | .130 | .143 | .127 | .145 |
| 5–7 | .107 | .133 | .141 | .114 |
| 8+ |  | .144 |  | .118 |

bearing. Nevertheless, these results suggest the need for a more rigorous multivariate analysis, found later in this chapter.

Religion again plays a significant role. The higher infant mortality rate among Catholics results in part from the larger size of their families, yet even when focusing on families with eight or more births, Catholic children faced worse survival prospects. Family size differences contributed to, but do not seem to have eliminated, the effect of the religious factor.

A short interval between childbearing may weaken a mother's condition, and thereby affect the health of subsequent offspring. The strain of caring for an infant or young child while pregnant might well heighten the risk of prenatal problems that could affect the health of the second child. Once the birth occurs, a mother will find her time divided between two small children both in need of a significant amount of care. The extent of these effects might also be influenced by the survival of the child born earlier. If the child dies prior to the next birth, the physical strain on the mother should be less. Moreover, the mother will have only one infant demanding her attention, and thus the negative effect of a short interval might well be reduced.[9]

Table 6.7 shows the probability of dying in infancy and early childhood based on the length of the interval between births and the survival status of the earlier-born child. Short intervals (less than eighteen months) were clearly associated with a higher risk of infant mortality for the later-born child. This was true for both religious groups and regardless of whether the first-born child survived. The probability of dying in infancy was lowest when the birth interval fell into the "normal" range of eighteen to twenty-nine months. When the interval was longer than thirty months, the risk of death increased, though not to

Table 6.7
Infant and child mortality by interval from previous birth, survival status of previous birth and religion

|  | Status of Previous Birth | | | |
|  | Catholics | | Lutherans | |
| Interval (in months) | Lives | Dies | Lives | Dies |
| --- | --- | --- | --- | --- |
| $1q_0$ | | | | |
| < 18 | .241 | .268 | .248 | .229 |
| 18–29 | .148 | .219 | .131 | .166 |
| 30+ | .179 | .246 | .157 | .209 |
| $4q_1$ | | | | |
| < 18 | .165 | .142 | .129 | .099 |
| 18–29 | .123 | .149 | .124 | .107 |
| 30+ | .110 | .118 | .121 | .104 |

the level observed in the case of short intervals. It is not entirely clear why this would be so, though it is possible that longer intervals were typical of women who were prone to miscarriages, which of course go unrecorded. Intervals also tend to increase with parity, and, as we have seen, mortality rates were higher among higher birth orders.

Contrary to expectations, the risk of death was greater when the earlier-born child died prior to the subsequent birth. This again suggests that some families, for a variety of reasons, suffered a higher risk of infant death. The pattern seems to have held for both Lutherans and Catholics. The Catholic rates are higher in almost all categories, but variation in the length of intervals and survival status operated in a similar fashion in both religious communities.

While the length of time between births influenced the risk of infant death, it did not seem to have any continuing effect on the survival prospects of the later-born child. Probability of death in early childhood bore only a loose relationship to the survival status of the previous child and interval length. Among Catholics, there was a weak negative association between interval length and the risk of mortality but none at all among Lutherans. The negative effect of bearing children in quick succession appeared, it would seem, in infancy or not at all.

OCCUPATIONAL DIFFERENTIALS

Parish and civil register data give us the information needed to examine quite precisely the effects of demographic factors such as age of mother, length of birth intervals, and sibship size on the risk of mortality. Unfortunately, the registers are less generous in supplying other pieces of information that would permit an examination of the influence of social factors. The only reasonably solid indicator of a family's social status is the occupation of the father, but even this has limitations. Inconsistency in the reporting of occupation is, as discussed in the appendix, one source of worry. A second centres on the varying nature of work in different settings. To take one example, weavers in the villages of Baldenheim and Mussig worked on their own or in small workshops, while those in Husseren plied their trade in a large factory. The farmers of Goxwiller and Avolsheim, most of whom were involved in the production of wine, experienced rather different conditions from the cereal producers of Baldenheim and Mussig. Moreover, given the evidence presented above that suggests a possible regional influence on mortality patterns, occupational differences may well reflect an underlying regional effect, in that the occupational structures of the villages differ significantly.

Table 6.8 presents infant and child mortality risks by occupation of the father separately for the two religious groups. The data used here are limited to children born after 1785, for two reasons. First, as already noted, there is evidence of under-registration of deaths in the years before 1785. In addition, occupation was much less likely to be recorded on the older death certificates. Second, since our primary purpose here is a comparison of occupational groups, it seemed best to look at comparative material based on all five villages. From 1785 on, all villages were providing cases to the file and the quality of the data was almost uniformly high. Given the reduction in the number of cases, we have limited the analysis to just two time periods, 1785–1835 and 1836–70.

The data indicate no significant occupational differences in infant mortality risks. Again, we find that Lutheran families from all occupational categories did better than their Catholic counterparts, but in neither community does occupation appear to be a decisive influence.

The situation is only slightly more complicated when looking at child mortality. Again, no consistent evidence points to occupational differences in the risk of juvenile mortality. The decline in the risk of child death in the Lutheran community observed above seemed to touch all occupational classes, and as a result, no clear differences by profession were evident in either the earlier or later period. Among the Catholics, this pattern had one exception: the risk of mortality for the children of farmers dropped significantly; while at the same time, the situation worsened slightly for the young children of both workers and artisans. It is possible that a growing crisis in the rural world may have accentuated class differences, giving a greater advantage to

Table 6.8
Infant and child mortality by religion, occupation of the father and period of birth

|  | Occupation of Father | | | |
|  | Farmer | Worker | Artisan | Total |
| --- | --- | --- | --- | --- |
| $1q_0$ |  |  |  |  |
| CATHOLICS |  |  |  |  |
| 1785–1835 | .208 | .183 | .186 | .187 |
| 1836–70 | .210 | .211 | .210 | .211 |
| LUTHERANS |  |  |  |  |
| 1785–1835 | .193 | .152 | .175 | .173 |
| 1836–70 | .159 | .187 | .197 | .178 |
| $4q_1$ |  |  |  |  |
| CATHOLICS |  |  |  |  |
| 1785–1835 | .133 | .111 | .130 | .120 |
| 1836–70 | .068 | .143 | .156 | .125 |
| LUTHERANS |  |  |  |  |
| 1785–1835 | .108 | .120 | .117 | .114 |
| 1836–70 | .084 | .067 | .078 | .075 |

those who owned land. Yet it is puzzling that this pattern emerged only in the Catholic community, while among Lutherans all social classes appeared to benefit from falling rates of child mortality. Still, it holds out the possibility that farmers, as a more privileged group, may have been the first to experience an improvement in child mortality, which was clearly slower in coming to the Catholic population.

MULTIVARIATE ANALYSIS

A full understanding of the factors affecting infant and child mortality is difficult to obtain by considering the effects of only a small number of variables at a time because many of the variables of interest are closely interrelated. Examining infant and child mortality rates separately for groups defined by religion, occupation, age of mother, size of family and so on quickly leads to a situation where each group contains only a very small number of cases. The calculated rates for such groups will then be subject to large random fluctuations. It is therefore essential to use an approach that allows an assessment of the effects of individual variables while statistically controlling for

Table 6.9
Hazards regression results for models of infant mortality

| Variable | All Infants | | First-Born Excluded | |
|---|---|---|---|---|
| | Coefficient | Risk Ratio | Coefficient | Risk Ratio |
| SEX OF CHILD | | | | |
| Female | −.301*** | 0.740 | −.350*** | 0.705 |
| BIRTH ORDER | | | | |
| 2–4 | −.310*** | 0.734 | — | — |
| 5–7 | −.309** | 0.734 | +.015 | 1.015 |
| 8+ | −.052 | 0.949 | +.250** | 1.284 |
| FAMILY SIZE | | | | |
| 1–4 children | +.130 | 1.139 | +.127 | 1.135 |
| 9+ children | +.134* | 1.144 | +.118 | 1.126 |
| MARRIAGE ORDER | | | | |
| 2nd marriage | +.071 | 1.074 | +.160 | 1.173 |
| AGE OF MOTHER | | | | |
| Mother < 22 | +.015 | 1.015 | +.131 | 1.140 |
| Mother 30–39 | +.063 | 1.065 | +.073 | 1.075 |
| Mother 40+ | +.180 | 1.198 | +.189 | 1.208 |
| STATUS OF PREVIOUS CHILD | | | | |
| Survived | — | — | −.334*** | 0.716 |
| INTERVAL BETWEEN BIRTHS | | | | |
| < 18 months | — | — | +.277** | 1.320 |
| > 29 months | — | — | +.200** | 1.221 |
| COHORT | | | | |
| 1750–99 | −.113 | 0.893 | −.135 | 0.873 |
| 1850–70 | −.065 | 0.937 | −.036 | 0.965 |
| RELIGION | | | | |
| Catholic | +.224*** | 1.250 | +.184*** | 1.202 |
| REGION | | | | |
| Baldenheim/Mussig | −.293*** | 0.746 | −.233*** | 0.792 |
| Husseren | −.398*** | 0.672 | −.407*** | 0.666 |
| OCCUPATION | | | | |
| Farmer | +.222 | 1.249 | +.201 | 1.223 |
| Worker | +.224* | 1.252 | +.270* | 1.310 |
| Unknown | −.085 | 0.919 | −.207 | 0.813 |
| LOG LIKELIHOOD | −12864.8*** | | −9138.2*** | |
| N | 8351 | | 6545 | |

* p < .10    ** p < .05    *** p < .01

the influence of other factors. To do this, I have employed a proportional hazards model, the results of which are presented in tables 6.9 and 6.10. Like the more familiar life table approach used in demography, the proportional hazards method examines the risk of death for a group of individuals. However, the technique also indicates how characteristics of the individuals increase or decrease the risk of infant or child death. In that sense, it operates more like a regression technique.

The actual format of the analysis is complex. It begins by looking at the risk of infant death, or the probability of dying between birth and exact age one. This is done first by examining all infants, and then by looking separately at children other than the first-born. The reason for this is to include variables that deal with the effects of the previous confinement, in this case the interval in months between the previous birth and the birth of the index child, and whether the previous child was still alive at the birth of the index child.

The results of the proportional hazards analysis show the risk of death for a given category of individuals relative to those in another category that has been arbitrarily chosen as the reference group. Thus, for example, male children have been selected to be the reference category, and the parameter estimate for female children has a negative sign, indicating that females faced a lower risk of infant death. The risk ratio figure indicates that the risk for female babies was approximately 74% of the risk faced by male children.

The model for all children, shown in column 1 of table 6.9, points, as we would expect, to a significant role for several demographic factors. As noted above, male children faced a substantially higher risk of early death. Birth order also influenced survival prospects. Using first-born children as the reference group, the coefficients are negative and statistically significant for birth orders two through seven, but not for infants of birth orders eight and higher. These findings point to a curvilinear relationship between birth order and the risk of infant death, with first-borns and those of the highest birth orders experiencing the greatest risk. The effect of sibsize appears to have been important only in the case of very large families. With families of size five through eight chosen to be the reference category, the coefficient for smaller families is not significant. For children from families with more than eight births, however, the risk of infant death was some 14% higher. After controlling for such related factors as sibsize and birth order, age of mother has no significant effect on the risk of infant death.

Having taken account of the influence of a wide variety of demographic variables, it is striking to see that several social factors continue to be important in determining mortality risks. The findings suggest that religion and region of residence were clearly linked to the risk of infant death. For Catholic children, the relative risk of early death was 25% higher than that faced by infants in Lutheran families. In addition, babies born in the two agricultural villages (Avolsheim and Goxwiller) located in the wine-producing central region were at a distinct disadvantage. Infants in the other two regions, whether from the villages along the Rhine or from the industrial town of Husseren, faced a significantly lower risk of premature death. Indeed, for children in Husseren, the risk was about one-third lower than in the agricultural villages.

Occupational differentials in the risk of infant mortality appear to have been modest. The children of workers and servants were at a greater risk of infant death. However, the coefficients for the other occupational groups are non-significant, and there is no evidence of any dramatic change over time in risk of infant death. The relative risk of death for those born before 1800 and those born after 1850 does not differ significantly from that of the 1800–49 group that served as the reference category. This supports the earlier finding that no substantial progress against infant mortality was achieved during the 120-year period of this study.

The results in the second column of table 6.9 exclude first-borns and include two measures relating to a previous birth: the length of time between the earlier birth and that of the index child, and the survival status of the earlier child. The results for the previously included variables do not change dramatically, but the new variables do play an important role. For example, an interval between births of less than eighteen months increased the risk of infant death for the index child by almost 35%. Longer intervals (of thirty months or more) were also associated with a higher risk of early death, although the increase was not as pronounced as was true for short intervals. As we have noted before, a number of these longer intervals may be a function of pregnancies during the interval that resulted in miscarriages or stillbirths that went unrecorded. If so, women with unusually long intervals may have been at a generally higher risk of suffering infant deaths. The other additional variable tries to tap this issue. The negative coefficient for the variable indicating whether the earlier child survived until the birth of the index child suggests a tendency for infant death to run in families. While one might have expected that the continued presence of the earlier child in the household would have increased the demands on the mother, it appears that after controlling for other factors, especially the length of the birth interval, the survival of the previous child increases the survival prospects of the index child. The most plausible interpretation of this finding is that some families, for reasons that are hard to identify, provided an environment more conducive to good health among infants.

The addition of these demographic measures, while significant in themselves, did not alter the results for the sociological variables. Especially important is the continued role of religion. Although Catholic women experienced, on average, shorter birth intervals, controlling for length of interval and survival status of the previous child did not eliminate the effect of religion. After holding constant the effects of both demographic and sociological variables, Catholic infants still faced a significantly higher risk of dying. As well, the regional variable continued to exert an important effect, suggesting again that geographic and environmental factors, while difficult to measure directly, influenced the health of children.

Table 6.10 shows the results of the analysis of child mortality. The focus here is on the probability of dying between exact ages one and five for children who have celebrated their first birthday. The analysis proceeds in the same way, looking first at all children who survived infancy, and then narrowing the focus by excluding first-born children. In contrast to infant mortality, the results suggest that demographic variables are of little help in explaining variation in the risk of early childhood mortality. Interestingly, there was no significant difference in risk between male and female children. The only statistically significant coefficient among the demographic variables is for large family size, indicating that the risk of death in childhood was greater among children from families with more than eight children, and, somewhat anomalously, for children of birth order five through seven. However, even the effect of this variable becomes non-significant when first-born children are excluded and an indicator of the status of the previous sibling is included. The higher risk of death that some families faced seems to have had its impact largely through an elevated risk of infant rather than childhood mortality.

Adding the social factors into the model, however, strengthens the findings noticeably. The statistically significant coefficient for the variable indicating that the child was born in the period 1750–1800 makes clear the improvement in the risk of childhood mortality that occurred over time. Children born before 1800 faced a markedly higher risk of early childhood death. There is also evidence of a clear regional effect. Children who lived in the centrally located villages of Avolsheim and Goxwiller not only faced higher risks in infancy, but even those who survived the first year of life continued to suffer from

Table 6.10
Hazards regression results for models of early childhood mortality

| Variable | All Children | | First-Born Excluded | |
|---|---|---|---|---|
| | Coefficient | Risk Ratio | Coefficient | Risk Ratio |
| SEX OF CHILD | | | | |
| Female | +..083 | 1.087 | +..059 | 1.060 |
| BIRTH ORDER | | | | |
| 2–4 | +.150 | 1.162 | — | — |
| 5–7 | +.229* | 1.257 | +.091 | 1.095 |
| 8+ | +.225 | 1.253 | +.120 | 1.128 |
| FAMILY SIZE | | | | |
| 1–4 children | −.074 | 0.929 | −.100 | 0.904 |
| 9+ children | +.187* | 1.207 | +.126 | 1.134 |
| MARIAGE ORDER | | | | |
| 2nd marriage | +.147 | 1.158 | +.049 | 1.050 |
| AGE OF MOTHER | | | | |
| Mother < 22 | +.196 | 1.216 | +.204 | 1.227 |
| Mother 30–39 | +.109 | 0.896 | −.127 | 0.881 |
| Mother 40+ | +.040 | 0.961 | −.031 | 0.970 |
| STATUS OF PREVIOUS CHILD | | | | |
| Survived | — | — | +.102 | 1.107 |
| INTERVAL BETWEEN BIRTHS | | | | |
| < 18 months | — | — | +.130 | 1.139 |
| > 29 months | — | — | −.060 | 0.942 |
| COHORT | | | | |
| 1750–99 | +.424*** | 1.529 | +.362** | 1.436 |
| 1850+ | +.026 | 1.026 | +.075 | 1.078 |
| RELIGION | | | | |
| Catholic | +.144* | 1.155 | +.154* | 1.166 |
| REGION | | | | |
| Baldenheim/Mussig | −.396*** | 0.673 | −.439*** | 0.645 |
| Husseren | −.463*** | 0.629 | −.479*** | 0.620 |
| OCCUPATION | | | | |
| Farmer | −.196 | 0.822 | −.098 | 0.907 |
| Worker | +.050 | 1.051 | +.142 | 1.152 |
| Unknown | −.109 | 0.896 | −.174 | 0.840 |
| LOG LIKELIHOOD | −7355.0 | | −5793.3 | |
| N | 6912 | | 5495 | |

$*\,p < .10$    $**\,p < .05$    $***\,p < .01$

a greater chance of death during the early years of childhood. Again of central concern is the role of religion, although its effect here is weaker than was true for infant mortality. The relative risk of death for Catholic children was about 16% higher than for Lutheran children, though the coefficient was statistically significant only at the .10 level. Nevertheless, while it appears that the effect of religion on survival prospects was greatest in infancy, it did exert a continuing effect through the early childhood years as well.

## SUMMARY AND CONCLUSION

Throughout the years 1750–1870, Alsace experienced relatively high rates of infant and child mortality and, with one exception, saw little evidence of improvement. Overall, approximately one in five infants died in their first year of life and between one-fourth and one-third of children died before their tenth birthday. As was often the case, the region's experience placed it between the relatively low rates found in France and the very high rates of southern Germany throughout much of the nineteenth century (Poulain and Tabutin 1980). However, while little or no progress was made against infant mortality, evidence suggests a decline in childhood mortality among the Lutheran population of Alsace. In the Catholic community, on the other hand, no significant progress was achieved on either front, and when the Treaty of Frankfurt was signed in 1871 and the region passed under the control of Germany, the Catholic community continued to experience high levels of both infant and child mortality.

Reports from public health officials, which date from the early nineteenth century, make the high level of infant and child mortality in the region appear unsurprising. Doctors appointed to these positions filed regular reports on the health and living conditions of the population, as well as special reports when epidemics occurred.[10] Their comments show that while the great crises of mortality that had decimated the population in the seventeenth and early eighteenth centuries had disappeared, periodic outbreaks of infectious diseases continued to strike both rural and urban populations in the region.[11] The province was regularly ravaged by typhus, smallpox, and dysentery, as well as malarial infections in the marshy regions near the Rhine. In the nineteenth century, cholera appeared as a new threat to the populace, with major outbreaks occurring in 1832, 1849, and 1854.

The spread of disease was aided by the poor quality of nutrition, contaminated sources of water, and a general lack of hygiene at both the individual and community level. The average rural family ate meat rarely and survived on a diet that relied heavily on bread and vegetables, often consumed in the form of soup. A number of officials noted that during times of near famine, impoverished families would dig up the potatoes before they had ripened, a habit they associated with outbreaks of diarrhoea among both children and adults (ADBR 5M 127). Water drawn from stagnant pools or shallow wells was frequently cited as a source of disease, and some doctors applauded the increasing reliance on wine as the main beverage even among children (ADBR 5M 48). Housing was of poor quality, and families often lived in desperately crowded conditions. One doctor reported visiting a household stricken by an outbreak of typhoid fever in which six family members, all sick with the disease, were gathered in one room, two to a bed (ADBR 5M 127). Perhaps the most regular complaint of these officials concerned the lack of attention to cleanliness in the public spaces of the villages. Piles of garbage and human waste left to fester, streets with no drainage, and pools of stagnant water were most commonly cited as threats to public health. Despite their advice to local officials to take action on these problems, little seems to have been done.[12] Reports from the 1850s echo the same comments recorded in the first decades of the century.

Medical care apparently had little impact on the health of the rural population, though doctors felt they could have made a difference if only villagers had heeded their advice. An aggressive campaign of vaccination against smallpox was initiated in the early nineteenth century. As late as the 1850s, however, doctors still claimed that parents attempted to avoid having their children vaccinated, and in this they were abetted by local officials.[13] When epidemics broke out, some doctors complained, people would not call on their services, or when they did so would not follow their advice. Popular remedies – inducing vomiting or ingesting *schnapps* (ADBR 5M 127) – were more likely to aggravate than alleviate the patient's condition. It is not clear how useful the treatments prescribed by physicians would have been in the face of bacterial and viral infections, though at least some of their advice – particularly to limit contact between the infected persons and others – would have helped prevent the spread of the diseases. One physician reported that masters would send servants who fell ill back to their families in neighbouring villages, spreading the disease in the process (ADBR 5M 121).

It is not surprising, then, that survival prospects, particularly for infants and children, remained poor throughout much of the nineteenth century. Our primary interest, though, is in the variability in mortality rates among groups in the population. The multivariate analysis pointed to significant regional and religious differences even after taking into account the effects of a wide range of demographic factors. The regional factor is especially surprising in that lower rates of mortality were found in the industrial village of Husseren and in the two villages located near the Rhine. One plausible reason for the better performance of Husseren, previously mentioned, involves the presence of a clean and abundant source of water from the Vosges Mountains (Dobson 1997). It is also possible that the rise in mortality that appears to have occurred in the village during the nineteenth century reflected a deterioration in the environment associated with greater population density and greater mechanization in the textile industry.

The lower mortality rates in the villages near the Rhine relative to those in the agricultural villages of the Plaine d'Alsace are more puzzling. The canton of Marckolsheim in which they are located was generally viewed as one of the poorer areas of Alsace. Before large-scale drainage efforts were undertaken in the nineteenth century, the land was marshy and its people experienced periodic outbreaks of malarial infections.[14] On the other hand, the population density, lower in this area than in the more heavily populated region of the interior, may have slowed the transmission of disease. Clearly, environmental variables require far more detailed investigation.

Most intriguing, given the major interest of this book, is the significant difference between Catholics and Lutherans, a difference that is not erased by controlling for a range of demographic variables. The more rapid pace of childbearing in the Catholic community would lead us to expect a higher level of infant mortality. Yet, as the multivariate analysis has shown, controlling for differences in family size and length of birth interval does not account for all of the difference between the two groups. Several reasons for this differential can be suggested. First, the longer intervals between births in the Lutheran population likely reflected greater reliance on breastfeeding and later weaning. This may have conferred a qualitative advantage on infants, the effect of which is not fully captured by holding constant the length of time between births. Second, the Lutheran population was more affluent (Dreyfus 1979; Wahl 1980) and perhaps, as a result, better nourished. The proportion of the population that was indigent was significantly lower among Lutherans (Muckensturm 1988).[15] And data on recruits into the army for the canton of Marckolsheim show that young men from the predominantly Lutheran villages were on average some two centimetres taller and a smaller proportion were rejected for health reasons.[16]

There are two other possible reasons for the advantage enjoyed by Lutheran infants and children, though the evidence to support them is more speculative. One concerns the higher level of hygiene in the Protestant communities. It is a factor noted in passing by scholars in the region even though hard evidence to prove it is all but impossible to obtain. Juillard and Kessler (1952) drew attention to it in their comparative analysis of Lutheran and Catholic villages in the fertile Kochersberg region, west of Strasbourg. Despite the obvious similarities between the two communities, they noted in their ethnographic study conducted in the 1940s the greater concern with cleanliness among Lutherans: "Saturday evenings each Protestant family sweeps the street and cleans the gutter in front of their house; among Catholics, there is less unanimity and the Protestant village, it is generally agreed, is cleaner" (1952, 50). This observation was made several generations after the end of our study period, of course, and it is risky to assume that such differences prevailed a century or more earlier. Yet even the cantonal doctor of Marckolsheim, commenting on the generally deplorable state of hygiene in the region, identified the Catholic village of Mussig as "holding the honour of being the most unhygienic in the whole canton ... so that a disease that presents little danger in another village, becomes in Mussig ... serious and dangerous" (ADBR 5M 44).

Finally, it is interesting to speculate on whether the generally higher level of literacy among Lutheran parents was associated with a higher standard of childcare. Research on currently developing societies has identified literacy and/or the educational level of mothers as an important correlate of infant and child mortality (Hobcraft 1993). The link is a complex one. More educated parents are likely to be wealthier and in a better position to obtain modern medical care. Some researchers have argued that the positive effect of literacy goes beyond these factors, however, and may promote better quality child care within the home as well. It is possible that a similar pattern prevailed in nineteenth-century Alsace, and that the children of Lutheran families benefitted indirectly from a culture that placed great value on literacy for both men and women.

The earlier success enjoyed by the Lutheran community in the struggle against mortality calls us to reexamine the question posed by demographic transition theory about the role of declining mortality in helping to bring about lower fertility. Taken together, the results presented in chapters 5 and 6 reveal an almost complete absence of change in the Catholic community. Rates of infant and child mortality remained high for all marriage cohorts. In light of this, the persistence of high levels of marital fertility in the Catholic community is not surprising. The situation of the Lutheran community is more interesting in this regard. Despite a disappointing absence of progress against infant mortality, both Lutheran communities did witness important declines in child mortality. And, though not conclusive, there is reason to believe that fertility control was spreading in the Lutheran communities throughout the nineteenth century. However, in contrast to the original transition theory argument, which pictured falling fertility rates as a response to improved mortality conditions, the history of the Lutheran population of Alsace leaves the impression that the two changes occurred more or less simultaneously. As such, the Lutheran experience provides little support for the view that couples made note of the improving prospects for young children (their own or their neighbours') and adjusted their childbearing behaviour accordingly. On the other hand, it is not inconsistent with the view that smaller family size led to improved care for young children and thus lower death rates. In the absence of more detailed information on the sources of declining childhood mortality, it would be premature to push such an interpretation too far. We need better data on change in the causes of death among children in order to evaluate the role parental care may have played, directly or indirectly, in the process. Happily, new work in both historical demography and the history of medicine (Dobson 1997; van Poppel and van der Heijden 1997) may equip us to provide better answers to these questions in the future.

# CHAPTER SEVEN

# Conclusion

In the period from 1750 to 1870, the Catholic and Lutheran populations of Alsace were governed by two different demographic regimes. The Catholic pattern was marked by restricted marriage, high marital fertility, and high levels of infant and child mortality. This pattern changed remarkably little over the 120 years we have studied. The middle decades of the nineteenth century saw further tightening of the marriage system, brought on in part by increasing population density in the rural areas. Illegitimacy and bridal pregnancy also increased significantly. On the whole, however, the Catholic demographic regime was surprisingly stable in the face of considerable economic and political change.

In the Lutheran community, a different pattern prevailed. Marriage occurred earlier than among Catholics and a smaller part of the population remained permanently celibate. Marital fertility was consistently lower as were rates of infant and child mortality. The years from 1750 to 1870 also saw much greater demographic change in the population. There was some restriction of marriage in the mid-years of the nineteenth century, and for many of the same reasons as in the Catholic community. More important is the clear evidence of change in rates of marital fertility and child mortality. Fertility control began to take hold amongst the cohorts married in the early nineteenth century, and among these same couples, premarital conceptions and births became noticeably more common as well. And, while infant mortality rates remained stubbornly high (though still below the level in the Catholic community), progress was made against mortality in early childhood.

Although the two religious denominations had quite different demographic regimes, the differences partly offset one another such that the rate of population growth was not so different in the two

Table 7.1
Estimated effect of variations in nuptiality, marital fertility and child survival rates on differences in the mean number of legitimate children surviving to age five by religion and period of marriage

| Religion | Period of Marriage | Mean Number of Survivors to Age Five | Percentage Difference in Mean Number of Survivors | Nuptiality | Children Ever Born | Survival Rates to Age Five |
|---|---|---|---|---|---|---|
| | | | | Percentage Difference Expected Due to Observed Differences in | | |
| Catholics | 1750–1815 | 4.76 | +21.8 | –0.8 | +24.8 | –0.6 |
| Lutherans | 1750–1815 | 3.69 | –5.5 | +6.2 | –11.5 | –0.7 |
| Catholics | 1816–60 | 4.14 | +5.9 | –6.9 | +18.1 | –2.7 |
| Lutherans | 1816–60 | 3.18 | –18.6 | +0.8 | –24.4 | +7.4 |

Note: Based on legitimate births to first marriages only. Percentage difference in mean number of survivors compares the particular cohort to the entire sample.

communities. Following Knodel (1988, 364), we have computed the mean number of children surviving to age five, by religion, for two marriage cohorts. The findings, contained in table 7.1, show that Catholic families produced a larger number of children who survived to age five. For both cohorts the difference amounted to about one child. However, this method overstates the difference between the Catholic and Lutheran communities in that the proportion never marrying was higher among Catholics and the rate of remarriage lower. Both these factors would have worked to reduce the gap in population growth rates. Interestingly, while the mean number of children surviving to age five declined for both religious groups over time, the interval between the two (in absolute terms) remained nearly constant.

The table also presents the results of a simple decomposition technique, suggested by Knodel (1988), to assess the effect of variations in nuptiality, marital fertility and childhood mortality on the number of surviving children. To do this, the mean number of children surviving to age five is first computed for the total sample. The value for a given demographic component is then substituted into the equation. Thus, for example, using the data on number of children ever born for Catholic women married 1750–1815, along with the data on nuptiality and survival for the entire sample, produces a mean number of surviving children 24.8% higher than the mean for the sample as a whole.

The results of the analysis show that differences in marital fertility rates were most important in distinguishing between the two religious groups. However, the advantage enjoyed by the Catholic community as a result of its higher level of marital fertility was offset, in part, by lower nuptiality and slightly higher infant and child mortality. This was especially so for couples married between 1816 and 1860. Had their nuptiality and the survival prospects of their children been equal to that of the whole sample, the average number of children surviving to age five would have been 18.1% greater than for the sample as a whole. In fact, the number of surviving children was only 5.9% higher than the average for the sample. Among Lutherans, the opposite was true. The lower marital fertility of these women was counterbalanced in the older cohort by earlier marriage, and in the later cohort by better survival prospects. The end result of these two different demographic regimes, then, was a modest difference in the number of surviving children. While we cannot compute the rate of natural increase for the two communities, these data would lead us to expect that the rate was only moderately higher in the Catholic population. The result, as census data confirm, was that the religious balance of the population did not change greatly during the period of our study.

The data presented in table 7.1, as well as those discussed at length in earlier chapters, confirm the existence of important differences in demographic behaviour between the Lutheran and Catholic communities of Alsace. The challenge that remains is to explain the evolution of these differing demographic regimes. The introductory chapter identified three important elements to consider in assessing the likelihood that religion will influence social and demographic behaviour: first, the values and teachings of a group relevant to the behaviour in question; second, the institutional mechanisms through which religion can influence the behaviour of members; and, third, the importance of religious membership and identity for the members of the group. The remainder of this chapter shows that the Catholic and Lutheran communities followed quite different paths on these three dimensions, and that this, in turn, had important implications for the behaviour of the individuals who formed these two groups.

THE REFORMATION AND SOCIAL VALUES

The teachings of Luther and those who followed in his wake challenged the position of the old Church, and, I would argue, directly and indirectly created the basis for a substantial change in the lives of ordinary people. These changes included a gradual reshaping of the demographic regime of the Lutheran community. Perhaps most importantly, Luther and other early leaders of the Reformation introduced a new view of marriage. As we saw in chapter 3, for the new Protestant leaders marriage was the natural state to which men and women should aspire. Family life, centred on the bond between man and woman, was to be the cornerstone of the new Lutheran communities while celibacy came to be viewed with a combination of suspicion and disdain. This new view of marriage and family life provided the impetus for a different nuptiality pattern in the communities that accepted Protestantism.

It is less clear whether this new ideology of family life also opened the door to the practice of fertility control. To be sure, there is no direct support for limiting births in the teachings of the reformers. Luther was himself the father of six children and an ardent pronatalist. As Ozment notes (1992, 165), he encouraged women to produce large families: "Even if women bear themselves weary or ultimately bear themselves out, this is the purpose for which they exist." Yet, in celebrating the importance of the bond between husband and wife, the reformers implicitly provided a basis for behaviour that protected and strengthened the marital relationship.[1] From this perspective, if children (or an excessive number of children) posed a threat to the solidarity of husband and wife, fertility control might appear as an acceptable solution in order to protect and nourish the marital bond.

Focusing only on the specific teachings of Protestantism underestimates the influence of the Reformation on the values and beliefs of its followers, however. The argument offered here is that the development of Lutheran thought led as well to a different understanding of the social world, one that allowed for greater accommodation to innovation, and eventually made for far-reaching changes in the social and demographic patterns of the new Protestant communities. To understand how this emerged in Alsace requires following a rather circuitous route through the religious and social history of the province.

As the Protestant Reformation developed through the early decades of the sixteenth century, Luther and those who sympathized with his views gradually created a sweeping critique of Catholic teachings and traditions. In place of the elaborate rules and ceremonies of Catholicism, man-made creations in Luther's view, the reformers wished to rebuild the Christian Church on the word of God as presented in Scripture. From the earliest days of the Reformation, Luther and other leaders argued for the importance of Scripture over tradition and in favour of making accessible to the common people the word of God. This orientation had two important consequences. One concrete result was that the new Protestant Churches promoted literacy among the common people so as to allow individuals direct access to the substance of their faith (Strauss 1988). A second, more nebulous effect was the legitimation of a sceptical world-view, one that rejected many of the more mystical elements of the Christian tradition in favour of a more rationalist approach to religious belief. As Ozment (1992, 6) has succinctly put it: "Protestant faith promised to save people above all from disabling credulity."

The significance of literacy and education for demographic and social behaviour is now well established in social science (Caldwell 1980; Hobcraft 1993). It is essential, then, to underline the importance that was attached to literacy in the Lutheran communities that formed in the wake of the Reformation. From its beginnings, the Lutheran community in Alsace was committed to the development of schooling. As early as 1534, authorities in Strasbourg undertook to develop a network of schools that would concentrate on producing basic literacy and a knowledge of religious teaching (Vogler 1994). The war and chaos of much of the first half of the seventeenth century obstructed such efforts, and as soon as peace returned, Protestant authorities set among their highest priorities the reestablishment of religious education. At the end of the seventeenth century, they advanced the idea of compulsory schooling. Although this objective was not realized in practice, considerable progress was made even in rural areas.[2] The Lutheran community was thus considerably more advanced than the Catholic population in levels of literacy, a gap that was not closed until near universal levels of literacy were achieved in the nineteenth century.

Harder to conceptualize than the growth of literacy but, I would argue, no less important in the development of a distinctive Lutheran model of social life, was the increasing significance in Lutheran theology and teaching of a rationalist approach to religious belief. With the definitive break from the Roman Church, reformers were faced with the task of not only criticizing existing practice but of articulating their own beliefs and building a new set of traditions and rituals for their followers. At the same time, religious and civil authorities sought to communicate these new beliefs to the population and solidify the place of the new church in the regions where Protestantism held sway. This often required rooting out the vestiges of popular Catholicism still found among elements of the populace, and in Alsace, this entailed a major drive to eliminate religious practices that conflicted with Lutheran teachings (Vogler 1994, 89). Churches were stripped of elaborate decoration, devotions to local patron saints were suppressed, and such popular practices as processions and healing rituals were condemned as superstition. A more austere form of religious faith was promoted in their place, one in which the Bible held the central place and in which the faithful were encouraged to develop their knowledge and understanding of the central tenets of the faith. This new religious orthodoxy which gradually took root in the Protestant communities communicated two important ideas to its believers. First, in attacking many traditional practices that provided supernatural solutions to the problems of the natural world, Protestantism encouraged individuals to accept responsibility for handling the problems of everyday life. While religious faith remained the source of one's beliefs and a guide to moral behaviour, it was no longer a resource for solving life's difficulties. This orientation laid the basis for a greater engagement with the secular world and a greater openness to non-religious systems of thought on social problems. Second, Luther's stinging criticisms of the ways of the old Church, as well as the subsequent battles among the reformers themselves, may have encouraged greater scepticism about religious ideas and institutions generally. After all, if the structures that had so carefully regulated social life for so long could be so easily dismantled, did it make sense to view the new structures that replaced them as absolute? Might not future generations debunk the teachings and practices of Lutheranism as the reformers had done to Catholicism?

It would be inaccurate to say that the Lutheran Church in Alsace abandoned traditional Lutheran teachings in the centuries following the Reformation, but there was, without doubt, a considerable departure from the orthodoxy that prevailed among the earliest generations. By the eighteenth century, even the prince-bishop of Strasbourg, Cardinal de Rohan, was pointing out that the Lutheran Church had moved away from the beliefs contained in the Confession of Augsburg (Strohl 1950, 245). Chief among the new currents of thought that came to influence the Lutheran Church of Alsace was rationalism. The aim of the proponents of rationalism was to blend Lutheran principles with the new scientific and philosophical ideas of the era. In Strasbourg, Blessig, one of the leaders of the Lutheran Church, organized a series of seminars designed to explore the implications of the German *Aufklärung* for the church and society. Similar efforts were undertaken in Colmar and Mulhouse. Clubs of an officially secular nature, such as the *Deutsche Gesellschaft*, formed to discuss and propagate the ideas of the Enlightenment (Vogler 1994, 158). Although not explicitly denominational, their membership was entirely Protestant. The success of Enlightenment ideas in the Lutheran community was confirmed by the election in 1787 of

Philippe-Jacques Muller, a committed proponent of rationalism, as president of the Lutheran convention.

The growing influence of science and secular philosophies on Lutheranism found no parallel in the Catholic community. Preoccupied with combating the spread of Protestantism, the Catholic Church followed a very different intellectual path in the time from the Council of Trent to the French Revolution. In the immediate aftermath of the Reformation, the Church languished in a state of disorder. Weak leadership and a poorly educated and often corrupt clergy handicapped efforts to reform the Church along Tridentine principles (Vogler 1994, 96–9). This situation changed dramatically, however, with the arrival of the Jesuits. At the request of the bishop of Strasbourg, they took over a number of functions in the diocese including the visitation of abbeys, chapters and rural parishes to assess the state of Catholicism in the region (Châtellier 1981, 155). Under their intellectual leadership the Church in Alsace began to develop a response to Lutheranism that stressed traditional Catholic teaching and practices and, above all, fidelity to Rome. In contrast to other regions of France, Gallic ideas that argued for greater independence from Rome and a larger role for secular authorities found little favour in the region. The Church in Alsace was firmly committed to an ultramontane position (Châtellier 1981, 483).

In light of the strong attachment to traditional Catholic principles and papal authority, rationalist ideas of the Enlightenment encountered a cold reception among Alsatian Catholics. The keen interest shown by Protestant churchmen only heightened the suspicion and eventually the opposition of the Catholic Church to Enlightenment rationalism. As the new theories came to greater prominence in the second half of the eighteenth century, the Church found in them a prime target for attack. The Enlightenment became synonymous with deism at best, atheism at worst, and was held responsible for the collapse of traditional religious and social values. The only defense, Church leaders argued, was a return to the roots of Catholic teaching and practice (Châtellier 1981, 409).

Between the dawn of the Reformation in the early sixteenth century and the beginning of our period of demographic analysis in the mid-eighteenth century, the Lutheran and Catholic churches in Alsace developed markedly different theological positions. The differences went beyond purely religious or theological concerns; their contrasting philosophies presented different views of the secular world and provided the basis for different patterns of behaviour. Lutheranism was open to new ideas in the secular world, and had a rationalist orientation that favoured greater mastery of the material world. By contrast, Catholicism, stung by the losses endured as a consequence of the Reformation and finding itself in a continuous struggle for the hearts and minds of the faithful, rejected new developments in philosophy and science, and emphasized instead traditional dogma and practices. In doing so, it promoted a world-view that discouraged accommodation with new developments in secular thought and favoured an approach to the problems of the social world that was firmly rooted in the sacred.

Needless to say, these contrasting patterns of intellectual development did not guarantee that ordinary Catholics and Protestants would come to differ from one another in the ways they married, had sex or raised children. For that to occur, religious authorities needed institutional mechanisms to bring their teachings to the people and to promote compliance with them.

## THE INSTITUTIONAL BASIS OF RELIGIOUS IDENTITY

In the immediate aftermath of the Reformation, the differences between the old religion and the new were only dimly perceived by the great majority of the people. Over time, however, the churches worked to sharpen those differences in the minds of their followers through a process German historians have referred to as confessionalization (Schilling 1988a, 1988b; Hsia 1989). In their view, religious leaders, motivated by both ideological and practical concerns, strove to reshape the beliefs and behaviour of the laity. This often entailed relying on or cooperating with secular authorities to discipline their followers. Rulers and civic officials, though sometimes wary of being drawn into theological quarrels (Abray 1985), saw in the work of the churches an opportunity to strengthen their own grip on the people and to build among their subjects a greater sense of allegiance to the territorial domains they controlled. At the same time, confessionalization created a strong sense of religious identity and, I would suggest, increased the likelihood that religious values would influence the behaviour of the faithful.

In the centuries between the Reformation and the French Revolution, three elements, in particular, contributed to the growth of religious identity in Alsace: first, the ongoing political and military struggle that culminated in the Thirty Years War; second, the policies followed by the French government in its efforts to both promote Catholicism and integrate the newly acquired region into the kingdom; and third, the efforts of the two churches themselves to use both ecclesiastical and civil power to enforce conformity among their members.

It is not my intention here to retrace the history of political and religious conflict that followed in the wake of the Reformation. It is essential to point out, however, that Alsace as much as any region in central Europe was deeply affected by this conflict. The free city of Strasbourg, having converted to the Reform, was forced to play a tricky political game, balancing its commitment to the new religion with its position in the Holy Roman Empire, still ruled by a Catholic emperor (Abray 1985). The countryside was divided in the wake of the Peace of Augsburg in 1555 according to the principle *cuius regio, ejus religio,* with villages on both sides of the new religious divide experiencing a variety of depredations in line with the shifting political and military fortunes of the various protagonists (Vogler 1994, 112). During the Thirty Years War, Alsace was devastated by warfare and the populace suffered horribly at the hands of troops from the various factions that passed through the area. Most important for our concerns, however, was that religious identity became a basis for better or worse treatment. Imperial troops wreaked havoc on Lutheran communities, particularly in some of the smaller towns of the region. The arrival of Swedish troops brought similar devastation to the Catholic community. It was a pattern that would be repeated later in the century during the war with Holland (1672), and it inevitably strengthened the sense of religious identity of the population (Vogler 1994, 112).

When France acquired Alsace, a new element entered into the struggle between the region's two religious communities. As was related earlier, although the French authorities were remarkably gentle in their approach to the traditions and institutions of the province (Livet 1956), the new regime gradually adopted policies that strengthened the position of the Catholic Church to the detriment of Lutheranism. These policies are described in chapter 2; perhaps the most wearing for the Lutheran community were the *alternation,* requiring that, in Protestant areas, many civil offices alternate between Protestants and Catholics (Strohl 1950, 198); a decree that illegitimate children were be automatically baptized in the Catholic faith, even where both parents were Protestant; and, perhaps most significant of all, the *simultaneum,* which dictated that in Protestant communities where as few as seven Catholic families lived, the church building was to be shared between the two faiths.[3] Before long, Catholic leaders stood accused of encouraging the movement of Catholic families into Protestant communities in order to stake a claim to use of the church (Vogler 1994, 129). This practice became the source of persistent conflict between the two communities over the next two centuries.

In this context of continuing conflict, the Lutheran and Catholic churches took positive steps to solidify their positions and to exert influence over the lives of their faithful. The new Protestant elites, especially in the cities, worked hard to extend their control over both religious institutions and the general population. The late sixteenth century saw the publication of numerous *Kirchenordnung* intended to both codify doctrine and establish rules for ceremonies, schooling and public behaviour. This period also saw the establishment of visitations whereby church officials examined the practices of local churches in an effort to insure conformity (Vogler 1994, 74). In the short run, their efforts often met with resistance from the common people. Although many had been disturbed by the failings of the old church, they did not necessarily rally to the new.[4] Many clung to old religious practices that the new religious authorities sought to eliminate. Even the clergy in the Alsatian countryside often mixed together elements of Protestant and Catholic liturgy. And, although the evidence is often limited, there is some basis for thinking that mixed marriages between adherents of Catholicism and those of the Reformed faith were not uncommon in the aftermath of the Reformation (Châtellier 1981, 146).

Gradually, however, differences started to solidify. The new Lutheran clergy took over the apparatus of the old Church and added elements of its own. Luther had developed a catechism of the new faith and it became the basis for teaching the faithful. The growth of religious instruction for the young was one critical part of the Lutheran strategy for defending the Reformation (Strohl 1950; Strauss 1978). At the same time, Lutheran ministers frequently encouraged civil authorities to use the power of the state to enforce elements of Lutheran doctrine (Abray 1988, 231; Hsia 1989).

The Catholic Church, of course, developed a strategy of its own to prevent the spread of Protestantism and to reverse its gains where possible. Led by a Jesuit outpost in the small town of Molsheim, just twenty kilometres from the Lutheran fortress of Strasbourg, the Church launched a vigorous Counter-Reformation. Missions into Protestant territories succeeded in "recapturing" whole villages, while in other areas significant numbers converted back to the old faith (Châtellier 1981, 290). In addition, the immigration of new administrative officials and military personnel, all Catholic, strengthened the position of Catholics in the region. Even Strasbourg, solidly Lutheran before the union with France in 1681, came to hold a significant Catholic population by the early eighteenth century (Dreyer-Roos 1969, 92). As was true in the Lutheran communities, the Catholic Church also set out to exert greater control over its followers. In the seventeenth century, in particular, increasing efforts were made to regulate behaviour. A 1629 ordinance, for example, compelled attendance at Sunday Mass and provided for a beadle to conduct a house-to-house search to identify violators (Châtellier 1981, 129). Such surveillance extended beyond religious duties to include family life as well. Infractions, especially when involving such practices as adultery, were reported to officials and resulted in both religious and civic penalties. Catholics also developed a strategy of visits to local communities by church officials to investigate the degree of compliance with officially approved procedures. The outcome was a greater uniformity of doctrine and practice throughout the rural communities of the province.

In this setting of interconfessional competition and conflict, a stronger sense of religious identity began to emerge, and with it, a sharpening of differences between the two faiths. Liturgical differences were now obvious (Vogler 1993). The centrality of Scripture and the use of Lutheran hymns and canticles came to mark Lutheran liturgy. Partly as an outgrowth of the Counter-Reformation, traditional Catholic practices such as processions, pilgrimages, and devotion to patron saints grew in importance. Now a passing glance at daily life in these villages would have allowed an observer to spot significant differences. As Châtellier concluded: "The evidence would suggest that it was, indeed, the notion of confession, with all that the term implies as a social characteristic, that should be applied to the Catholic and Lutheran communities, taken as a whole, in the eighteenth century. That which had, prior to 1650, only a general outline, especially for the simple faithful, took on a much sharper edge a century later"[5] (1981, 359).

The French Revolution further increased the divergence between the two groups on a number of economic, political, and, of course, demographic dimensions. In the early days of the revolutionary period, the Catholic community in Alsace moved to oppose the new regime, and much of this opposition centred on a rejection of the policies directed toward the Church. There was, to be sure, considerable antagonism towards the economic role of the Church in pre-revolutionary Alsace, even among the Catholic peasantry. The bishop of Strasbourg, the Abbey of Murbach, and other church institutions were leading landholders and, as often as not, were held in contempt for their efforts to extract rents and dues from the peasantry (Juillard 1953, Marx 1974). But the Catholic community remained devoutly religious, and the disgust many felt over the economic dealings of some church institutions did not translate into a rejection of the Church itself.

Opposition to the new order among the Catholic laity reflected the strong steps taken by the clergy. Lower Alsace (Bas-Rhin) led the country in the proportion of priests who refused to sign an oath in support of the Civil Constitution of the Clergy, passed in 1791

(Epp 1990). The bishop of Strasbourg fled to the right bank of the Rhine, outside French territory but still a part of the diocese of Strasbourg, and from there continued to exert influence over the operations of the Church in Alsace (Epp 1990, 238). The increasing radicalism of the revolutionary legislation on religion, culminating in the cult of reason during the Terror, hardened the rejectionist sentiment in the Catholic community.

The reaction to the Revolution in the Protestant community of Alsace was considerably different (Reuss 1906; Strohl 1950; Lienhard 1981; Vogler 1991). For the most part, Lutheran leaders welcomed with enthusiasm the changes, for the ideas expressed by early revolutionary leaders and the first legislative measures adopted fit well with the theology many Lutheran churchmen had developed in their efforts to harmonize traditional Lutheran teachings and the ideas of the Enlightenment. The Declaration of the Rights of Man, which some Lutheran writers saw as echoing traditional Protestant ideas, presaged the development of a society in which belonging to a minority religious group would no longer entail a different and often secondary status (Strohl 1950). Beyond this, the Lutheran community benefitted in a very practical way from revolutionary legislation. While laws allowing for the seizure of ecclesiastical property applied to the Catholic Church, Lutheran property was exempt. Though by no means a landholder on the scale of the Catholic Church, the Lutheran community gained by this differential treatment and saw in it, not without reason, evidence of a generally favourable view of Protestants among the leadership of the new regime. This broad-based support for the Revolution among the Lutheran community was temporarily weakened during the period of the Terror. A general hostility to organized religion combined with the extension of some punitive legislation to include the Protestant communities undercut what had been widespread support for the general thrust of social change associated with revolutionary ideals. The Terror was, of course, short-lived, and it seems clear that, in contrast to the situation among Catholics, the long-term judgment of the Lutheran community of Alsace on the Revolution and its effects was positive.

The very different responses of Catholics and Lutherans to the Revolution profoundly influenced the development of the two communities in the nineteenth century. The Catholic Church set about repairing the devastation brought on by the Revolution. Religious orders had been disbanded and the secular clergy was bitterly divided between those who had signed the oath of allegiance to the Civil Constitution and those who had not. With the fall of Napoleon and the reestablishment of the monarchy, the Church began to find its feet, rebuilding key institutions that exerted substantial control over the faithful. Once again, the civil authority, through a series of policies, provided support to the Church in its conflict with Protestantism, and church leaders used their newly strengthened position to advance the interests of the Catholic community. Priests tainted by past support for the revolutionary regime were gradually eliminated from active roles. Religious orders, including the Jesuits, were invited back into the region. A more effective method of recruitment and control over the clergy markedly improved the quality and character of recruits. Concubinage, common in the seventeenth and eighteenth centuries, was all but eliminated and reports of "moral failings" among the clergy declined (Muller 1986, 360).

On the ideological level, the hierarchy aligned the Church in Alsace with its most conservative trends. Strong links to the Catholic Church in Germany continued and, with the appointment of Andreas Raess, the first Alsatian to become bishop of Strasbourg since the fourteenth century, the Church in Alsace stood as a leading supporter of papal authority and the primacy of Rome.

Most important for our concerns, however, is that the Church was effective in bringing its conservative message to the people of the villages. After a serious decline during the Revolution and Napoleon's First Empire, vocations increased sharply throughout the nineteenth century (Muller 1986, 233). There was no difficulty in placing a priest in even the smallest villages of the region. And in the village, the priest played a commanding role, using his position to act as moral watchdog. Pastors did not hesitate to oppose behaviour they considered immoral, often singling out from the pulpit those whose behaviour they considered unacceptable. They also played a positive role, however, leading the faithful to more active participation in the Church. The *confréries*, or spiritual organizations of the laity, were revived and expanded. Virtually every parish had its own groups, most often divided along lines of age, gender, and sometimes occupation, which drew together large numbers of ordinary people in settings that combined both a religious and a social function. As such, they provided a powerful opportunity for the Church to extend its influence over the lives of its parishioners (Muller 1986, 811). Parish priests and their superiors also worked to reinvigorate popular devotions, most of which had a strong public dimension. Festive celebrations surrounding religious holidays and frequently including public processions strengthened the sense of attachment and identification to the Church and, by extension, increased the sense of difference from Protestants. Supporting the local clergy were the efforts of the religious orders. Two dimensions of their involvement were especially important (Muller 1986, 387). First, they preached missions throughout the countryside that were an opportunity to solidify the faith and transmit the ideas of church leaders. Second, and perhaps most importantly, orders of nuns supplied teachers for the village schools, providing another opportunity for the Church to deliver its conservative message.

For the Catholic community of Alsace, the French Revolution did not usher in a period of secularization nor lead to what Lesthaeghe and Surkyn (1988) have called a "laxist" orientation as occurred in many other regions of France and Belgium. On the contrary, the community as a whole followed the lead of the hierarchy in its opposition to many of the reforms of the period, especially those that impinged on religion. The gradual elimination of those in the clergy sympathetic to the Revolution, especially priests who had signed the Civil Constitution, set the Church on a conservative and even reactionary path throughout the nineteenth century. Although the laity by no means followed every initiative of the clergy and at times rejected initiatives they felt too extreme, the Catholic community maintained a high level of devotion to religious practice throughout the nineteenth century. Continually preoccupied with the struggle against Lutherans and those who favoured greater secularization of society, religious affiliation became a fundamental element of personal identity for Catholics throughout the period.

The positive evaluation of the Revolution in the Lutheran community of Alsace paved the way for very different developments in the nineteenth century than had occurred among Catholics. Proponents of a liberal form of Lutheranism continued to hold sway within the Church, and the reactionary policies of civil authorities introduced under the Restoration had the effect of strengthening this current within the Lutheran community. The active policy of support offered to Catholicism by the Restoration raised all the old suspicions and worries of Protestants and led them to embrace the secular ideology of the Revolution. This, in turn, had important consequences for the organization of the Church. Lutherans developed a far greater openness to secular thought and ideas. Continuing the pattern of the eighteenth century, Lutheran theologians sought to reconcile science and religion. Institutionally, the Lutheran Church shied away from a purely sectarian position. Newspapers, such as the *Courrier du Bas-Rhin*, though staffed almost exclusively by Protestants, were not explicitly confessional, a sharp contrast with the situation in the Catholic community where publications such as the *Katholisches Kirchen- und Schullblatt* took an openly Catholic position (Vogler 1994, 208). It was one sign of a growing secularization of the Lutheran community. Information on religious attendance, though sketchy, points in a similar direction. Reports filed by rural pastors suggest that by the mid-nineteenth century no more than half of the faithful were attending services on a regular basis (Vogler 1994, 232)[6] and some ministers, including the pastor of Baldenheim, felt religious devotion in the home such as daily Bible reading was uncommon (ADBR 2G 19 9). Certainly there was no analogue to the *confréries* that played such an important role in stimulating religious participation in the Catholic villages.

By the middle of the nineteenth century, two contrasting cultures had evolved in the two religious communities. In both groups, people's basic identity was shaped by membership in their religious faith. The two groups had developed a set of social and religious institutions that helped to draw their members into social intercourse with their co-religionists and to limit interaction with members of other faiths. The almost continual conflict between the two communities intensified feelings of attachment and bred suspicion and hostility towards members of the other faith.

These differences in culture and identity took concrete shape in the differing behaviour patterns of the two communities. The Lutheran community, more urban-based to begin with, had always enjoyed an economic advantage. The advantage grew over time, however, and extended to the rural villages we have studied. Income levels were higher, landholdings typically larger, and Lutheran farmers showed an earlier and stronger interest in adopting new developments in agricultural technology (Wahl 1980).[7] The industrial sector of the province was largely in the hands of Protestant investors. The greater commitment to education was both a source and a result of the greater economic success of the Lutheran community (Vogler 1994). In the political sphere as well, Catholics and Lutherans moved in different directions. With the extension of voting rights under the Second Republic and the Empire, religious affiliation came to play a critical role in shaping voting patterns. Lutherans were drawn to the parties of the left, arguing for a more liberal, secularized model of society, while Catholics voted overwhelmingly for the parties of the right, parties that were often heavily influenced by the Church itself (Igersheim 1993).[8]

As the analysis presented in this book has documented, the two religious groups also developed different demographic regimes. In attempting to account for these differences, we are handicapped, as are most historical studies, by an inability to specify their proximate determinants. Direct information on breastfeeding, contraception, or childcare, the kind of information that can be obtained through modern survey techniques, is unavailable, and its absence demands caution in any attempt to explain the two contrasting demographic patterns. Still, though the specifics must remain in doubt, it seems reasonable to conclude that Catholics and Lutherans developed rather different orientations to social life. Lutheran theology, buttressed by a range of institutional supports, predisposed its followers to a greater openness to cultural innovations. The identification of new modes of thought and behaviour as the enemy of religious faith discouraged Catholics from adopting new forms of behaviour that would have reduced rates of fertility and mortality. Moreover, given the continuous conflict between the groups, the adoption of a different pattern of behaviour by one group was almost certain to discourage members of the other community from following suit. The language that characterized the relations between the communities underlines the tendency to devalue the actions of the other group. For Catholics, Lutherans were heretics and opponents of true religion as their openness to the ideas of atheists confirmed. For Lutherans, Catholics were "obscurantists," who, in rejecting the developments of science remained committed to superstition and backwardness (Vogler 1994, 252). Such negative characterizations extended to demographic behaviour as well. As it became clear that fertility control was spreading in the Protestant communities, this became new evidence of the nefarious character of the Lutherans. In the report of the diocese of Strasbourg, written in 1858, the anonymous author wrote: "Protestantism in Alsace is in decline, not due to emigration, but because of a system widely in use among the dissidents which constitutes a grave affront to Christian morality" (cited in Muller 1986, 1114).

## A LESSON FROM ALSACE?

The persistent differences in demographic behaviour between Protestants and Catholics in Alsace illustrate how religion can help to shape the demographic regime of a community. At the same time, our findings emphasize that differences in behaviour do not emerge automatically from differences in religious culture (Kertzer 1995, 46). Religious affiliation is most likely to influence behaviour, I have argued, when three conditions are present: first, the ideological orientation of the culture favours certain forms of demographic behaviour over others; second, institutional mechanisms are present to translate values into social pressures felt by ordinary people in the course of their lives; and, finally, social and political conditions favour a strong sense of attachment to the culture among a community's members. Such attachment is especially likely to emerge when religious affiliation constitutes an essential element of group identity, and when that sense of identity is heightened by contact and competition with a different ethnic or religious group occupying the same territory.

The central argument of this book is that all three of these conditions were met in Alsace and, as a result, religion played a crucial role in shaping the process of demographic change. The question arises, of course, whether the Alsatian situation was unique, or if the ideas put forward here can help us to understand demographic change in other settings. Oddly, despite the renewed interest in the impact of culture in demography, a number of recent works have downplayed the importance of religious influence. Guinnane (1997), for example, argues that Catholicism has been greatly exaggerated as a factor in Irish demographic development. Similarly, Obermeyer (1992) has questioned the significance of Islam as a direct or indirect factor in shaping the demographic patterns of the Arab world. Insofar as these works seek to debunk simplistic accounts of the role of religion that focus narrowly on theological teachings or that view individuals as reacting in lock-step conformity to the instructions of religious leaders, they are welcome. However, if we take seriously the idea that culture helps to determine human behaviour, it is important that demographers pay serious attention to the role religion can play. In many societies, after all, religious values form a vital part of the ideologies that people hold. Moreover, religious institutions are frequently in a position to influence the behaviour of individuals in a wide range of contexts. This is particularly so in settings where religion organizes those activities such as education, health, and social welfare that are increasingly controlled by secular institutions in modern Western societies.

Historically, Ireland would seem to be an ideal setting to evaluate the argument that has been developed here. Irish demographic patterns in the period from the Famine to the Second World War, including relatively late marriage, a high level of permanent celibacy, and high marital fertility, bear a strong resemblance to those of Alsatian Catholics (Guinnane 1997). It is true as well that this period saw a resurgence in the power and influence of the Catholic Church with a rising tide of vocations and an important role in social and political affairs (Larkin 1972). At the same time, some would argue, Catholicism became an essential component of what it meant to be Irish.

A third case of interest is the Canadian province of Quebec. Marital fertility rates in Quebec attained legendary levels in the seventeenth and eighteenth centuries (Charbonneau et al 1987), and high fertility persisted well into the twentieth century (Henripin and Peron 1972; Beaujot and McQuillan 1982). As in Ireland and Alsace, the Catholic Church possessed far-reaching institutional power, including almost exclusive control over education until the 1960s (Linteau et al 1979, 232–50). And, once again, Catholicism formed an important part of the identity of French-Canadians in their struggle to maintain their cultural distinctiveness in the face of English economic and political dominance.

The very different structure of Islam suggests caution in extending the argument of this book to the situation in contemporary Islamic nations. Nevertheless, the persistence of distinctive patterns of nuptiality and fertility in a number of Islamic nations, particularly in the Arab world, demands a serious consideration of the role played by religion (Mazrui 1994). The merger of religious and secular authority in some nations of the Middle East and the significance of Islam as a source of identity and as an expression of difference from the West hints at interesting parallels with the situation of Catholicism in the past.

It is especially important to extend research into the effect of religion in the modern world. Too often, as in the Alsatian case, the ethnographic data necessary to understand the role of religion are limited. The archival materials available are rich in their documentation of the evolving strategies of churches and civil authorities but are less informative on the behaviour and attitudes of ordinary people. Some sources provide a glimpse of their reactions – judicial archives, police files and other records of the interaction of the common people with the institutions of society. While more can certainly be drawn from this evidence than is usually the case in historical demographic studies, even the most diligent researcher bumps up against the limitations of such sources. It is vital, then, to merge the study of historical demography with analyses of present-day populations to arrive at a better theoretical understanding of the evolution of demographic behaviour.

# Issues of Data Quality and Method

The demographic analysis in this volume builds upon data collected by religious and civil authorities in Alsace from the late seventeenth century to the late nineteenth century. These data form the family histories from which our demographic measures are computed. The validity of the analysis depends on the quality of the basic data, and on the validity of the method used. This appendix presents an overview of the data used in this study and discusses some of the methodological strategies employed to deal with data limitations. Before addressing those issues, however, a brief description of the family reconstitution approach in historical demography, which forms the basis of the analysis in this book, is in order.

## THE METHOD OF FAMILY RECONSTITUTION

The study of historical populations was revolutionized by the method of family reconstitution. First outlined by the great French demographer Louis Henry (Henry 1956; Henry and Blum 1988), the method involves the creation of family histories by joining together the individual records of births, marriages, and deaths contained in parish and civil registers. All the vital records for a particular locality are compiled, and then the individual records that pertain to a particular couple are matched. Thus, the marriage record forms the basic unit from which the family history proceeds. For each couple that marries in the community, the demographer attempts to assemble a complete history of the vital events of the family members, including each birth that occurs to the couple (including births that may have preceded the marriage) as well as the death records of the spouses and their children. In ideal circumstances, the analyst is able to develop a complete history of the family that allows for the calculation of a wide variety of demographic measures, including the duration of the marriage, the number of children born to the couple, the average length of time between births, and the survival prospects of the children. Normally, the researcher will also search back in the records to locate the birth records for the two marriage partners. When this information can be found (or when an indication of the age of the bride and groom is given on the marriage certificate) it is possible to carry the analysis much further by including such questions as age at marriage and age differences between spouses. It is also possible to examine in far more detail aspects of fertility and mortality. We can, for example, study variation in the length of time between births according to the age of the mother and father, or compute sophisticated demographic measures such as age-specific marital fertility rates. Once the family record is complete, other demographic and social indicators that can be gleaned from the historical record can be added to the family record. It then becomes possible to examine remarriage patterns, for instance, by linking the marriage of a widow or widower to the family record of the first marriage. Marriage and birth records or census files often provide other pieces of information about individuals, such as their occupation. This type of data helps us to push the analysis further and to explore variations in demographic behaviour among different groups in the community.

To illustrate the approach, table A.1 shows a family history from the village of Mussig. The marriage of Francois Joseph Ottenwelter and Anne Marie Schneider[1] took place in the village on 15 February 1830 and was recorded in the civil register of marriages. Birth dates for the husband and wife were supplied on the marriage register. However, since they were both born in the village of Mussig, we also possess their birth certificates. This allows us to calculate the age at marriage of the spouses as well as the age difference between them, which was an unusually large nine years. Both died in the village and their death certificates are contained in the civil register. Anne Marie was the first to die, passing away in January 1861 at the age of fifty-six, while her husband lived as a widow for just over seven years, dying in October 1868. There is always some concern about missing information on remarriage. It is not impossible, for example, that Francois Joseph may have remarried in another village and returned to live in Mussig. In this case, however, there is clear evidence that this did not occur: his death certificate identifies him as the widower of Anne Marie Schneider. Moreover, the 1866 census also lists him as a widower. The material available in this case leads us to believe that this couple was in observation from the time of their marriage until

Table A.1
Family history of Francois Joseph Ottenwelter and Anne Marie Schneider of Mussig

| HUSBAND | WIFE | |
|---|---|---|
| Francois Joseph Ottenwelter | Anne Marie Schneider | |
| Date of birth: 26 March 1795 | Date of birth: 8 April 1804 | |
| Date of death: 7 October 1868 | Date of death: 26 January 1861 | |
| | | |
| Date of marriage: 2 February 1830 | End of union: 26 January 1861 | |

| CHILDREN | Date of birth | Date of death |
|---|---|---|
| Catherine | 29 March 1827 | 19 March 1841 |
| Anne Marie | 23 October 1831 | 9 May 1871 |
| Joseph | 22 January 1834 | |
| Therese | 21 April 1836 | |
| Marie Anne | 26 June 1838 | |
| Antoine | 3 September 1840 | |
| Ignace | 26 August 1844 | 6 October 1844 |
| Catherine | 12 September 1846 | |
| Helene | 22 May 1849 | |

their deaths. In that sense, this is the kind of "ideal" family record that historical demographers hope to find.

The second stage in the process involves searching the registers of births and deaths to identify the children that were born to the couple. In this case, there is an interesting twist. Anne Marie gave birth to a child on 29 March 1827, some three years prior to their marriage. The birth certificate indicates the father was unknown and the child Catherine carried the surname of her mother. However, the marriage certificate tells us that Francois Joseph acknowledged being the father of the child and indicates that Catherine would, from that point on, be known as Catherine Ottenwelter.[2] Eight other children were born to the couple after the marriage, the first coming some twenty months after the wedding, the last over nineteen years into the marriage when the wife was forty-five years of age. Three death records were found for the children of the couple. The first-born, Catherine, died in 1841. (Note that the eighth child, born in 1846, was also called Catherine. As will be explained later, the practice of "re-using" names allows us to monitor the completeness of death registration.) The second child, Anne Marie, died in 1871, and the seventh child, Ignace, died in 1844 at the age of six weeks. Although no other death certificates were found, we cannot assume the other children survived until the end of the period of our study. It is quite possible, even likely, that some left the village in adolescence or early adulthood and died elsewhere. As explained in chapter 6, we have assumed that, since the couple evidently lived their whole lives in the village of Mussig, their children remained in the village (and thus in observation) until at least age ten. Thus, we conclude that of the nine children born, eight survived to the age of ten.

If all the family records were as complete as the above example, analyzing demographic patterns in the past would be quite straightforward. Unfortunately, family reconstitution studies are often hampered by missing or incomplete data.[3] In a typical reconstitution study, a significant proportion of family records will remain incomplete. A couple may marry in the community, give birth to several children, and then vanish from the records. Should this family history be excluded from the analysis and, if so, how does this affect the accuracy of our results? Henry was concerned about the problem of bias caused by the use of incomplete family histories in the computation of demographic rates. In particular, he warned about the problems that may arise if researchers use data on the behaviour being studied to decide which families to include in the analysis. A simple example may help to clarify this point. Let us assume that in order to examine fertility patterns we decide to include all families that remained in observation until the wife's forty-fifth birthday, a date taken to signal the end of the reproductive period. Any couple for whom we have a death record for the first partner to die and an indication that the wife had celebrated her forty-fifth birthday prior to the date of the death will be included. However, perhaps no death record is found for a spouse, but a marriage record for one of their children indicates that the mother died at age fifty and the father was alive and present at the child's wedding. Is it fair to conclude the family was in observation throughout the childbearing period and therefore include them in the analysis of fertility? Henry's answer was no. By using the children's marriage records as a source of data, we are biasing our sample. Childless couples, for example, have no children who will marry and thus stand no chance of being included in this data source. To follow such a strategy would lead us to overestimate fertility levels because more fertile couples stand a greater chance of being included in our sample. Henry's rules, which we have followed in this book, minimize the problem of bias by dictating that the presence of a family or individual in the community must be established by a source independent of the phenomenon under study. This brilliant insight laid the basis for the calculation of vital rates in a statistically unbiased manner. At the same time, however, it raised another problem that has long troubled historical demographers. The practical effect of Henry's rules is to limit much of our analysis to the behaviour of families that spent all of their lives in the community under study. But what if these families differ in important ways from those who move on? Our findings are accurate in the sense that they correctly measure the behaviour of a particular group of people, but as an indicator of the demographic behaviour of people in the region or country being studied they may be misleading. The problem grows in importance, of course, as the population becomes more mobile. Although this problem has long been recognized and debated, little evidence is available to determine how large the differences are between the sedentary and mobile parts of the population. Desjardins (1995) has shown that estimates of average age at first marriage are not significantly influenced by limiting our focus to marriages that occur in the village being studied. Still, it is possible that differences on other demographic dimensions are greater (Hammel 1993), and we need to remember this when evaluating the results of a family reconstitution study such as this.

REGISTRATION OF VITAL EVENTS

Following Henry's rules of procedure will not produce an accurate analysis of population patterns unless the underlying data on which the analysis is based are themselves of high quality. Registration of births, marriages, and deaths has a long history in Alsace with the earliest registers still in existence dating from the late sixteenth century. But the turbulent political history of the province and the frequent military conflicts fought out on Alsatian territory left gaps in the registers for some parts of the region. Fortunately, for the five villages used in our reconstitution analysis, the registers, with one important exception, were well-preserved. The exception is the parish register of Avolsheim, which is missing for the period prior to 1788. For the other four villages, the registers dating back until at least the early eighteenth century are available in the Archives Départementales du Bas-Rhin/Haut-Rhin.

The quality of the registers is generally extremely high, particularly so for the two Lutheran villages, Baldenheim and Goxwiller. There are no gaps in either the older parish registers or the civil registers which date from the time of the French Revolution. Additionally, as documented in the following sections, the completeness of registration attained remarkably high levels. Indeed, the register for Goxwiller is almost a model for historical demographers. Registration of births and deaths was nearly complete and the entries were unusually detailed, allowing for a high degree of confidence in matching events, a significant feature in a population with relatively few surnames and

Christian names. While the registers of Baldenheim were not quite as complete, the problems are fewer than might be expected for the time period.

As noted, the analysis for Avolsheim is limited by the absence of the parish registers and thus is almost exclusively drawn from the civil registers which begin in 1792. For the other two Catholic communities, Husseren-Wesserling and Mussig, the parish registers are again of generally high quality, though some limitations need to be noted. Husseren was part of the parish of Mollau, a community two kilometres away. In and of itself, this need not lead to under-registration, but it may have complicated the process of registration and possibly led to some events being missed or registered in another parish. More serious, however, was the fact that deaths of infants and young children were seldom registered prior to the late 1770s, and registration was not complete until approximately 1785. As noted in chapter 6, this means that analysis of mortality in the Catholic villages prior to 1785 is based exclusively on the village of Mussig.

In the case of Mussig, only two gaps existed. The marriage registers for 1790 and 1791 are missing. Additionally, the register of births dates back only to 1722. As a result, age at marriage for some couples married in the middle decades of the eighteenth century had to be taken from data provided on the marriage certificate or on their death certificates, both sources subject to some degree of error.

From 1792 on, the civil registers were used as the source of data, though in the early years of civil registration it was sometimes possible to check data against the parish registrations as well. On the whole, civil registration for the five villages was of exceptional quality, with very little evidence of under-registration of either births or deaths. The only exception was the revolutionary period when local officials took some time to master the registration process. There is some evidence of missed events and some inaccuracy in the recording of data. A particular problem was the revolutionary calendar, introduced in 1793, which remained a mystery to many local officials. Fortunately, some of the errors could be easily corrected (officials often confused the months of Vendémiaire and Ventôse, for example).[4] By the late 1790s, the system seems to have been functioning well, and our analysis of the data suggests very few problems throughout the nineteenth century.

## UNDER-REGISTRATION OF DEATHS

As was discussed in chapter 6, the family reconstitution approach is poorly suited to the analysis of mortality in the adult population. As a result, we are not directly concerned here with the completeness of death registration for adults.[5] The completeness of registration of infant and child deaths is, however, critical for the analysis in chapter 6, and we will discuss some of the problems encountered.

Assessing the completeness of registration requires using several indirect methods to detect the frequency with which deaths go unrecorded. One method follows on the approach suggested by Henry (Henry and Blum 1988, 145) and Houdaille (1970) and involves the registration of deaths for siblings bearing the same Christian name. If it is common practice to give the same name to more than one child, this information can be used to estimate the extent of under-registration of deaths in infancy and childhood. The procedure involves examining pairs of siblings with the same name and classifying them into three categories according to their fate. The first possible outcome is that the first-born child dies and a death certificate is found. The second possibility is that the first child survives and evidence exists to indicate that the family has two living children with the same name. Finally, the third possible outcome involves cases in which the fate of the first-born child of the pair is unknown. The extent of under-registration can then be estimated by comparing the frequency of name repetition in these different circumstances. If name repetition was more frequent in "fate unknown" circumstances than in situations where the first-born was known to have survived, it would be reasonable to conclude that registration was deficient. In the Alsatian case, the situation was simpler. There is no evidence that parents gave the same first name to a child if an older sibling who carried that name was still living. We could not find a single case where clear evidence existed that the first-born of a pair of siblings carrying the same name survived.[6] Thus, an indication of under-registration can be obtained by examining the frequency of cases of name repetition in which a death certificate for the first-born of the pair is missing.

Using this method to assess completeness of registration in the parish registers points to village-level differences in data quality. As explained above, only three villages – Baldenheim, Goxwiller and Mussig – are included in the analysis prior to 1785. In the case of the two Lutheran villages, registration was very nearly complete. Table A.2 shows the results of cases where siblings shared a common name. For Goxwiller, we found a total of 115 cases where two children in the same family were given the same Christian name. In every case, a death certificate was found for the first-born child. This finding underlines the extraordinary quality of the Goxwiller registers. In Baldenheim, a death certificate for the older sibling was missing in only 4% of cases. In Mussig, however, the problem was greater. The

Table A.2
Percentage of cases where the death certificate is missing for the first-born child of a
pair of siblings with the same first name, Mussig, Baldenheim and Goxwiller, 1750–89

| Village | % of Cases with Missing Death Certificate | Number of Sibling Pairs |
|---|---|---|
| Mussig | 15.4 | 26 |
| Baldenheim | 4.0 | 100 |
| Goxwiller | 0.0 | 115 |

tendency to reuse a name was less common in this village than in the
other two, which limits the usefulness of the technique. Nevertheless,
there is evidence of some under-reporting of infant and child deaths,
particularly in the period before 1780. As noted in chapter 6, this
problem should lead us to exercise caution in interpreting the data on
mortality for the Catholic population of the eighteenth century. In the
nineteenth century, registration in all five villages was of high quality.
For the period 1793–1870, 564 pairs of siblings with the same given
name were found. In eleven cases (1.95% of the total), a death certificate for the first-born child could not be located. Although obviously
not complete, this figure gives us considerable confidence in the data
drawn from the civil registers.

This positive conclusion was further supported by use of a second
technique, which took advantage of the fact that the nominal census
records for the five villages have been preserved. We examined all
births occurring in the two years preceding the 1836 census and
searched both the death registers and the manuscript censuses for
evidence that the children had either died (in which case a death
certificate should be available), or were still living and should thus be
recorded in the census. Again, the results were extremely encouraging. In only a handful of cases was there a suspicion that a child may
have died without the death being recorded. The method is not foolproof – a surviving child may be missed in the census. In the case of
Baldenheim, for example, three children born between 1 July 1834
and 30 June 1836 were not listed in either the census or the death register. In two of the cases, however, the child was listed in a subsequent census, suggesting the census-taker forgot to record the infant.
In sum, then, both methods give us a high degree of confidence in the
completeness of registration of infant and child deaths in the period
1793–1870.

The methods described above deal with the completeness of registration of deaths of children whose birth has been recorded. The
remaining aspect of the problem concerns infants whose birth and
death went unrecorded, which opens up a number of issues touching

not only on the registration process but on the perception of demographic events by local populations. Arguably, the birth and death of a child go unrecorded most often when the child dies very soon after birth. In such cases, the child may not be baptized and there may then be little point to recording the infant's death and burial. In most Christian populations, however, the baptism of a child takes on cultural and religious importance. For Catholics, in particular, baptism was seen as essential in order that the child might enter heaven. Midwives were thus permitted to baptize children at the time of birth if the child was thought to be in imminent danger of death. The registers for the Catholic villages indicate that some such "emergency" baptisms were recorded in the parish records though we cannot, of course, be sure that all were. Protestants have not always accorded the same degree of urgency and importance to infant baptism, and this has been a stumbling block to demographic analysis in many Protestant communities. Fortunately, in the case of Alsatian Lutherans, baptism seems to have taken place as rapidly as was true in the Catholic population. Using a sample of 182 births in the village of Baldenheim between 1750 and 1789, only four or 2.2% of baptisms occurred more than two days after the birth. While we cannot be sure, then, about the proportion of early infant deaths that were missed in this way, it seems likely the number was small. As a result, no adjustments to the data have been made.

Another issue concerns the identification and recording of stillbirths. Even in modern populations, recording systems have difficulty in distinguishing between a live birth followed by death and a stillbirth. The variation in recording practices among villages in nineteenth-century Alsace suggests that local tradition and idiosyncratic factors played a considerable role in decisions about registration. Results from our larger sample based on aggregate data suggest huge differences in the ratio of stillbirths to neonatal deaths. Among Lutheran villages, the ratio ranged from a low of .34 to a high of 1.21. Given the concern among Catholics with baptizing children, we would expect to find fewer stillbirths in Catholic villages, parents and midwives counting the child as born alive if any sign of life could be assumed to be present. And indeed the ratio of stillbirths to neonatal deaths was lower in the Catholic villages. Yet even here, there was enormous variation. For the period 1811–70, Mussig, one of the reconstituted villages, recorded only sixteen stillbirths versus 212 neonatal deaths, while Hilsenheim, a Catholic village located only five kilometres away, registered 232 stillbirths and 356 neonatal deaths. When we add together the stillbirths and early infant deaths and express them as a percentage of all infant deaths, we find that 51.4% of Hilsenheim's infant deaths were neonatal (defined here to include stillbirths), while for Mussig the figure was 52.8%. It seems likely that much of the variability in the number of stillbirths reflected local traditions of recording early infant deaths. As a result, in virtually all of the mortality analysis, stillbirths have been included in the total of infant deaths. This does not, of itself, resolve the problem of unreported neonatal deaths but may help to eliminate what would be significant differences among communities.

## BIRTH REGISTRATION

As was true in the case of death registration, we have good reason to believe that the registration of births, particularly in the nineteenth century, was of very high quality. Using the 1836 census again as a check, only one case was uncovered of a child age two or under who was listed in the census as belonging to a family believed to be living in the village at the time of the child's birth, but for whom no birth certificate could be found. Similarly, examining the marriage and death registers for evidence of individuals who were born to families residing in the village at the time of their birth but who lacked a birth certificate suggests under-registration of births in the nineteenth century was minimal. Finally, sex ratios at birth do not differ significantly from an expected level of 105 for either religious community. This would suggest that there was no differential under-registration by sex.

Prior to the establishment of the civil registration system, birth registration (or, more accurately, baptismal registration) also was of high quality, though there is evidence of some missed events. Using Henry's technique to estimate the proportion of missing births on the basis of subsequent marriages points to under-registration of 1.4% in the Lutheran villages and 2.7% in the Catholic villages for the period 1750–89 (Henry and Blum 1988, 75–9; Poulard et al 1991, 84).[7] The age-specific marital fertility rates presented in chapter 5 have been corrected for this shortfall. Other aspects of the fertility analysis, such as the computation of birth intervals, are affected by this problem, however, and this needs to be kept in mind when evaluating the results.

## SELECTION OF FAMILIES FOR MARRIAGE AND FERTILITY ANALYSIS

As discussed above, care is essential in selecting the families to be included in the calculation of demographic rates to insure that the results of the analysis are unbiased. This study has followed the rules set down by Henry in the calculation of almost all indicators, and the analysis differs from a classic family reconstitution study in only one important way. Vital registers for the villages studied are available only up until 1892. This would place a serious limitation on analysis of trends in the nineteenth century since many couples marrying even in the 1850s would still be alive in 1892.[8] In the absence of a recorded death, such families would have to be considered "open," and thus would be excluded from much of the analysis. We have taken advantage of the fact that the 1885 nominal census is available for four of the five villages reconstituted (I was unable to locate the census of Husseren). For purposes of fertility analysis, then, we counted as closed files cases where the family was listed in the 1885 census as resident in the village, and where the wife was at least forty-five years of age at the time of the census. As the census is a measure of exposure independent of the vital registers (for example, a childless couple will be as likely to be included as a couple that has had children), this approach should not bias our measures. This strategy allows us to include all couples who married before 1856 and remained in the village. In each case, the couple should either appear in the census if both parties are still alive, or a death certificate for one or both parties should be found. It would be inappropriate to include couples married after 1855 since only couples where one partner died prior to the wife's forty-fifth birthday would stand a chance of being included, and this would introduce a bias into the analysis. In practice, however, we have extended the terminal date to 1860. This has the effect of excluding four couples married between 1856 and 1860 where the wife was less than twenty at the time of marriage: such couples could not be included because the wife would not have reached the end of the childbearing period by the date of the 1885 census. Since so few cases were excluded by this criterion it seemed worth following this strategy in order to extend the analysis somewhat further in time.

Table A.3 summarizes the number of unions available for study depending on the type of restriction that was imposed. These data provide only a baseline for the various analyses; specific types of analysis, as explained throughout the text, demanded further restrictions.

## SELECTION OF INDIVIDUALS FOR MORTALITY ANALYSIS

As powerful a tool as family reconstitution has proven to be for historical demographers, the technique has its limitations when addressing the issue of mortality. We cannot calculate accurate measures of mortality unless we are certain that the population at risk of dying

Table A.3
Number of unions available for analysis by village

| Village | All unions with marriage certificate | Unions occurring prior to 1861 | Unions prior to 1861 with an end date | Unions prior to 1861 with end date where wife was 45+ |
|---|---|---|---|---|
| Avolsheim | 420 | 338 | 361 | 179 |
| Husseren | 640 | 557 | 343 | 193 |
| Mussig | 523 | 459 | 326 | 194 |
| Baldenheim | 906 | 789 | 604 | 392 |
| Goxwiller | 639 | 562 | 446 | 298 |
| Total | 3128 | 2705 | 1980 | 1256 |

remains in observation throughout the life cycle. Since the focus in this and other reconstitution studies is on one or more distinct communities, this condition cannot be met. As people who were born in the village move out, they pass from observation. We not only remain ignorant of their death date but we normally do not even know how long they remained in the community being studied, and thus at risk of dying and having their death recorded.

It is, however, usually possible to examine death rates for infants and children, though even here it is necessary to restrict the focus in a way that produces a certain inaccuracy. Following Knodel (1988), we have decided to limit the analysis to children born in the five villages to couples who married in the village and where the first spouse to die passed away in the village. The assumption here is that the couple spent their entire married life in the community, and thus the children remained in observation throughout childhood.[9] To further reduce the risk of including children who had left the village, we restrict the analysis of mortality risks to the years from birth to age ten.

The approach used here is a "safe" one in the sense that we can be fairly certain that the population studied was under observation for at least the first ten years of life. However, it needs to be pointed out once again that families who qualify do not constitute a representative sample of the village population as a whole. One group that is excluded, for example, consists of children born outside marriage to mothers who do not subsequently marry the father of the child. What evidence we have from this and other studies suggests that these children suffered a higher risk of premature death. In general, it seems likely that the more sedentary population included in the analysis enjoyed somewhat lower risks of mortality. If so, our calculated mortality rates would underestimate the general level of mortality. This is unfortunate but unavoidable. On the positive side, there is no particular reason to believe this strategy would significantly distort comparisons between groups or over time.

## CLASSIFICATION OF OCCUPATION

As we have argued in the text, there are important reasons for examining differences in demographic behaviour among families that occupied different economic statuses. Unfortunately, parish registers seldom provide much information about a family's economic position. Other sources of data – wills, voters lists, land ownerships records – hold much of value but in many cases only a portion of the population is included. Moreover, an enormous amount of work would be necessary to search such documents and link the data to the demographic sources. Thus, in the current work as in many others, we have relied on occupational data contained on the birth, marriage and death certificates.

There has been much debate over appropriate methods for classifying occupational data from historical sources (Katz 1975; Armstrong 1972). In this case, however, we have adopted a very simple set of categories. Given the relatively small number of cases, a refined system of categories would make little sense. In most of the analysis, we have generally used only five categories: farmers, day-labourers, artisans, wage-workers, and (when numbers permit) professionals.

Even such a simple set of categories entails problems, however. Ideally, people would be sorted on the basis of their economic position within the community, allowing us to examine whether wealth, class position, or the conditions of work influenced demographic behaviour. Occupational data take us some way in this direction but it must be admitted that the measure is a crude one. Several problems should be kept in mind when considering the results using the occupational data. First, there is considerable heterogeneity within categories. The category of farmer includes both small-holders and some very substantial landowners who were leading figures in the village. Perhaps most significant, the wage-worker category contains both employees of the factory in Husseren and the small weavers who plied their trade at home or in a small workshop in Baldenheim or Mussig. Second, the reporting of occupational status for individuals can be inconsistent over time. A man may be classed as a *journalier* at the time of marriage, a farmer when his first children are born, and a *journalier* once again at the time of his death. In some cases, the inconsistency reflects real change in the circumstances of the individual. A significant number of men moved from the status of *journalier* to

Table A.4
Occupational distribution of husbands in all marriages and in marriages
with an end-of-union date

| | All Marriages | | | Marriages with End-of-Union Date | | |
|---|---|---|---|---|---|---|
| Occupation | N | % of Total Cases | % of Valid Cases | N | % of Total Cases | % of Valid Cases |
| Farmer | 786 | 25.1 | 29.4 | 608 | 30.7 | 35.1 |
| Journalier | 372 | 11.9 | 13.9 | 270 | 13.6 | 15.6 |
| Artisan | 748 | 23.8 | 28.0 | 443 | 22.4 | 25.6 |
| Worker | 593 | 18.9 | 22.2 | 350 | 17.7 | 20.2 |
| Professional | 103 | 3.3 | 3.9 | 31 | 1.6 | 1.8 |
| Other | 73 | 2.3 | 2.7 | 29 | 1.5 | 1.7 |
| Missing | 462 | 14.7 | — | 249 | 12.6 | — |
| Total | 3137 | 100.0 | 100.1 | 1980 | 100.1 | 100.1 |

farmer at some point, perhaps as a result of inheritance or the purchase of land. For others, it may also reflect temporary changes related to the unstable economic situation in which people often combined different types of work. It may also, of course, reflect inattention on the part of the officials who recorded the data, perhaps going on the basis of memory or second-hand information. The rule we have followed here is to use the designation of occupation given on the marriage certificate. In cases where no occupation was given on the marriage certificate, we used the occupation first given for the subject on a subsequent record.

Table A.4 shows the distribution of husbands by occupational status first for all cases where a marriage certificate was available, and then for marriages that occurred prior to 1860 and for which we have an end-of-union date (from a death certificate of the husband or wife, or from the 1885 census). In just under 15% of cases from the larger file no occupational information was available, but this drops to just 12.6% for the file of completed unions. It is not surprising that farmers constitute a larger share of the restricted sample that includes only families with a beginning and end date. Farmers, as owners of property, were less likely to migrate from the village. It is interesting, though, that *journaliers* also form a larger share of the file of complete families. By contrast, the share of both artisans and workers declines somewhat, the latter a function of the considerable degree of movement in and out of the industrial village of Husseren. The small professional group also shrinks significantly. Although 103 marriages involved a man with a professional occupation (generally, notaries, merchants, ministers, and several managers from the factory in Husseren), these families were highly mobile. It is disappointing that we cannot examine their situation more closely, especially with respect to fertility. Overall, however, the data do permit some assessment of the effect of economic status on demographic behaviour.

# Notes

1 As is explained in the following chapter, small but significant communities of Calvinists, Jews, and Anabaptists also lived in the area. Few resided in the communities we have chosen, and thus the analysis is restricted to the Catholic and Lutheran populations.

2 The development of demographic transition theory is complex (Chesnais 1992). The model used here derives largely from Notestein's 1945 statement.

3 It should be noted that a growing literature in social history touches on the origin and spread of values. Among the most important examples for demography are the debate over the impact of the Reformation on marriage patterns, discussed in chapter 3, and the extensive literature on the legal treatment of birth control and abortion (McLaren 1978; Brodie 1994).

4 By this I mean to exclude situations in which religious groups exhibit distinctive patterns largely as a result of other social characteristics that describe their situation such as higher income levels or urban residence (Goldscheider 1971). A recent reappraisal of this issue can be found in Goodkind (1995).

5 This, of course, follows in the tradition of Weber's analysis of the relationship between Protestantism and the rise of capitalism.

6 Chapter 3 contains a fuller discussion of the changing view of marriage introduced by the Reformation.

7 The Catholic Church's refusal to permit burial in consecrated ground of persons believed to have violated various ordinances was a continuing source of controversy in Alsace. See the documents in ADBR 1V 112.

8 This idea has deep roots in sociology, extending notably to the work of Simmel (1955) [1923]. Barth (1969) has developed these ideas further in the special case of ethnic competition.

9 This is the central conclusion of the literature on confessionalization that is discussed in the conclusion.

CHAPTER TWO

1 This view was echoed by the pastor of the village of Goxwiller who, in 1860, noted that there was little point in reading Scripture to children at Sunday school in French: "It goes without saying that it would not be understood" (ADBR 2V 86).

2 For a fuller discussion of the method of family reconstitution, see the appendix.

3 The pastor noted only one mixed marriage during his long tenure in the village (ADBR 2G 19 9).

4 A detailed history of the factory is presented in Schmitt (1980), from which much of the detail that follows has been taken.

5 As a result, many family members worked together in the factory. For example, an 1822 document (ADHR 9M 21) lists as employees a Jacques Nehr along with his four sons, aged sixteen, fourteen, ten and seven.

CHAPTER THREE

1 While the Reformation clearly developed a new theology of marriage, it is important not to exaggerate the differences between Catholic and Protestant views. See, for example, Wendel's 1928 analysis of the pre- and post-Reformation views of clerics in Strasbourg. More generally, Harrington (1995) argues that Catholic and Protestant theologians favoured many similar types of reform in the sixteenth century.

2 Although concern has been expressed about the possibility of bias in using family reconstitution data to estimate age at marriage (Ruggles 1992), there is a growing consensus that the problem is not as serious as was believed. See the discussion in Desjardins (1995) and Wrigley et al (1997, 160–4).

3 Kertzer and Hogan (1989, 128) found a similar pattern in Casalecchio, Italy.

4 Interestingly, such marriages appear even less frequent if we use the occupation of the groom rather than that of his father. Some of the sons of farmers who marry the daughters of *journaliers* were themselves *journaliers*. Men who listed their own occupation as farmer and whose father was also a farmer almost never married a woman from a lower social group.

5 Knodel (1988) and Van Poppel (1995b) obtained similar results for Germany and the Netherlands respectively.

CHAPTER FOUR

1 The ordinance was not always observed, and there is evidence that baptisms of illegitimate children occurred in Lutheran parishes. See, for example, Peter (1995, 180).

2 Dupâquier (1979a, 27) has noted similar problems for other regions of France that contained a significant Protestant population.

3 Pastors often made explicit mention of the status of even prenuptially conceived children in the baptismal register. Peter quotes an example from the village of Preuschdorf in which the pastor noted the infant was "an early baby [*ein fruhkind*] (as the mother gave birth only eight weeks after the wedding)" (1995, 177).

4 The analysis extends to 1875 because the 1871 census, disrupted by the transition to German rule, is defective.

5 The lack of an expected relationship between delayed marriage and higher illegitimacy has been noted by Laslett (1977) for England and Van De Walle (1980) for France.

6 For present purposes, we do not distinguish between situations where the mother bore more than one child before the marriage so long as at least one child was acknowledged by the husband.

7 Interestingly, Todd (1985) has argued that Alsace was a region in which the "authoritarian family" form prevailed, a family type he sees as associated with male-female relationships that are unstable and relatively equal. Typical of such systems are small age differences between spouses and high rates of illegitimacy, a pattern that prevailed in Alsace (LeBras and Todd 1981, 62). These data suggest the two characteristics go together at the individual level as well.

8 The time pattern of these prenuptially conceived births places Alsace closer to the English model than it does to the French. See Smith, 1986.

9 Readers will recall from chapter 3 that the extent of seasonality can be measured by summing the absolute deviations from 100 (where the average number of marriages per month is set to 100) for each month and dividing by twelve. The higher the result, the more pronounced the seasonal variation.

10 Given clothing styles and perhaps poor nourishment among expectant mothers, women may have been able to hide evidence of pregnancy for some time. It is striking to read the reports of many cases of infanticide in which the woman seemed able to hide evidence of her pregnancy for almost all nine months of her confinement.

11 Again, this contrasts with the pattern observed for most regions of France (Smith 1986).

12  Peter (1995, 179) notes, however, that the churches and, sometimes, civil authorities struggled to suppress such practices.

13  It is an interesting question whether the practice of infanticide was limited to unmarried mothers. Among the more than fifty cases uncovered in the police and court files for the region, I found only one involving a married mother. It is possible, of course, that antipathy towards unmarried mothers made them more frequent targets for suspicion and investigation. In one striking case, an unmarried woman investigated on suspicion of infanticide was found to be in the seventh month of her pregnancy (ADBR 3M 888 [Boersch]).

14  For example, Migneret's (1868, 67) data for Strasbourg in 1853 indicate that while 5.5% of births to married women ended in a stillbirth, the figure was 9.5% among unmarried mothers.

15  It should be emphasized that many of those who bore more than one illegitimate child married the father of those children.

CHAPTER FIVE

1  This need not be the case, however. Societies with a "grandmother taboo" – the belief that it is inappropriate for a woman to continue to bear children once she has become a grandmother – in effect create what could be called an "unconscious" mechanism for stopping childbearing.

2  The rates were corrected for the effects of premarital conceptions by following the technique suggested by Knodel (1988, 264), which involves adding to the denominator, woman-years of exposure, the difference between the average interval from marriage to first birth for those not pregnant at marriage and those who were.

3  For a full discussion of the computation and limitations of the Coale indices, see Coale and Treadway (1986, 153–62). The Coale index of marital fertility shown here is a modified version designed for use with family reconstitution data (Knodel 1988, 249). The standard population used was taken from the 1851 census of the Bas-Rhin. See Weir (1993) for another discussion of the use of the index with reconstitution data.

4  The data presented here are based on women who gave birth to at least one child and exclude those with either a premarital birth or a child premaritally conceived.

5  Denis (1978) reports a mean interval from marriage to first birth of 15.46 months for the Lutheran village of Bosselshausen, very similar to that for the Lutheran population of Goxwiller and Baldenheim.

6  As these measures are now well established in demographic analysis, no account of their derivation is presented. Readers unfamiliar with them should refer to Bongaarts (1975) and Coale and Trussell (1974).

7  See the discussion of these data in chapter 6.

8 Again, this fits well with the findings of Denis (1978). She computes an average age at last birth for Lutheran women married in Bosselshausen between 1737 and 1837 of 38.46.

9 Knodel (1988, 368) suggests limiting the comparison to women with at least one birth past age thirty or thirty-five. Obviously, the higher the age used, the weaker the relationship. In Alsace, imposing such a limitation does not erase the difference between the two religious communities. For Catholic women married 1815–60, mean age at last birth for those with a birth after age thirty ranged from 40.2 to 41.2; for Lutheran mothers the range was from 37.2 to 41.3.

10 The mean for Tourouvre-au-Perche was 25.3 months (Charbonneau 1970) while for the pioneer couples of New France, the average interval was 23 months (Charbonneau et al 1987).

11 The pattern observed in Alsace is similar to that found among other Protestant populations in the region. See Zschunke 1984; Perrenoud 1988; Head 1988.

12 Again, it should be noted that the number of cases for this cohort is limited, in part, because an increasing proportion of couples had less than four children.

13 Figures refer to completed fertility (*descendance finale* in Henry's terms) based on the age at marriage distribution for the full reconstitution sample.

14 Boehler (1995, 1747), citing a doctor who toured the region in the early eighteenth century, identifies Alsace as an area of early weaning, and one in which wet-nursing was unknown. No information is available on differences between the two religious communities.

15 Peter (1995, 181) reports a very similar episode involving an adulteress.

16 While not taking a direct position on this issue, Wrigley et al (1997, 493) caution against assuming that the relatively long intervals between births in their English study were the result of deliberate efforts to space births.

17 Van de Walle (1998), however, has recently extended his argument concerning withdrawal to the practice of abortion, claiming that effective methods of abortion were seldom used by married women.

18 Santow (1995, 42) makes a similar observation, arguing that experience with spacing may have paved the way for the adoption of parity-dependent forms of control.

CHAPTER SIX

1 These examples draw on the civil registers for Baldenheim (ADBR 4E 19).

2 More recently, Perrenoud (1991, 1994) has pointed to the simultaneity of mortality declines in different European settings as evidence for the autonomous nature of mortality change.

3 The experience of Husseren was not unique even in Alsace. Two of the villages in our aggregate sample that were also located in mountainous regions had relatively low mortality rates despite the fact that the canton in which they were located (Villé) was generally thought to be among the poorest in Alsace. This fits with the pattern observed in southeast England by Dobson (1997, 505).

4 An increase in the years 1850–70 has been noted for many parts of Europe by a number of observers. See, for example, Vallin (1991). For the whole sample, $_1q_0$ for the period 1850–70 was .203 and for the Catholic population it was .221.

5 In the calculations, the length of a month was taken to be (365.25/12) or 30.43 days.

6 Rather than a precise calendar month, the risks actually refer to two over-lapping months, e.g. January-February. In the discussion, we refer to the data as reflecting the experience of the first month of the pair.

7 There was no relationship in the data between age of mother and the like-lihood of early childhood mortality. To simplify the presentation, we have not included this figure.

8 The risk was higher for the babies of very young mothers, aged fifteen to nineteen. Since the number of births is so small and virtually all involved first-born children, we have not included these data in the figure.

9 There is, of course, a link between survival status and the length of the birth interval. An early death will lead to the end of breastfeeding and increase the likelihood of a new conception.

10 Their reports are contained in the series 5M in the Archives Départemen-tales du Bas-Rhin.

11 Peter (1995, 158) argues that crises of mortality disappeared from the region around 1725. Boehler's data (1995, 471) for a sample of rural parishes seem to support this view.

12 Dr André Ritzinger commented: "Since I directed the attention of the administration to the terrible state of the streets in the communes, and especially those in Mussig, as well as the roads in the surrounding areas, things have only gotten worse." See ADBR 5M 44, report for the canton of Marckolsheim, 1st trimester 1812.

13 A report by a Dr Bierck dated 16 July 1855 notes strong resistance in the canton of Marckolsheim.

14 The situation seems to have been strikingly similar to that of the marshy areas of southeast England discussed by Dobson (1997).

15 Migneret (1871), citing data from the 1856 census, reports that 8.6% of the Catholic population of the Bas-Rhin (excluding the city of Stras-bourg) was classified as indigent compared to only 4.4% of the Lutheran population.

16 The data on height are drawn from the recruitment registers of 1836 and can be found in ADBR 1R 567. See also the analysis of recruitment data by Selig (1988).

CHAPTER SEVEN

1 Gugerli (1992), in his study of Protestant pastors in the Zurich region, has suggested this view. It is important to note that other historians have argued that the Reformation served to strengthen the patriarchal character of the Christian family (Roper 1989).

2 A school was established in Baldenheim in the late seventeenth century (Bopp 1963, 133).

3 The *simultaneum* was introduced in Goxwiller in 1685 and in Baldenheim in 1749 (Bopp 1963).

4 It is important to underline the fact that the common people did not passively accept the efforts at indoctrination by the churches. Abray (1985, 1988) stresses this point in the case of Strasbourg. They were also capable of using the religious conflict to their advantage. In one instance, when the curé of the parish of Bergholtz punished a young boy for misbehaving at Mass, the boy's father threatened to convert to Lutheranism (ADBR 1V 369). Dixon (1996) makes a similar point in his study of Brandenburg. The efforts of pastors to discipline often failed, especially when opposed by the village elite.

5 Müller (1995) has made a similar point in his study of Oldenburg, arguing that only in the eighteenth century did the new teachings take firm root.

6 Vogler quotes one minister who identified the growth of rationalism as a source of the decline in religious belief and activity.

7 Golde (1975) has found a similar pattern in the German region of Baden.

8 Igersheim (1993, 163) reports that the correlation between percentage of Protestants by canton and the percentage of the vote going to the Social Democratic party in the 1849 election was +0.66.

APPENDIX

1 The civil register "francicizes" the first names of the individuals. The husband's signature on the form indicates his first name as Josef. It was common in the region for individuals with compound Christian names to use the second name.

2 Of course, we cannot be sure that Catherine was indeed his child. However, since many husbands did not acknowledge children born to their wives prior to the marriage, it seems likely that he was her biological father.

3 As a number of detailed treatments of family reconstitution methods are now available, this appendix provides only a basic introduction to the strengths and weaknesses of the method. More extensive treatments are available in Henry and Blum (1988), Knodel (1988) and Wrigley et al (1997).

4 To further complicate matters, some regions used German translations for the month names, e.g. Brumaire was translated to Nebelmonat.

5 Of course, completeness of registration for adult deaths is important for completing family histories.

6 This contrasts with the situation in England where evidence from wills suggests families had more than one surviving child with the same first name. See Wrigley et al (1997, 98–100).

7 Henry (Henry and Blum 1988, 79) points to the need for a further correction to account for the proportion of infants who die before baptism. As baptism in both religious communities occurred rapidly and there is no good basis for estimating the percentage of births that would have been missed, we have not further corrected the figures for births.

8 Indeed, in order not to bias the selection of couples towards those who died at younger ages, it would be necessary to exclude couples from perhaps 1842 on.

9 If the first spouse to die does so while some of the children are still young, it is possible the surviving spouse may leave the village with the children. Knodel (1988, 537) has compared the results using his method and the more traditional method used by the Cambridge group and found little difference.

# References

Abray, Lorna Jane. 1985. *The People's Reformation: Magistrates, Clergy and Commons in Strasbourg, 1500–1598.* Ithaca: Cornell University Press.

– 1988. The Laity's Religion: Lutheranism in Sixteenth Century Strasbourg. In *The German People and the Reformation*, edited by R. Po-Chia Hsia. Ithaca: Cornell University Press.

Alter, George. 1992. Theories of Fertility Decline: A Nonspecialist's Guide to the Current Debate. In *The European Experience of Declining Fertility, 1850–1970: The Quiet Revolution*, edited by John R. Gillis, Louise A. Tilly, and David Levine. Cambridge, MA: Blackwell.

Anderson, Barbara. 1986. Regional and Cultural Factors in the Decline of Marital Fertility in Western Europe. In *The Decline of Fertility in Europe*, edited by Ansley J. Coale and Susan C. Watkins. Princeton: Princeton University Press.

Ariès, Philippe. 1981. Introduction in *Marriage and Remarriage in Populations of the Past*, edited by Jacques Dupâquier et al. London: Academic Press.

Armstrong, W.A. 1972. The Use of Information about Occupation. In *Nineteenth-Century Society: Essays in the Use of Quantitative Methods for the Study of Social Data*, edited by E.A. Wrigley. Cambridge: Cambridge University Press.

Barth, Frederik. 1969. *Ethnic Groups and Boundaries: The Social Organization of Cultural Difference.* London: Allen and Unwin.

Beaujot, Roderic and Kevin McQuillan. 1982. *Growth and Dualism: The Demographic Development of Canadian Society.* Toronto: Gage Publishing.

Bernardin, Edith. 1990. La loi d'état-civil dans le Bas-Rhin. Son application de 1793 à 1799. *Revue d'Alsace* 116:119–36.

Blaikie, Andrew. 1993. *Illegitimacy, Sex, and Society, Northeast Scotland, 1750–1900.* Oxford: Clarendon Press.

Boehler, Jean-Michel. 1995. *Une société rurale en milieu rhénan: La paysannerie de la plaine d'Alsace, 1648–1789.* 3 vols. Strasbourg: Presses Universitaires de Strasbourg.

Bongaarts, John. 1975. A Method for the Estimation of Fecundability. *Demography* 12:645–59.

Bongaarts, John and Robert C. Potter. 1983. *Fertility, Biology and Behavior.* New York: Academic Press.

Bopp, Marie Joseph. 1963. *Die evangelischer Gemeinden und Hohen Schulen in Elsass und Lothringen von der Reformation bis zur Gegenwart.* Neustadt: Verlag Degener.

Bourgeois-Pichat, Jean. 1951. La mesure de la mortalité infantile. *Population* 6:233–48.

Brinton, Crane. 1936. *French Revolutionary Legislation on Illegitimacy, 1789–1804.* Cambridge: Harvard University Press.

Brodie, Janet Farrell. 1994. *Contraception and Abortion in Nineteenth-Century America.* Ithaca: Cornell University Press.

Broström, Göran. 1985. Practical Aspects of the Estimation of the Parameters in Coale's Model of Marital Fertility. *Demography* 22:625–32.

Caldwell, John C. 1980. Mass Education as a Determinant of the Timing of the Fertility Decline. *Population and Development Review* 6:225–55.

– 1986. Routes to Low Mortality in Poor Countries. *Population and Development Review* 12:171–220.

Caldwell, John C. and Pat Caldwell. 1987. The Cultural Context of High Fertility in sub-Saharan Africa. *Population and Development Review* 13:409–37.

Carlson, Eric Josef. 1994. *Marriage and the English Reformation.* Oxford: Blackwell.

Charbonneau, Hubert. 1970. *Tourouvre-au-Perche aux XVII^e et XVIII^e siècles.* Paris: Presses Universitaires de France.

Charbonneau, Hubert, Bertrand Desjardins, André Guillemette, Yves Landry, Jacques Légaré, and François Nault. 1987. *Naissance d'une population: Les Français établis au Canada au XVIII siècle.* Paris: Presses Universitaires de France (INED: Travaux et Documents, Cahier 118).

Châtellier, Louis. 1981. *Tradition chrétienne et renouveau catholique dans le cadre de l'ancien diocèse de Strasbourg 1650–1770.* Paris: Ophrys.

– 1989. *The Europe of the Devout: The Catholic Reformation and the formation of a new society.* Cambridge: Cambridge University Press.

Chesnais, Jean-Claude. 1992. *The Demographic Transition: Stages, Patterns, and Economic Implications.* Oxford: Clarendon Press.

Cleland, John and Christopher Wilson. 1987. Demand Theories of the Fertility Transition: An Iconoclastic View. *Population Studies* 41:5–30.

Cleland, J.G. and J.K. van Ginneken. 1988. Maternal Education and Child Survival in Developing Countries: The Search for Pathways of Influence. *Social Science and Medicine* 27:1357–68.

Coale, Ansley J. 1973. The Demographic Transition Reconsidered. In *International Population Conference, Liège, 1973, Volume 1.* Liège: International Union for the Scientific Study of Population.

Coale, Ansley J. and Roy Treadway. 1986. A Summary of the Changing Distribution of Overall Fertility, Marital Fertility, and the Proportion Married in the Provinces of Europe. In *The Decline of Fertility in Europe*, edited by Ansley J. Coale and Susan Cotts Watkins. Princeton: Princeton University Press.

Coale, Ansley J. and T. James Trussell. 1974. Model Fertility Schedules: Variations in the Age Structure of Childbearing in Human Populations. *Population Index* 40:195–258.

Coale, Ansley J. and Susan Cotts Watkins, eds. 1986. *The Decline of Fertility in Europe*. Princeton: Princeton University Press.

Condran, G. and S.H. Preston. 1994. Child Mortality Differences, Personal Healthcare Practices, and Medical Technology: The United States, 1900–1930. In *Health and Social Change*, edited by Lincoln Chen, Arthur Kleinman and Norma C. Ware. Cambridge: Harvard University Press.

Desjardins, Bertrand. 1995. Bias in Age at Marriage in Family Reconstitutions: Evidence from French-Canadian Data. *Population Studies* 49:165–9.

Denis, Marie-Noele. 1977. Un problème de moeurs dans l'Alsace rurale traditionelle: les naissances illégitimes à Bosselshausen de 1738 à 1838. *Revue des sciences sociales de France de l'Est* 6:114–19.

– 1978. Composition des familles à Bosselshausen au XVIII$^e$ siècle. *Revue des sciences sociales de France de l'Est* 7:125–44.

Dixon, C. Scott. 1996. The Reformation and Parish Morality in Brandenburg-Ansbach-Kulmbach. *Archiv für Reformationsgeschicte* 87:255–86.

Dobson, Mary J. 1997. *Contours of Death and Disease in Early Modern England.* Cambridge: Cambridge University Press.

Dreyer-Roos, Suzanne. 1969. *La Population Strasbourgeoise sous l'Ancien Régime.* Strasbourg: Istra.

Dreyfus, François-Georges. 1979. *Histoire de l'Alsace.* Paris: Hachette.

Dupâquier, Jacques. 1979a. *La population française aux XVII$^e$ et XVIII$^e$ siècles.* Paris: Presses Universitaires de France.

– 1979b. L'analyse statistique des crises de mortalité. In *The Great Mortalities: Methodological Studies of Demographic Crises in the Past*, edited by Hubert Charbonneau and André Larose. Liège: Ordina.

Dupâquier, Jacques, Etienne Hélin, Peter Laslett, Massimo Livi-Bacci, and S. Sogner, eds. 1981. *Marriage and Remarriage in Populations of the Past.* London: Academic Press.

Easterlin, Richard. 1978. The Economics and Sociology of Fertility: A Synthesis. In *Historical Studies of Changing Fertility*, edited by Charles Tilly. Princeton: Princeton University Press.

Ellis, Geoffrey. 1981. *Napoleon's Continental Blockade: The Case of Alsace.* Oxford: Clarendon Press.

Epp, René. 1990. Le Bas-Rhin, département français au pourcentage du prêtres jureurs le plus faible. *Revue d'Alsace* 116:237–44.

Ewbank D. and Preston, S.H., 1990. Personal Health Behaviour and the Decline in Infant and Child Mortality: The United States, 1900–1930. In *What We Know about Health Transition: The Cultural, Social and Behavioural Determinants of Health*, edited by John Caldwell. Canberra: Australian National University.

Fildes, Valerie A. 1986. *Breasts, Bottles and Babies: A History of Infant Feeding*. Edinburgh: Edinburgh University Press.

Flandrin, Jean-Louis. 1979. *Families in Former Times: Kinship, Household and Sexuality*. Cambridge: Cambridge University Press.

– 1983. *Un Temps pour Embrasser. Aux origines de la morale sexuelle occidentale (VIᵉ–XIᵉ siècle)*. Paris: Seuil.

Fohlen, Claude. 1956. *L'industrie textile au temps du Second Empire*. Paris: Librairie Plon.

Forste, Renate. 1994. The Effects of Breastfeeding and Birth Spacing on Infant and Child Mortality in Bolivia. *Population Studies* 48:497–512.

Fuchs, Rachel. 1984. *Abandoned Children: Foundlings and Child Welfare in Nineteenth-Century France*. Albany: State University of New York Press.

– 1992. *Poor and Pregnant in Paris*. New Brunswick, NJ: Rutgers University Press.

Gélis, Jacques. 1984. *L'arbre et le fruit*. Paris: Fayard.

Gerst, Hermann. 1975. *Histoire de Hunspach*. Strasbourg: Editions Oberlin.

Gillis, A.R. 1996. So Long as They Both Shall Live: Marital Dissolution and the Decline of Domestic Homicide in France, 1852–1909. *American Journal of Sociology* 101:1273–305.

Golde, Günter. 1975. *Catholics and Protestants: Agricultural Modernization in two German villages*. New York: Academic Press.

Goldscheider, Calvin. 1971. *Population, Modernization and Social Structure*. Boston: Little, Brown.

Goodkind, Daniel M. 1995. The Significance of Demographic Triviality: Minority Status and Zodiacal Fertility Timing among Chinese Malaysians. *Population Studies* 49:45–55.

Goody, Jack. 1983. *The Development of the Family and Marriage in Europe*. Cambridge: Cambridge University Press.

Goody, Jack, Joan Thirsk, and E.P. Thompson. 1976. *Family and Inheritance: Rural Society in Western Europe, 1200–1800*. Cambridge: Cambridge University Press.

Greenhalgh, Susan. 1990. Toward a Political Economy of Fertility: Anthropological Contributions. *Population and Development Review* 16:85–106.

– 1995. Anthropology Theorizes Reproduction: Integrating Practice, Political Economic, and Feminist Perspectives. In *Situating Fertility: Anthropology and Demographic Inquiry*. Cambridge: Cambridge University Press.

Gugerli, David. 1992. Protestant Pastors in Late-Eighteenth Century Zurich: Their Families and Society. *Journal of Interdisciplinary History* 22:369–85.

Guinnane, Timothy W. 1997. *The Vanishing Irish. Households, Migration, and the Rural Economy in Ireland, 1850–1914*. Princeton: Princeton University Press.

Guinnane, Timothy W., Barbara S. Okun, and James Trussell. 1994. What Do We Know About the Timing of Fertility Transitions in Europe? *Demography* 31:1–20.

Hajnal, John. 1953. Age at Marriage and Proportion Marrying. *Population Studies* 7:111–32.

– 1965. European Marriage Patterns in Perspective. In *Population in History: Essays in Historical Demography*, edited by D.V. Glass and D.E.C. Eversley. London: Edward Arnold.

– 1982. Two Kinds of Preindustrial Household Formation Systems. *Population and Development Review* 8:449–94.

Haliczer, Stephen. 1996. *Sexuality in the Confessional: A Sacrament Profaned*. New York: Oxford University Press.

Hammel, Eugene. 1990. A Theory of Culture for Demography. *Population and Development Review* 16:455–85.

– 1993. Incomplete Histories in Family Reconstitution: A Sensitivity Test of Alternative Strategies with Historical Croatian Data. In *Old and New Methods in Historical Demography*, edited by David S. Reher and Roger Schofield. Oxford: Clarendon Press.

Harrington, Joel F. 1995. *Reordering Marriage and Society in Reformation Germany*. Cambridge: Cambridge University Press.

Hau, Michel. 1987. *L'industrialisation de l'Alsace (1803–1939)*. Strasbourg: Presses Universitaires de Strasbourg.

Hau, Michel and Nicole Hau. 1981. La croissance du produit agricole alsacien, 1815–1975. *Revue d'Alsace* 107:133–52.

Head, Anne-Lise. 1988. Le contrôle de la fécondité en milieu préalpin: l'exemple de paroisses protestantes dans le pays glaronais (XVIIᵉ–XIXᵉ siècles). *Annales de démographie historique* 99–109.

Henripin, Jacques and Yves Peron. 1972. The Demographic Transition of the Province of Québec. In *Population and Social Change*, edited by D.V. Glass and R. Revelle. London: Edward Arnold.

Henry, Louis. 1953. Fondements théoriques des mesures de la fécondité naturelle. *Revue de l'Institut International de Statistique* 21:135–51.

– 1956. *Anciennes familles génévoises, étude démographique: XVIᵉ–XXᵉ siècles*. Paris: Presses Universitaires de France (INED: Travaux et Documents, Cahier 26).

– 1979. Concepts actuels et résultats empiriques sur la fécondité naturelle. In *Natural Fertility*, edited by Henri Leridon and Jane Menken. Liège: Ordina.

Henry, Louis and Alain Blum. 1988. *Techniques d'analyse en démographie historique. Second edition*. Paris: Editions de l'institut national d'études démographiques.

Hobcraft, John. 1993. Women's Education, Child Welfare and Child Survival: A Review of the Evidence. *Health Transition Review* 3:159–75.

Houdaille, Jacques. 1970. La population de Remmesweiler en Sarre aux XVIIIᵉ et XIXᵉ siècles. *Population* 25:1183–92.

– 1980. La mortalité des enfants en Europe avant le XIXᵉ siècle. In *La mortalité des enfants dans le monde et dans l'histoire*, edited by Paul-Marie Boulanger and Dominique Tabutin. Liège: Ordina.

Hsia, Ron Po-Chia. 1989. *Social Discipline in the Reformation: Central Europe 1550–1750*. London: Routledge.

Hufton, Olwen. 1974. *The Poor of Eighteenth-Century France, 1750–1789*. Oxford: Clarendon Press.

– 1979. The French Church. In *Church and Society in Catholic Europe of the Eighteenth Century*, edited by William J. Callaghan and David Higgs. Cambridge: Cambridge University Press.

– 1981. Women, Work and Marriage in Eighteenth-Century France. In *Marriage and Society: Studies in the Social History of Marriage*, edited by R.B. Outhwaite. London: Europa Publications.

– 1996. *The Prospect Before Her. A History of Women in Western Europe, 1500–1800*. New York: Alfred A. Knopf.

Hull, Isabel V. 1996. *Sexuality, State, and Civil Society in Germany, 1700–1815*. Ithaca: Cornell University Press.

Igersheim, François. 1993. *Politique et Administration dans le Bas-Rhin (1848–1870)*. Strasbourg: Presses Universitaires de Strasbourg.

Imhof, Arthur. 1981. Unterschiedliche Säuglingssterblichkeit in Deutschland, 18. bis 20. Jahrhundert – Warum? *Zeitschrift für Bevölkerungswissenschaft* 7:343–82.

Juillard, Etienne. 1953. *La Vie Rurale dans la Plaine de Basse-Alsace*. Strasbourg: F.X. LeRoux.

Juillard, Etienne and Philippe Kessler. 1952. Catholiques et Protestants dans les campagnes alsaciennes. *Annales: Economies, Sociétés, Civilisations* 7:49–54.

Karant-Nunn, Susan C. 1986. The Transmission of Luther's Teaching on Women and Matrimony: The Case of Zwickau. *Archiv für Reformationsgeschicte* 77:31–46.

Katz, Michael B. 1975. *The People of Hamilton, Canada West. Family and Class in a Mid-Nineteenth-Century City*. Cambridge: Harvard University Press.

Kephart, William M. and Davor Jedlicka. 1988. *The Family, Society, and the Individual*. New York: Harper and Row.

Kertzer, David I. 1995. Political-Economic and Cultural Theories of Demographic Behavior. In *Situating Fertility: Anthropology and Demographic Inquiry*, edited by Susan Greenhalgh. Cambridge: Cambridge University Press.

Kertzer, David I. and Dennis P. Hogan. 1989. *Family, Political Economy, and Demographic Change: The Transformation of Life in Casalecchio, Italy, 1861–1921*. Madison: University of Wisconsin Press.

Kintz, Jean-Pierre. 1977. *Paroisses et Communes de France. Bas-Rhin.* Paris: École des hautes études en sciences sociales.

- 1981. XVII<sup>e</sup> siècle: du Saint Empire au Royaume de France. In *Histoire de Strasbourg des origines à nos jours. Volume 3*, edited by Georges Livet and Francis Rapp. Strasbourg: Istra.

- 1984. *La Société Strasbourgeoise du milieu du XVI<sup>e</sup> siècle à la fin de la guerre de trente ans, 1560–1650.* Paris: Ophrys.

- 1993. Une enquête administrative sur l'émigration en Amerique sous la monarchie de Juillet: Le cas des Alsaciens. In *Mesurer et comprendre: Mélanges offerts à Jacques Dupâquier*, edited by Jean-Pierre Bardet, François Lebrun, and René Le Mée. Paris: Presses Universitaires de France.

Knodel, John. 1974. *The Decline of Fertility in Germany, 1871–1939.* Princeton: Princeton University Press.

- 1988. *Demographic Behaviour in the Past. A Study of Fourteen German Village Populations in the Eighteenth and Nineteenth Centuries.* Cambridge: Cambridge University Press.

Knodel, John and Steven Hochstadt. 1980. Urban and Rural Illegitimacy in Imperial Germany. In *Bastardy and its Comparative History*, edited by Peter Laslett, Karla Oosterveen and Richard M. Smith. London: Edward Arnold.

Knodel, John and Hallie Kintner. 1977. The Impact of Breastfeeding Patterns on the Biometric Analysis of Infant Mortality. *Demography* 14:391–409.

Knodel, John and Etienne Van De Walle. 1979. Lessons from the Past: Policy Implications of Historical Fertility Studies. *Population and Development Review* 5:217–45.

Kreager, Philip. 1986. Demographic Regimes as Cultural Systems. In *The State of Population Theory*, edited by David Coleman and Roger Schofield. London: Basil Blackwell.

- 1993. Anthropological Demography and the Limits of Diffusionism. *IUSSP International Population Conference, Montreal*, vol. 4:313–26.

Kriedte, Peter, Hans Medick, and Jürgen Schlumbohm. 1993. Proto-Industrialization Revisited: Demography, Social Structure, and Modern Domestic Industry. *Continuity and Change* 8:217–52.

Kunitz, Stephen J. and Stanley L. Engerman. 1992. The Ranks of Death: Secular Trends in Income and Mortality. *Health Transition Review* 2(supplement):29–46.

Landers, John. 1992. Historical Epidemiology and the Structural Analysis of Mortality. *Health Transition Review* 2(supplement):47–76.

- 1993. *Death and the Metropolis: Studies in the Demographic History of London 1670–1830.* Cambridge: Cambridge University Press.

Landes, David S. 1970. *The Unbound Prometheus: Technological Change 1750 to the Present.* Cambridge: Cambridge University Press.

Larkin, Emmet. 1972. The Devotional Revolution in Ireland, 1850–1870. *American Historical Review* 77:625–52.

Laslett, Peter. 1977. Long-term Trends in Bastardy in England. In *Family Life and Illicit Love in Earlier Generations*. Cambridge: Cambridge University Press.

– 1980. The Bastardy Prone Sub-Society. In *Bastardy and its Comparative History*, edited by Peter Laslett, Karla Oosterveen, and Richard M. Smith. London: Edward Arnold.

LeBras, Hervé and Emmanuel Todd. 1981. *L'invention de la France*. Paris: Librairie Générale Française.

Lee, Robert. 1981. Family and 'Modernisation': The Peasant Family and Social Change in Nineteenth Century Bavaria. In *The German Family: Essays on the Social History of the Family in Nineteenth- and Twentieth-Century Germany*, edited by Richard J. Evans and W.R. Lee. London: Croom Helm.

LeGrand, Thomas K. and James F. Phillips. 1996. The Effect of Fertility Reduction on Infant and Child Mortality: Evidence from Matlab in rural Bangladesh. *Population Studies* 50:51–68.

Lesthaeghe, Ron. 1983. A Century of Demographic Change in the West. *Population and Development Review* 9:411–36.

– 1989. Production and Reproduction in sub-Saharan Africa: An Overview of Organizing Principles. In *Reproduction and Social Organization in sub-Saharan Africa*, edited by R. Lesthaeghe. Berkeley: University of California Press.

Lesthaeghe, Ron and Johan Surkyn. 1988. Cultural Dynamics and Economic Theories of Fertility Change. *Population and Development Review* 14:1–45.

Leuilliot, Paul. 1959. *L'Alsace au début du XIX$^e$ siècle*. 3 volumes. Paris: S.E.V.P.E.N.

Levine, David. 1977. *Family Formation in an Age of Nascent Capitalism*. New York: Academic Press.

Levy, Robert. 1912. *Historie économique de l'industrie cotonnière en Alsace: Étude de sociologie descriptive*. Paris: Librairie Felix Alcan.

L'Huillier, Fernand. 1970. L'évolution dans la paix (1814–1870). In *Histoire de l'Alsace*, edited by Philippe Dollinger. Toulouse: Privat.

Lienhard, Marc. 1981. *Foi et Vie des Protestants d'Alsace*. Strasbourg: Editions Oberlin.

Linteau, Paul-André, René Durocher, and Jean-Claude Robert. 1979. *Histoire du Québec Contemporain: De la Confédération à la crise*. Montreal: Boréal.

Livet, Georges. 1956. *L'Intendance d'Alsace sous Louis XIV*. Paris: Les Belles Lettres.

– 1970a. La guerre de trente ans et les traités de Westphalie: la formation de la province d'Alsace (1618–1715). In *Histoire de l'Alsace*, edited by Philippe Dollinger. Toulouse: Privat.

– 1970b. Le XVIII$^e$ siècle et l'esprit des lumières. In *Histoire de l'Alsace*, edited by Philippe Dollinger. Toulouse: Privat.

Livi-Bacci, Massimo. 1986. Social-Group Forerunners of Fertility Control in Europe. In *The Decline of Fertility in Europe*, edited by Ansley J. Coale and Susan Cotts Watkins. Princeton: Princeton University Press.

Macfarlane, Alan. 1986. *Marriage and Love in England: Modes of Reproduction 1300–1840*. Oxford: Basil Blackwell.

McKeown, Thomas. 1976. *The Modern Rise of Population*. New York: Academic Press.

McKeown, T. and R.G. Brown. 1955. Medical Evidence Related to English Population Changes in the Eighteenth Century. *Population Studies* 9:115–41.

McKeown, T. and R.G. Record. 1962. Reasons for the Decline of Mortality in England and Wales During the Nineteenth Century. *Population Studies* 16:94–122.

McLaren, Angus. 1978. *Birth Control in Nineteenth Century England*. London: Croom Helm.

McNicoll, Geoffrey. 1992. Changing Fertility Patterns and Policies in the Third World. *Annual Review of Sociology* 18:85–108.

– 1994. Institutional Analysis of Fertility. In *Population, Economic Development, and the Environment*, edited by Kersten Lindahl-Kiessling and Hans Landberg. Oxford: Oxford University Press.

McQuillan, Kevin. 1984. Modes of Production and Demographic Behaviour in Nineteenth Century France. *American Journal of Sociology* 84:1324–46.

– 1989. Economic Structure, Religion, and Age at Marriage: Some Evidence from Alsace. *Journal of Family History* 14:331–46.

Marx, Roland. 1970. De la pré-revolution à la restauration. In *Histoire de l'Alsace*, edited by Philippe Dollinger. Toulouse: Privat.

– 1974. *La Révolution et les classes sociales*. Paris: Bibliothèque National.

Mason, Karen Oppenheim. 1992. Culture and the Fertility Transition: Thoughts on Theories of Fertility Decline. *Genus* 48:1–13.

Mazrui, Ali A. 1994. Islamic Doctrine and the Politics of Induced Fertility Change: An African Perspective. *Population and Development Review* 20(supplement):121-36.

Medick, Hans. 1981. The Structures and Function of Population-Development under the Proto-industrial System. In *Industrialization Before Industrialization*, edited by Peter Kriedte, Hans Medick and Jurgen Schlumbohm. Cambridge: Cambridge University Press.

Medick, Hans and David Warren Sabean, eds. 1984. *Interest and Emotion: Essays on the Study of Family and Kinship*. Cambridge: Cambridge University Press.

Mendels, Franklin. 1972. Proto-industrialization: The First Phase of the Industrialization Process. *Journal of Economic History* 32:241–61.

– 1984. Des industries rurales à la protoindustrialization: Histoire d'un changement de perspective. *Annales: Économies, Sociétés, Civilisations*. 39:977–1008.

Meuvret, Jean. 1946. Les crises de subsistances et la démographie de la France de l'Ancien Régime. *Population* 1:643–50.

Michel, Patrick. 1991. *Politics and Religion in Eastern Europe: Catholicism in Hungary, Poland and Czechoslovakia.* Oxford: Polity Press.

Migneret, Stanislas. 1868. *Description du Département du Bas-Rhin.* Volumes 1–2. Strasbourg: Berger-Levrault.

– 1871. *Description du Département du Bas-Rhin.* Volume 3. Strasbourg: Berger-Levrault et Fils.

Moch, Leslie Page. 1983. *Paths to the City: Regional Migration in Nineteenth-Century France.* Beverly Hills: Sage Publications.

Muckensturm, Stephan. 1988. L'indigence révélatrice des faiblesses d'une société: l'exemple bas-rhinois au XIX$^e$ siècle (1790–1870). *Revue d'Alsace* 114:127–54.

Muller, Claude. 1986. *Dieu est catholique et alsacien.* Strasbourg: Société d'Histoire de l'Église d'Alsace.

Müller, Siegfried. 1995. Die Konfessionalisierung in der Grafschaft Oldenburg – Untersuchungen zur "Sozialdisziplinierung" einer bäuerlichen Gesellschaft in der Frühen Neuzeit. *Archiv für Reformationsgeschicte* 86:257–319.

Notestein, Frank. 1945. Population – The Long View. In *Food for the World*, edited by Theodore Schultz. Chicago: University of Chicago Press.

Oberlé, Raymond. 1985. *Mulhouse ou la genèse d'une ville.* Strasbourg: Éditions du Rhin.

Oberman, Heiko A. 1992. *Luther: Man Between God and the Devil.* New York: Image Books.

Obermeyer, Carla Makhlouf. 1992. Islam, Women, and Politics: The Demography of Arab Countries. *Population and Development Review* 18:33–60.

Okun, Barbara S. 1994. Evaluating Methods for Detecting Fertility Control: Coale and Trussell's Model and Cohort Parity Analysis. *Population Studies* 48:193–222.

Ozment, Steven. 1983. *When Fathers Ruled: Family Life in Reformation Germany.* Cambridge: Harvard University Press.

– 1992. *Protestants: The Birth of a Revolution.* New York: Doubleday.

Palloni, Alberto. 1989. Effects of Inter-birth Intervals on Infant and Early Childhood Mortality. In *Differential Mortality: Methodological Issues and Biosocial Factors*, edited by Lado Ruzicka, Guillaume Wunsch and Penny Kane. Oxford: Clarendon Press.

Palmer, R.R. 1969. *Twelve Who Ruled: The Year of the Terror in the French Revolution.* Princeton: Princeton University Press.

Parker, Geoffrey. 1984. *The Thirty Years' War.* London: Routledge and Kegan Paul.

Perrenoud, Alfred. 1974. Malthusianisme et protestantisme: un modèle démographique wéberien. *Annales: Économies, Sociétés, Civilisation* 29:975–88.

- 1988. Espacement et arrêt dans le contrôle des naissances. *Annales de démographie historique* 59–78.
- 1991. The Attenuation of Mortality Crises and the Decline of Mortality. In *The Decline of Mortality in Europe,* edited by R. Schofield, D. Reher, and A. Bideau. Oxford: Clarendon Press.
- 1994. La mortalité des enfants en Europe francophone. *Annales de démographie historique,* 79–96.
Peter, Daniel. 1995. *Naître, vivre et mourir dans l'Outre-Forêt (1648–1848).* Cercle d'histoire et d'archéologie de l'Alsace du Nord.
Pfister, Ulrich. 1985. *Die Anfänge von Geburtenbeschränkung: Eine Fallstudie (ausgewählte Zürcher Familien im 17. und 18. Jahrhundert).* Berne: Lang.
- 1988. Mobilité sociale et transition de la fécondité: le cas de Zurich (Suisse) au XVIIᵉ Siècle. *Annales de démographie historique* 111–25.
Phillips, Roderick. 1988. *Putting Asunder: A History of Divorce in Western Society.* Cambridge: Cambridge University Press.
Pinto Aguirre, Guido, Alberto Palloni, and Robert E. Jones. 1998. Effects of Lactation on Post-partum Amenorrhoea: Re-estimation Using Data from a Longitudinal Study in Guatemala. *Population Studies* 52:231–48.
Pollak, Robert A. and Susan Cotts Watkins. 1993. Cultural and Economic Approaches to Fertility: Proper Marriage or a Mésalliance. *Population and Development Review* 19:467–95.
Post, John D. 1985. *Food Shortage, Climatic Variability, and Epidemic Disease in Preindustrial Europe.* Ithaca: Cornell University Press.
- 1990. Nutritional Status and Mortality in Eighteenth-century Europe. In *Hunger in History,* edited by Lucile F. Newman. Oxford: Basil Blackwell.
Poulain, Michel and Dominique Tabutin. 1980. La mortalité aux jeunes ages en Europe et en Amérique du Nord du XIXᵉ siècle à nos jours. In *La Mortalité des Enfants dans le Monde et dans l'Histoire,* edited by Pierre-Marc Boulanger and Dominique Tabutin. Liège: Ordina.
Poulard, Serge, Evelyne Heyer, André Guillemette, and Guy Brunet. 1991. *SYGAP: Système de Gestion et d'Analyse de Population.* Lyon: Programme Rhône-Alpes, Recherches en Sciences Humaines.
Preston, Samuel H., ed. 1978. *The Effects of Infant and Child Mortality on Fertility.* New York: Academic Press.
Preston, Samuel H. and Michael R. Haines. 1991a. *Fatal Years: Child Mortality in Late Nineteenth Century America.* Princeton: Princeton University Press.
- 1991b. Response to Comments on Fatal Years. *Health Transition Review* 1:240–4.
Reuss, Rodolphe. 1906. *Les églises protestants d'Alsace pendant la Révolution.* Paris: Librairie Fischbacher.
Robisheaux, Thomas. 1989. *Rural Society and the Search for Order in Early Modern Germany.* Cambridge: Cambridge University Press.

Rollet, Catherine. 1994. La mortalité des enfants dans le passé: au-delà des apparences. *Annales de démographie historique* 7–22.

Rollet-Echalier, Catherine. 1990. *La politique à l'égard de la petite enfance sous la IIIᵉ République*. Paris: Presses Universitaires de France (INED, Travaux et Documents, Cahier 127).

Roper, Lyndal. 1989. *The Holy Household: Women and Morals in Reformation Augsburg*. Oxford: Oxford University Press.

– 1994. *Oedipus and the Devil: Witchcraft, Sexuality and the Devil in Early Modern Europe*. London and New York: Routledge.

Ruggles, Steven. 1992. Migration, Marriage, and Mortality: Correcting Sources of Bias in English Family Reconstitutions. *Population Studies* 46:507–22.

Sabean, David Warren. 1990. *Property, Production, and Family in Neckarhausen, 1700–1870*. Cambridge: Cambridge University Press.

Santow, Gigi. 1987. Reassessing the Contraceptive Effect of Breastfeeding. *Population Studies* 41:147–60.

– 1995. *Coitus interruptus* and the Control of Natural Fertility. *Population Studies* 49:19–43.

Sarg, Freddy. 1977. *En Alsace, du berçeau à la tombe: rites, coutumes et croyances*. Strasbourg: Editions Oberlin.

Schilling, Heinz. 1988a. Between the Territorial State and Urban Liberty: Lutheranism and Calvinism in the County of Lippe. In *The German People and the Reformation*, edited by R. Po-Chia Hsia. Ithaca: Cornell University Press.

– 1988b. Die Konfessionalisierung im Reich: Religiöser und gesellschaftlicher Wandel in Deutschland zwischen 1555 und 1620. *Historische Zeitschrift* 246:1–45.

– 1992. *Religion, Political Culture and the Emergence of Early Modern Society: Essays in German and Dutch History*. Leiden: E.J. Brill.

Schmitt, Jean-Marie. 1980. *Aux Origines de la Révolution Industrielle en Alsace: Investissements et relations sociales dans la vallée de Saint-Amarin au XVIIIᵉ siècle*. Strasbourg: Istra.

Schmitt, Louis. 1983. Les conséquences démographiques de la guerre de Trente Ans en Basse-Alsace. In *Histoire de l'Alsace rurale*, edited by Jean-Michel Boehler, Dominique Lerch and Jean Vogt. Strasbourg: Istra.

Schneider, Peter and Jane Schneider. 1995. High Fertility and Poverty in Sicily: Beyond the Culture vs. Rationality Debate. In *Situating Fertility: Anthropology and Demographic Inquiry*, edited by Susan Greenhalgh. Cambridge: Cambridge University Press.

Schofield, Roger. 1985. English Marriage Patterns Revisited. *Journal of Family History* 10:2–20.

Schrader-Muggenthaler, Constance. 1989. *The Alsace Emigration Book*. Apollo, CA: Closson Press.

Seccombe, Wally. 1993. *Weathering the Storm: Working-Class Families from the Industrial Revolution to the Fertility Decline*. London: Verso.

Segalen, Martine. 1980. *Mari et femme dans la société paysanne*. Paris: Flammarion.

– 1981. Mentalité populaire et remariage en Europe occidentale. In *Marriage and Remarriage in Populations of the Past*, edited by Jacques Dupâquier et al. London: Academic Press.

Selig, Jean-Michel. 1988. Misère et malnutrition dans les campagnes alsaciennes du XIX<sup>e</sup> siècle. *Revue d'Alsace* 114:155–69.

Shorter, Edward. 1975. *The Making of the Modern Family*. New York: Basic Books.

Shorter, Edward, Etienne Van De Walle, and John Knodel. 1971. Illegitimacy, Sexual Revolution and Social Change in Modern Europe. *Journal of Interdisciplinary History* 2:237–72.

Simmel, Georg. [1923] 1955. *Conflict and The Web of Group-Affiliations*. Reprint, New York: The Free Press.

Smith, Helmut Walser. 1995. *German Nationalism and Religious Conflict*. Princeton: Princeton University Press.

Smith, Richard M. 1986. Marriage Processes in the English Past: Some Continuities. In *The World We Have Gained: Histories of Population and Social Structure*, edited by Lloyd Bonfield, Richard M. Smith and Keith Wrightson. Oxford: Basil Blackwell.

Stoskopf, Nicolas. 1987. *La petite industrie dans le Bas-Rhin, 1810–1870*. Strasbourg: Editions Oberlin.

Strauss, Gerald. 1978. *Luther's House of Learning*. Baltimore: Johns Hopkins University Press.

– 1988. The Reformation and Its Public in an Age of Orthodoxy. In *The German People and the Reformation*, edited by R. Po-Chia Hsia. Ithaca: Cornell University Press.

Stroh, Louis. 1914. *Les petites industries rurales en Alsace*. Agen: Maison d'Édition et Imprimerie Moderne.

Strohl, Henri. 1950. *Le Protestantisme en Alsace*. Strasbourg: Editions Oberlin.

Swidler, Ann. 1986. Culture in Action: Symbols and Strategies. *American Sociological Review* 51:273–86.

Szreter, Simon. 1988. The Importance of Social Intervention in Britain's Mortality Decline *c.* 1850–1914: A Re-interpretation of the Role of Public Health. *Social History of Medicine* 1:1–38.

– 1996. *Fertility, Class and Gender in Britain, 1860–1940*. Cambridge: Cambridge University Press.

– 1997. The Politics of Public Health in Nineteenth-Century Britain. *Population and Development Review* 23:693–728.

Tentler, Thomas N. 1977. *Sin and Confession on the Eve of the Reformation*. Princeton: Princeton University Press.

Tilly, Charles. 1984. Demographic Origins of the European Proletariat. In *Proletarianization and Family History*, edited by David Levine. Orlando: Academic Press.

Todd, Emmanuel. 1985. *The Explanation of Ideology: Family Structures and Social Systems*. Oxford: Basil Blackwell.

Vallin, Jacques. 1991. Mortality in Europe from 1720–1914: Long-term Trends and Changes in Patterns by Age and Sex. In *The Decline of Mortality in Europe*, edited by Roger Schofield, David Reher and Alain Bideau. Oxford: Clarendon Press.

Van de Walle, Etienne. 1980. Illegitimacy in France during the Nineteenth Century. In *Bastardy and Its Comparative History*, edited by Peter Laslett, Karla Oosterveen and Richard M. Smith. London: Edward Arnold.

– 1998. Pour une histoire démographique de l'avortement. *Population* 53:273–90.

Van De Walle, Etienne and Helmut V. Musham. 1995. Fatal Secrets and the French Fertility Transition. *Population and Development Review* 21:261–80.

Van Poppel, Frans. 1995a. Seasonality of Work, Religion and Popular Customs: The Seasonality of Marriage in the Nineteenth- and Twentieth-Century Netherlands. *Continuity and Change* 10:215–56.

– 1995b. Widows, Widowers and Remarriage in Nineteenth-Century Netherlands. *Population Studies* 49:421–41.

Van Poppel, Frans and Cor van der Heijden. 1997. Les effets controversés de l'adduction d'eau sur la santé des populations. Bilan des recherches et expérimentation sur une ville des Pays-Bas (Tilburg). *Annales de démographie historique* 157–204.

Viazzo, Pier Paolo. 1986. Illegitimacy and the European Marriage Pattern: Comparative Evidence from the Alpine Area. In *The World We Have Gained*, edited by Lloyd Bonfield, Richard M. Smith and Keith Wrightson. Oxford: Basil Blackwell.

– 1989. *Upland Communities: Environment, Population and Social Structure in the Alps since the Sixteenth Century*. Cambridge: Cambridge University Press.

– 1994. Les modèles alpins de mortalité infantile. *Annales de démographie historique* 97–117.

Vogler, Bernard. 1983. Les campagnes protestants: une première approche. In *Histoire de l'Alsace rurale*, edited by Jean-Michel Boehler, Dominique Lerch and Jean Vogt. Strasbourg: Istra.

– 1991. Les protestants d'Alsace et la Révolution. *Revue d'Alsace* 116:197–205.

– 1993. La famille dans les recueils de prières luthériens 1550–1700. In *La vie, la mort, la foi, le temps: Mélanges offerts à Pierre Chaunu*, edited by Jean-Pierre Bardet and Madeleine Foisil. Paris: Presses Universitaires de France.

– 1994. *Histoire des Chrétiens d'Alsace des origines à nos jours*. Paris: Desclée.

Wahl, Alfred. 1980. *Confession et Comportement dans les campagnes d'Alsace et de Bade 1871–1939*. Strasbourg: Editions Coprur.

Watkins, Susan Cotts. 1990. The Transformation of Demographic Regimes in Western Europe, 1870–1960. *Population and Development Review* 16:241–72.

– 1991. *From Provinces into Nations: Demographic Integration in Western Europe, 1870–1960.* Princeton: Princeton University Press.

Weber, Eugen. 1976. *Peasants into Frenchmen: The Modernization of Rural France, 1870–1914.* Stanford: Stanford University Press.

Weber, Max. [1904–5] 1958. *The Protestant Ethic and the Spirit of Capitalism.* Reprint, New York: Charles Scribner's Sons.

Weigel, George. 1992. *The Final Revolution: The Resistance Church and the Collapse of Communism.* New York: Oxford University Press.

Weir, David. 1984. Rather Never than Late: Celibacy and Age at Marriage in English Cohort Fertility. *Journal of Family History* 9:340–54.

– 1993. Family Reconstitution and Population Reconstruction: Two Approaches to the Fertility Transition in France, 1740–1911. In *Old and New Methods in Historical Demography,* edited by David S. Reher and Roger Schofield. Oxford: Clarendon Press.

Wendel, François. 1928. *Le mariage à Strasbourg à l'époque de la Réforme 1520–1692.* Strasbourg: Imprimerie Alsacienne.

Wiesner, Merry. 1986. *Working Women in Renaissance Germany.* New Brunswick, NJ: Rutgers University Press.

Woods, Robert I. and P.R.A. Hinde. 1985. Nuptiality and Age at Marriage in Nineteenth-Century England. *Journal of Family History* 10:119–44.

Wrigley, E.A., R.S. Davies, J.E. Oeppen, and R.S. Schofield. 1997. *English Population History from Family Reconstitution 1580–1837.* Cambridge: Cambridge University Press.

Wuthnow, Robert. 1987. *Meaning and Moral Order: Explorations in Cultural Analysis.* Berkeley: University of California Press.

Wuthnow, Robert and Marsha Witten. 1988. New Directions in the Study of Culture. *Annual Review of Sociology* 14:49–67.

Zschunke, Peter. 1984. *Konfession und Alltag in Oppenheim: Beiträge zur Geschichte von Bevölkerung und Gesellschaft einer gemischtkonfessionellen Kleinstadt in der frühen Neuzeit.* Wiesbaden: Franz Steiner.

# Index

abortion, 99, 129, 130, 197, 201

Abray, Lorna, 29, 46, 78, 81, 170, 172, 203

abstinence, 104, 120

acknowledgment. *See* paternity, illegitimacy

*acte de reconnaissance*, 87

adultery, 130, 173

age at marriage, 13, 44, 48–54, 60

age differences (between spouses), 44, 54–9, 89

age of mother: and age at marriage, 200; at last birth, 115–17, 127–8, 201; and infant death, 142–4, 153–4, 202

agriculture: in Avolsheim, 35; in Baldenheim, 38; in Goxwiller, 36–7; organization, 23–6; productivity, 25, 26. *See also* farmers, land ownership

Alter, George, 4

*alternation*, 30, 171

Anabaptists, 40, 197

Anderson, Barbara, 4

Ariès, Philippe, 75

Armstrong, William, 193

army. *See* military

artisans: age at marriage, 53–4; age difference (between spouses), 58–9; bridal pregnancy, 94–5;

infant and child mortality, 150–2; marital fertility, 126–7; mate selection, 65–7

*Aufklärung. See* Enlightenment

authoritarian family, 199

Austria, 134

Avolsheim, 33, 36; age at marriage, 49, 50; child mortality, 137–9, 151, 156–7; data quality, 185–6, 192; illegitimacy, 83; infant mortality, 137–9, 151, 153, 155; local conditions, 35–6; marital fertility, 109, 116; origin of spouses, 69; population, 35; religious identity, 36; stopping behaviour, 116

Baden, 31, 203

Baldenheim, 33, 36; age at marriage, 49, 53; child mortality, 137–9, 151, 157; data quality, 185–6, 187–8, 189, 192, 193, 201; illegitimacy, 83; infant mortality, 137–9, 151, 153; intermarriage, 64; local conditions, 38–9, 48; marital fertility, 108–9, 116, 200; origin of spouses, 69; population,

37; religious situation, 38–9, 177, 203; stopping behaviour, 116, 127; textile industry in, 38, 48

baptism, 11, 80, 83, 171, 189; of illegitimate children, 30, 86, 87, 198

Barr, 37, 67

Barth, Frederik, 197

Bas-Rhin (*département du*): clergy in, 30, 173; creation of, 16, 19; industry in, 28; literacy in, 27; migration from, 26

Basel, 19, 26, 41

Basque region, 78

bastardy-prone subsociety, 90–1, 99–100

Bavaria, 100, 134

Beaujot, Roderic, 179

Belgium, 176

Bergholtz, 203

Bernardin, Edith, 23

Bernardswiller, 86

Bernolsheim, 33

*biens nationaux*, 19

bilingualism, 21

Bindernheim, 33

biometric analysis, 140–1

birth control. *See* contraception

birth intervals, 110, 120–5, 128, 134; and infant death, 122–3, 145, 149–50, 153–5, 160; inter-

Volumes in the McGill-Queen's Studies in the History of Religion have been supported by the Jackman Foundation of Toronto.

SERIES ONE
G.A. Rawlyk, Editor

1 Small Differences
Irish Catholics and Irish
Protestants, 1815–1922
An International Perspective
Donald Harman Akenson

2 Two Worlds
The Protestant Culture of
Nineteenth-Century Ontario
William Westfall

3 An Evangelical Mind
Nathanael Burwash and the
Methodist Tradition in Canada,
1839–1918
Marguerite Van Die

4 The Dévotes
Women and Church in
Seventeenth-Century France
Elizabeth Rapley

5 The Evangelical Century
College and Creed in English
Canada from the Great Revival
to the Great Depression
Michael Gauvreau

6 The German Peasants' War and
Anabaptist Community of
Goods
James M. Stayer

7 A World Mission
Canadian Protestantism and
the Quest for a New
International Order, 1918–1939
Robert Wright

8 Serving the Present Age
Revivalism, Progressivism, and
the Methodist Tradition in
Canada
Phyllis D. Airhart

9 A Sensitive Independence
Canadian Methodist Women
Missionaries in Canada and the
Orient, 1881–1925
Rosemary R. Gagan

10 God's Peoples
Covenant and Land in South
Africa, Israel, and Ulster
Donald Harman Akenson

11 Creed and Culture
The Place of English-Speaking
Catholics in Canadian Society,
1750–1930
Terrence Murphy and
Gerald Stortz, editors

12 Piety and Nationalism
Lay Voluntary Associations
and the Creation of an Irish-
Catholic Community in
Toronto, 1850–1895
Brian P. Clarke

13 Amazing Grace
Studies in Evangelicalism in
Australia, Britain, Canada, and
the United States
George Rawlyk and Mark A.
Noll, editors